FROM GENERATION
TO
GENERATION

SBN 7050 0005 2
Printed in Gt. Britain for The Research Publishing Co. (Fudge & Co. Ltd.), London.

Henry Garstang's Chantry in Cirencester Church
(*by kind permission of the Vicar, the Revd. Rowland E. Hill*)

photograph by Wm. Barrett of Silver St., Cirencester

FROM GENERATION TO GENERATION

The Story of a Lancashire Clan

BY

S. GAMZU GURNEY, M.B.E.

WITH A FOREWORD BY

G. D. SQUIBB, Q.C.

Norfolk Herald Extraordinary

LONDON:

THE RESEARCH PUBLISHING CO.

52 LINCOLN'S INN FIELDS, W.C.2.

"The Great Danish Earls, Agmund, Orme, and Gair, have all left memorials of their existence, if not of their exploits, in the names of the hundreds, towns and villages of Lancashire."

From Baines and Fairbairn's
Lancashire and Cheshire Past and Present.
vol. I. p.313.

FOREWORD

Surnames, such as Garstang, derived from place names can have come into existence in two ways. Sometimes the name of the place where a man lived, his address, came to be used with his Christian name so frequently that it became part of his name and then as surnames began to be hereditary it came to be used by his descendants whether they lived at the place in question or not. More frequently, a man who had moved to another place would be known by the name of the place whence he came as a sort of nickname and that also could develop into a surname to be passed on to his descendants. While the "address" type of surname would for practical reasons be unlikely to be acquired by more than a few people at any one time, that used to designate a man who had originated in another place could be adopted by or applied to immigrants in a large number of different places. It was therefore possible for persons who were in no way related to each other to acquire the same place name as a surname.

No doubt this frequently happened with names derived from large areas or populous towns, such as Cornwall or Lincoln. However, in the case of a village or a small town it was more than likely that there was some relationship between most of the people who lived there. Parish registers show how frequently this has been the case in recent centuries, and there is no reason to believe that it was any less so in the days before there were parish registers when surnames were coming into being.

It is, therefore, highly probable that, while the surname of Garstang came to be used by a number of men in various places at about the same time, these men were related to each other in some way. It is unlikely that they were all agnatically related, but cognatic relationships between them were probably common. Garstang was quite a small place. By 1831 its population had only grown to 936. In the period when surnames were coming into being it must have been much smaller.

Mrs. Gurney has endeavoured to collect information regarding all the persons bearing the surname of Garstang whom she could trace. Her sub-title, "The Story of a Lancashire Clan", seems to indicate precisely what they are. In addition to the probability that there was some sort of relationship between the original bearers of the name, the pages of this book disclose a number of cases in which a Garstang has married a Garstang. Often there is no apparent relationship between the parties to these matches, so their descendants may combine the blood of more than one Garstang line. To call all Garstangs a family would imply that they were all descended in the male line from a

5

common ancestor and would not be justified by the evidence. To call them a clan is to use just the right word.

The clanship of Garstangs in this sense dates from the period between 1250 and 1450, during which most English surnames came into being. There is, however, a sense in which their clanship may go back to a much remoter period. The eponymous Gair, who is said to have been a Norseman, no doubt brought with him followers of his own race. These men (and perhaps their womenfolk as well) formed an enclave among the original inhabitants of the area in which they settled. They were Gair's men in the same way that the followers of a Scottish highland chief were his men. Although not literally born of the same mother by the same father, they were a band of brothers. This notional relationship underlies the Scottish clan system. No one (or perhaps one should say no Englishman) really believes that all Campbells or all MacGregors are in fact descended from a single forefather, but through their common allegiance and, in many cases, intermarriage they have from time immemorial regarded themselves as members of one clan. We are accustomed to regard the clan as a Scottish institution, but given the circumstances which prevailed at the time when Gair the Norseman gave his name to Garstang there must have been something very similar in some parts of England.

The feeling of belonging to one clan comes out very clearly in some of the letters from Garstangs printed in this book. One of the fascinating features of Mrs. Gurney's story is the way in which she has let members of the clan tell what they know of their family histories in their own words. This is source material for the collection and recording of which future generations of Garstangs will be grateful to Mrs. Gurney. Those of them who are so minded will be able to obtain information about their ancestors from public records, either in print or still in manuscript. To search the records for all references to members of the clan would have been impracticable. The value of this book is it makes clear many matters about which records are silent. This is the human knowledge which makes the records make sense.

There are many ways of writing family histories. I am always attracted by the author who explains how and where he searched for information, not omitting the stones which he turned and the avenues which he explored without success. This is what Mrs. Gurney calls the Quest and she tells us all about it. Then when she writes of her own near relations, for whom no quest was necessary, she puts flesh onto the dry bones of the pedigree and brings the past alive with the human details stored in her long memory which embraces members of seven generations of her family. This is a book which only Mrs. Gurney could have written.

G. D. SQUIBB
Norfolk Herald Extraordinary

PREFACE

IN 1907 when my brother Walter's name appeared in various newspapers on his appointment to the Professorship of Zoology in Leeds University he received letters from Garstangs in all parts of the world including many villages and towns of Lancashire. My father, another Walter Garstang, was a physician and had lived in Blackburn all his life; we had all heard how our ancestors had landed in the Wyre valley and founded the town of Garstang The Garstangs who wrote to Walter, however, were filled with curiosity at this cropping up of their own name in Leeds University, and the letters for the most part were something like this:

> My father had come to live here before I was born, and he is now dead. I have never met any other Garstang, but I often wonder if we have any connexion with the town of Garstang. I hope that one day I shall see it, and it gives me a great thrill to be writing to you as it may lead me to being put in touch with some of my kith and kin.

Walter therefore studied afresh our grandfather's papers about his family connexions, and asked for any information the unknown Garstangs might have about their uncles and aunts or grandparents. Our cousin Adelaide's daughter Bessie married George Squibb (later Q.C.) in 1936 and they delved into the histories and records of Lancashire to make lists of births, marriages, and deaths of as many Garstangs as possible.

This was made difficult by the fact that in the survey of Lancashire in Domesday Book the district between Mersey and Ribble is placed under Cheshire, and the Hundreds of Amounderness and Lonsdale are included under Yorkshire; while Preston, Garstang, and Lancaster were linked with Carlisle by the northern part of the Roman road Watling Street. Also Lancashire had been in the ancient ecclesiastical diocese of York, but from 1541 until recently it had been in the diocese of Chester, divided between the two archdeaconries of Richmond and Chester, and had been very thinly populated until the era of coal-mining.

The chief sources of information, such as wills, therefore had to be sought either in Chester or Preston, and many of the parish registers had been lost or destroyed.

Wills and marriage certificates can now be obtained from either the Preston Record Office, or from Somerset House in London. The following have also yielded much information:

Calendars of documents in the Public Record Office.
The Victoria County History of Lancashire.
The Record Society of Lancashire and Cheshire.
The Lancashire Parish Register Society.
The Chetham Society.

For all the information thus collected I now wish to thank George Squibb, without whose help this story could not have been written.

Since the writing of the story passed to me I have been greatly helped by my near relations of "the next generation" whose mothers or fathers were born Garstangs or had married Garstangs.

My thanks are also due to Mr. R. Sharpe France, M.A. the archivist in the Lancashire Record Office at Preston, also to Mr. W. W. Yeates, F.L.A. when Curator and Librarian of the Blackburn Museum, and to the vicars, town-clerks, and secretaries of the various Societies who have frequently helped in my researches.

                                                            S.G.G.

Oxford, September 1969.

CONTENTS

Chapter

ILLUSTRATIONS

PLATES

IN THE TEXT

PEDIGREES

CHAPTER I

GRANDPARENTS, PARENTS, AND COUSINS

FROM OUR earliest days our imaginations had been fired by romantic pictures of the origin of the Garstang Clan: high-prowed Scandinavian long-boats tossing over the rough seas from the barren rock shores of Norway towards the fertile green banks of Norfolk rivers and sloping coasts of Sussex.

We could picture a few of the adventurers turning westward under the secret orders of three daring Vikings, Gair, Orme, and Agmund, their kinsfolk straining at the heavy oars as they rowed to seek shelter in the rock-bound lochs of Scotland where two on the west coast still bear the name of "Gair".

They would move from loch to loch exchanging amber for their stores until at last they reached the mouth of the river Wyre in the district of the forsaken Roman fortress at Lancastra on Lune. There the land-locked narrow entrance to the estuary promised a calm anchorage, and as they tied their boats to the trunks of willow trees on the staithe, they had only a group of British fisherfolk to placate before they moved up the winding river, past a religious community of British Christians, until having found a clearing in the forest at a wide bend in the river, our hero Gair planted his "Stange" or staff on the bank as a sign that there he would build his homestead with the huts of his followers clustering round.

Agmund settled with his men where fertile ground met the empty marshlands between the Wyre and Ribble, while Orme trekked farther still among the Brigantes, bequeathing their names to Amounderness and Ormskirk. Built into the east wall of the church at Ormskirk can be seen two roughly carved stone figures taken from an earlier church sepulchre, and traditionally representing two sisters of the name of Orme who caused the first Christian church to be built in Orme's settlement.

A few years ago when my niece, Joan Elliot, happened to be going to Ormskirk I asked her to visit the church to see if there remained anything to connect it with the Norsemen, and she came back having seen these figures about which I had heard nothing previously.

During the next hundred years after the landing of the Norsemen they settled down to till the ground and breed flocks of sheep, marrying the daughters of British or Scandinavian citizens, and bringing up their families in Over Wyresdale between Garstang and Lancaster under the influence of the Abbot of Cistercian Monks at Abbeystead[1]. The Abbot owned the vast forests where herds of wild deer ranged across the moorlands in which

[1] See the *New Lancashire Gazetteer* by Stephen Reynolds Clarke, London 1830. A. L. Rowse: *The Spirit of English History*, Cape 1947.

13

Abbeystead was situated. With the hunting and game laws under his control the Abbot was practically the ruler of the land, so that from him the settlers learned to obey law and order. Even the fishing rights were also granted by him, from the sources of the Wyre in Brinan Tarn through Abbeystead and Garstang to the river's junction with the West Calder below Gair's settlement; beyond that point the river was joined by the stream Myer at St. Michaels and became tidal, flowing westward through Poulton to form the wide estuary of Wyre Water.

Excitement spread through the whole Danelaw when their great leader Canute was acknowledged as King of all the country. Having sent back to Scandinavia the soldiers who had established him upon the throne and keeping only the Huscarls about his person, he was solemnly crowned in London with all ancient ceremonies, and at a Witenagemot at Oxford he vowed to God that he would rule justly and piously, administering justice to all his subjects with impartial equality: "If heretofore," he declared, "I have done aught beyond what is just, I am ready with God's help to amend it utterly."

A new wave of enthusiasm for Christianity spread across the land: abbeys and churches dedicated to the Apostles and to more recent local Saints were built with eager devotion in Amounderness and the districts round Garstang and Ormskirk. The later passing of the throne to William of Normandy made little difference to the inhabitants of the County of Lancaster, the scene of this story.

Gair's landing took place about the year A.D. 832. Precisely eight centuries elapsed from that time until the year 1632 when our ancestor, a yeoman of Northbank in Whittle, died and left his property to a long line of master blacksmiths. This James Garstang had married a daughter of William Garstang of Brindle (see Pedigree II below). The great grandson of this yeoman, another James, left the home of his ancestors and the forges to his eldest son Lawrence, and with his wife Ruth and younger son Thomas, migrated to Beardwood Fold near Blackburn and took to farming and hand-loom weaving, a necessary skill which was practised at that time in the homes of many citizens.

In 1937 my cousin Bessie and her husband George Squibb were travelling round Lancashire to discover more about the conditions in which our ancestors had passed their lives, and afterwards they told my brother Walter about their discoveries:

> From Whittle we went to Northbank where your ancestor James had lived. Some rooms in the house seem to have been left as they were in his day, and the present tenant's wife showed us a part of the house which had been used for hand-loom weaving.
>
> This is very interesting because the inventory made of James's goods after his death included spinning wheels and the workrooms belonging to the mill.
>
> James's son, the blacksmith William who died in 1680, had two smithies, but we could not find anybody in Whittle who knew of a second.
>
> The farmer's wife at Northbank knew the last of the Garstangs who had worked as blacksmiths there.

Pedigree I.
Thomas of Blackburn
(Beardwood Fold)
The Garstangs of Whittle-le-Woods (blacksmiths)

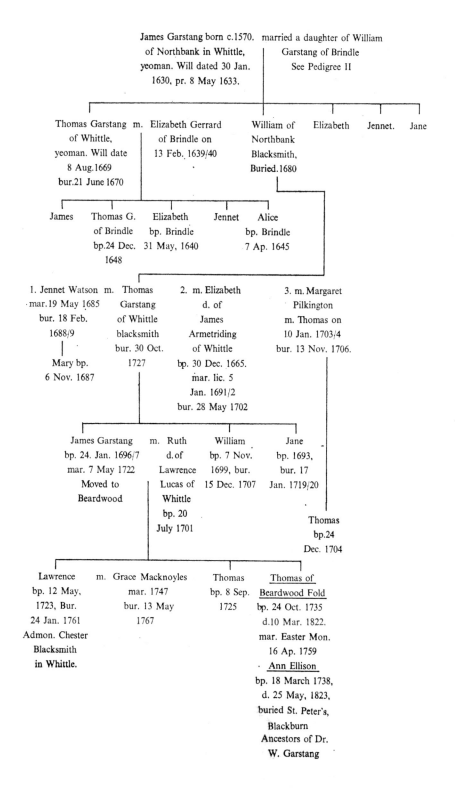

James Garstang born c.1570. married a daughter of William
of Northbank in Whittle, Garstang of Brindle
yeoman. Will dated 30 Jan. See Pedigree II
1630, pr. 8 May 1633.

Thomas Garstang m. Elizabeth Gerrard William of Elizabeth Jennet. Jane
of Whittle, of Brindle on Northbank
yeoman. Will date 13 Feb. 1639/40 Blacksmith,
8 Aug.1669 Buried.1680
bur.21 June 1670

James Thomas G. Elizabeth Jennet Alice
of Brindle bp. Brindle bp. Brindle
bp.24 Dec. 31 May, 1640 7 Ap. 1645
1648

1. Jennet Watson m. Thomas 2. m. Elizabeth 3. m. Margaret
mar.19 May 1685 Garstang d. of Pilkington
bur. 18 Feb. of Whittle James m. Thomas on
1688/9 blacksmith Armetriding 10 Jan. 1703/4
  bur. 30 Oct. of Whittle bur. 13 Nov. 1706.
Mary bp. 1727 bp. 30 Dec. 1665.
6 Nov. 1687 mar. lic. 5
  Jan. 1691/2
  bur. 28 May 1702

James Garstang m. Ruth William Jane
bp. 24. Jan. 1696/7 d. of bp. 7 Nov. bp. 1693,
mar. 7 May 1722 Lawrence 1699, bur. bur. 17
Moved to Lucas of 15 Dec. 1707 Jan. 1719/20
Beardwood Whittle
  bp. 20
  July 1701   Thomas
      bp.24
      Dec. 1704

Lawrence m. Grace Macknoyles Thomas Thomas of
bp. 12 May, mar. 1747 bp. 8 Sep. Beardwood Fold
1723, Bur. bur. 13 May 1725 bp. 24 Oct. 1735
24 Jan. 1761 1767 d.10 Mar. 1822.
Admon. Chester mar. Easter Mon.
Blacksmith 16 Ap. 1759
in Whittle. Ann Ellison
  bp. 18 March 1738,
  d. 25 May, 1823,
  buried St. Peter's,
  Blackburn
  Ancestors of Dr.
  W. Garstang

When James, the grandson of this William, married Ruth, the daughter of Lawrence Lucas of Whittle, he had inherited the family forges and he insisted that his elder son Lawrence should continue to manage them himself when he and his wife migrated to Blackburn. They bought the property at Beardwood Fold on the right hand side of the new road from Blackburn to Preston. I remember them well as we often passed them on our childhood walks. There were two charming little houses, the one nearer to Blackburn was thatched and had a beautiful flowery garden round it, the other was white with black beams and a wooden gate leading to a grassy paddock surrounded by a stone wall. This was the fold used by James and his younger son Thomas who had gone there with his parents from Whittle.

One day during one of our walks my brother Walter surprised us younger children by saying that the Beardwood property really belonged to Father, but he could not claim it for some mysterious reason, and the uncertainty only made the little houses more desirable. When I was six years old I remember sitting by the table to draw and paint the cottage with the black beams to send to Walter while he was an undergraduate in Oxford. I found the picture put away with Walter's family papers. There also I have found the reason for Father's reluctance to claim the property. Walter inherited the following information:

On 27 February 1756 James made his will leaving everything he possessed in Whittle and Beardwood Fold to his wife Ruth on certain conditions. She must remain as a widow, unmarried, or receive only 1/-. At her death all the property in both places must go to their two sons Lawrence and Thomas equally. Lawrence must continue the business of blacksmith and have the smithy in Whittle entirely to himself without letting it to any other.

The signature "James" was written boldly with a quill pen. On the 31 January 1761 Ruth made her own will: 'I Ruth Garstang of Beardwood in Blackburn do hereby promise, consent, and agree that my Grandsons Will and James Garstang, sons of my son Lawrence shall have one half or moiety of all the lands that belonged to my late husband.' At this point Lawrence added the following:

At the same time I Lawrence Garstang on condition that my two sons or one of them that may happen to be alive at the decease of their Grandmother have the said moiety, do hereby give and assign my title of the other moiety or half of the said lands lately belonging to my late father unto my brother Thomas Garstang.

Ruth and Lawrence's wife Grace signed their initials, R and G, the will was witnessed by Ralph Low, so both Ruth and Lawrence had agreed that the Beardwood property should belong to Thomas.

Lawrence died in 1761 and Grace in 1767. Thomas married Ann Ellison on Easter Monday 16 April 1759 and they lived in the White House at Beardwood, while the widow Ruth ended her life in the thatched cottage and never changed her will except to leave some 'leper houses' to her father William Lucas in an addendum.

In Pedigree IV. 24 the sons of Thomas and Ann are seen to have the names

James and Lawrence, and this is where some confusion arose about the ownership of Beardwood Fold. Lawrence wanted to farm and kept his sheep in
the fold; he remained a bachelor and lived in the White House having a
housekeeper. Ann, his widowed mother with her daughters lived in the
thatched cottage, and when the eldest son James married he lived with his
wife Alice in 'Tythe Barn House' at Lane End on Revidge Hill. James worked
as a miller and also at hand-loom weaving, using the Tythe barn. He had
written family details in a note book the way his father had done; this was
passed on to his eldest son Thomas who had accompanied him to Lane End
and wrote:

> Lawrence Garstang of Beardwood died 27 Feb. 1852 aged 80 years.
> James Garstang of Tythe Barn, Lane End, died 27 Feb. 1853, aged 89
> years.

So James was alive when his brother died, and we could not understand
why Grandfather Thomas did not go to live at Beardwood. Then Walter
found a letter from Father who was the eldest son of Thomas and clearly
owned the property:

> Lawrence's housekeeper (he being a bachelor) was a woman named
> Morris. Old Morris (presumably her father) brought a will from Man-
> chester maintaining that Lawrence had left Beardwood to his housekeeper.
> Then a man called Horsfield married another daughter of old Morris and
> seized the property.

As the property had been entailed it could not have been willed away
legally from the elder brother James. But James was an old man of 88 years
and probably had forgotten the facts of the entail, and his son Thomas had
probably never heard about it, so nothing was done to keep the property.

Now that we knew that it really should have been Walter's we all wanted
him to claim it, but he very wisely wrote to Uncle John, Father's younger
brother, and he replied:

> I think you will be wise to drop any idea re Beardwood as we dropped
> it after investigations. . . . Old Lawrence Garstang had not the right to
> will it away, the property being entailed and freehold; consequently it fell
> to your grandfather as heir at Law. Unfortunately my father did not lay
> claim to it, not understanding the situation. Our solicitor thought that the
> great lapse of time was sufficient to bar the claim. The mistake was made
> by my father in not claiming it legally when old Lawrence died, so my
> advice now is that you do not spend money or time or thought on the
> matter.

And so ended our hopes of living at Beardwood!

All the Garstangs who wrote to Walter about their ancestors believed that
originally their forefathers' home town had been Garstang, and Cecil Garstang
of London knew the date A.D. 832 for the arrival of the Viking Gair on the
banks of the Wyre. Cecil's grandfather had been the grandson of the
Lawrence (then spelt Lorance) who had stayed in Whittle to manage the

smithy when our ancestor Thomas went with their father James to Beardwood.

Another link with the same Lawrence is Winifred Garstang also of London, whose ancestor we found to be Lawrence's son William. See pp. 162-171.

A grandson of Lawrence was Thomas Garstang of Leyland about whose family we shall hear more later, and his great grand-daughter Alice reminded us of a legend published in a novel *The Garstangs of Garstang Grange,* by T. Adolphus Trollope in 1869. He claimed that the family had been known in Garstang before the families of Norman blood had settled in that neighbourhood, and their tendency to marry mates of the same Clan had inspired the theme of the story. He described one family inhabiting a lone grim stone-built house standing on a bleak cliff overlooking the sea to the west of Garstang. On the block of stone stretching across the chimney above the great kitchen fire was cut the dreadful verse of a curse;

When Garstang shall with Garstang mate,
The curse shall fall however late.

We had not read the book as children but we knew about the curse. I often wondered if the curse accounted for the fact that the little houses at Beardwood Fold could not belong to Father. It so happened that the grandson of the boy Thomas, who had been taken from Whittle to live in Beardwood Fold with his parents had married Hannah Garstang of Moss Fold in Lower Darwen on June 7th 1829, and their eldest son was my father "Walter" born in 1832, then John and James followed after intervals of two years, and one daughter Alice. On April 2nd 1837 Hannah and her fifth child born prematurely both died. We have her hymn book, with her name signed on August 20th 1820, the year the book was published in Blackburn as a *Supplement to Psalms and Hymns* by Dr. Watts. Many of them were my mother's favourite hymns, especially "Jesus, Lover of my Soul". (Pedigree III).

We did not know then that James, the yeoman of Whittle had already married a Garstang of Brindle, and that future marriages of two Garstangs would sometimes take place, as we shall now see. So I could have been comforted by the fact that the power of the curse must have been destroyed!

Granny's father, Roger, had worked as a miller after his elder brother had inherited the Moss Fold farm. He made his own clay pipes for smoking tobacco and also candles. We still used candles as children: wax candles in the bedrooms and on the piano, and tallow candles in the kitchen. These were all sold in bundles tied together by their wicks. Great Grandfather, Roger, had entered all these expenses very carefully in his note-book which came to Walter after Father's death:

3 loads of best meal at 35/-	5	5	0
85lbs. flour		14	10
169lbs. meal	1	9	9
Pipe clay			5½
1 gross pipes		1	9
3 doz. 2½ candles		18	5½
Wax			10½
7½lbs. tobacco	1	4	9
Tallow cakes			5½

Pedigree II

For wife of James Garstang of Whittle, a daughter of William G.

Garstang, bur. at Brindle; born c. 1530

born c. 1560. William Garstang
of Brindle, husbandman
Will dat. 23 Aug. 1622;
pr. 10 Oct. 1622

| John Garstang of Brindle, tanner. Will dat. 16 Mar. 1635; pr. 8 Jul. 1635; bur. B. 22 June 1635 | = Agnes Cowper Mar. B. 13 Jan. 1601/2 living 1635 | George Garstang bp. B. 25 June 1580; living 1635 | = ?Anne bur. B. 21 Jul. 1649 | James Garstang bp. B. 10 Feb. 1582/3 | Roger Garstang m. Alice Hacking. bur. B. 6 Dec. 1646 | Daughter Mar. James Garstang of Whittle See Ped. 1 |

| Thomas Garstang of Brindle, Tanner bp. B. 10 Feb. 1604/5; Will dat. 23 Aug. 1670; pr. 9 Nov. 1670; bur. B.* | William Garstang bur. B. 1 Feb. 1606/7 | William Garstang bp. B. 2 Feb. 1607/8; living 1635 ? mar. Margaret G. Nov. 30 1631 (B.) | John Garstang bp. B. 4 June 1612 | Alice bp. B. 4 June 1621. m. James Gerrard of St. Ellin Well. living 1635 |

"yeoman"
William
Garstang
living 1635.
m. 1644

William bp. 13 Oct. 1647	George bp. 29 Dec. 1648	Ann b. ca. 1645 m. Ch. Black. bur. Leyland 1711				
Elizabeth 23 May, 1656			William Garstang bp. B. 30 Jul. 1599	John Garstang bp. B. 26 Jul. 1602. living 1622	George Garstang living 1622	William Garstang bp. B. 15 Jan. 1610/11; bur. 12 June 1638
	Janet bp. Sept. 1677 (B.)					

Janet bp. B. 28 Sep. 1600 bur. 31 Jan. 1600/1

Margaret bp. B. 15 Sep. 1608; bur. 3 May 1636

* Thomas the Tanner 1604 - 1670 was fined for recusancy

One of his sons, Grandmother's brother John (1811-1876) (Pedigree III), was much respected by the townspeople of Blackburn, his obituary and photograph being printed in the Weekly Times:

> He was a Schoolmaster, and also held an official position at the Blackburn Savings Bank for upwards of 20 years. All who knew him will regret his removal from amongst us, his genial disposition endearing him to a large number of friends, and his admirable business qualities eminently fitting him for the post of Actuary, which he occupies at the Bank, and since his appointment in 1867 the posts of Actuary and Manager have always been combined.
>
> His conduct was ever that of a straight forward man, who observed the strictest integrity in all his dealings. He taught a private Academy in Paradise Lane, and when he received the Savings Bank appointment he gave his school a half-holiday on Wednesdays as well as Saturdays, for those were Savings Bank days. In forty years his salary had increased from £20 to £200.
>
> In 1843 he was also Mathematical Master at the Blackburn Grammar School.

Towards the end of 1837 (after the death of Hannah), my grandfather married Susanna Pilkington, their children being one daughter, Eliza, and one son, Luke. Luke's daughter Adelaide was the mother of my cousin Bessie who, with her husband George Squibb, discovered the births, marriages, and deaths, of many Garstangs round Leyland and Whittle.

One of the friends of my father and his brothers and sisters was a great grand-daughter of Thomas Garstang who had married Ann Ellison in 1759. Ann was the daughter of a well-known Blackburn townsman and had received as wedding presents, not only £100 from her father, but a beautiful China tea-service, although tea at that time cost a guinea for 1lb. One of these cups was shewn to us when it must have been a hundred years old. This old Thomas, as well as looking after his sheep at Beardwood Fold had been appointed Surveyor of Highways for the Parish of Blackburn, thus following in the footsteps of Anthony Garstang who in 1598 held a similar post in nearby Amounderness. In his old note-book Thomas had written many of the medical prescriptions handed down from his father James Garstang, all this group of the Clan being very interested in medicine, e.g.

For rheumatism
Take of white Mustard seed three teaspoonful a day, one in the morning at 7 o'clock, another in the forenoon at 11, and another at night; so continue to use it for 3 or 4 months. Also bathe the parts affected every night with Ling Liver oil.

For Burns
Put $\frac{1}{2}$lb. of Camphor broken into 1 pint good rum. Keep it well corked up in a bottle. Apply it with a linen rag to the part affected and the pain will entirely disappear.

There were many other useful remedies probably used by Ann, as they had a large family of two sons and seven daughters, the second child being my great-grandfather James.

This James was interested in recording the exact time as well as the date of all events connected with his family, such as:

Thomas, my father, son of James and Ruth Garstang, was baptised 24th October 1738. Ann, his wife, was baptised 18th March, 1738.

Jane, one of my grandfather's aunts, had lived with her mother and sisters after the death of her father in the thatched house at Beardwood Fold, while her brother Lawrence kept the White House. When Jane married Robert Diggles she went to live at Moulden Water on the banks of a small tributary of the river Darwen, then a picturesque clear stream about four miles to the south-west of Blackburn. Robert used the water power to grind wheat and kept the flour till sold in a large barn. This business appealed to James when he bought the Tythe Barn, and he also had become a miller, keeping the flour in the great barn, but there is no record of his manner of grinding it; perhaps he used a wind-mill as there is certainly no stream along the ridgeway. One of his note books contained transactions in sacks of flour, while my grandfather was interested also in the buying and selling of property.

1849 purchased premises in Blakey Street from Mrs. Green.
1849 purchased a house from Geo. Haworth of Burnley for £20.
1849 purchased a house from trustees of late John Hartley.
1854 purchased a house in St. Paul's St. from Jonathan Brocklehurst £141.
1855 commissioned J. Kershaw to erect 3 dwelling houses and shop in Bond Street for £200 on ground of Joseph Fielden, Esq.
1862 Bought John Ward's house in Mellor for £50.

Tythe Barn South side wants repairs, over the little door some side bricks wanting.
North corner about a yard and a quarter wants three or four brick posts.
The North-west slates want pointing.

Then would follow recipes, prescriptions, and amusing poems or anecdotes, while on the fly-leaf he wrote:

Thomas Garstang's Book
November 10th 1822.
Whatever distress
Awaits us below
Such plentiful Grace
Will Jesus bestow
He still will support us
And silence our fear
For nothing can hurt us
While Jesus is near.   END

The following poem which Grandfather had copied reminds me of the way my brother John used to use letters to stand as words in writing notes to me:

Lines addressed to a Lady on seeing the cipher U X L engraved on her seal.

UXL in all you tell, in all U take in hand
What e'er it be U let us see
That you can praise command.
What e'er U do
Is matched by few
U always do XL
Merit doth lurk
In all your work
U always do it well.
These lines to U addressed, are true,
No flattery lurketh here,
And I can tell that U X L
And all your friends revere.

This is copied from a newspaper-cutting pasted into the diary:

Dean Jackson, passing one morning through Christ Church quadrangle, Oxford, was met by some Under Graduates, who walked along without *capping;* the Dean called one of them, and asked,
"Do you know who I am?" "No, Sir."
"How long have you been in College?" "Eight days, Sir."
"Oh, very well," said the Dean, walking away, "puppies don't open their eyes till the ninth day."

.   .   .   .

This is pasted on another page:

A parent, anxious for his little boy to obtain promotion at school, asked him one day how he ranked in his class.
"Oh, Pa," said he, "I am the top but two."
"That's a darling," said the fond parent, "and tell me how many scholars your class consists of?"
"Three, Sir," whispered the little prodigy.
Like many previous Garstangs Grandfather was also intensely interested in the churches of the neighbourhood, and recorded in his diary the dates when foundation stones were laid for various new churches to be built at the end of William IV's reign and in the early years of Queen Victoria's:

Feniscowles Church, first stone laid by Mr. Fielden, Esq., M.P. for Blackburn, on Thursday Feb. 5th 1835.
Witton Church, the first stone laid by Joseph Fielden on Oct. 8th 1836.

The Fielden family owned most of the land in and around Blackburn, and the General lived in a large house in Witton Park. We always went there for Church field-days when the town brass-band played while we as children amused ourselves with all sorts of games, and in the evening young men and maidens danced to their music. The Blackburnians were invited to walk any where over the grass lands in the park, and over beautiful Billinge Hill nearby until the people began to damage trees and leave untidy litter.
To continue with Grandfather's notes:

On October 5th 1837, the first stone laid in Trinity Church Blackburn by the Bishop.

Trinity Church Blackburn opened for Divine Service the first time on Sunday January 11th 1846.

His accounts were also carefully kept and prices are surprising:

April 10th 1828, paid to John Palmer for a suit of clothes making 16/-.

April 14th 1841, bot. a cage of Cunliff for 4/- and paid 2/3 for knobbing the same, and 7d. for glass front.

March 10th 1841, bot. a Chist of Drawers for £-16s.-0d. at a sale in Northgate.

The next entries seem to show that watches were still rare and difficult to repair. Even my father's gold watch was very large and was wound up by a separate key like a clock:

June 17th 1833, bot. a watch of Thomas Brodrick's at Preston for £2-11s.-0d., name inside Henry Holme, West Preston 1797.

April 1st 1844, exchanged a watch value £2-11s.-0d. for a lever watch and gave £2-6s.-0d. in exchange, which makes the said watch to cost £4-17s.-0d.

June 27th 1859, exchanged the above watch with Mr. Brown, watch-maker of Preston, and gave £5 which makes the present watch to cost £7-17s.-0d.

Although Grandfather's note book was beautifully bound in good leather, still sound after all these years, it had cost only 1s. The last entry in his accounts is:

Paid 8/6 for my Father's Will, and £26-17s.-6d. in Tythe.

The rest of the book is filled with prescriptions for various ailments after the manner of Great-Grandfather's recipes already mentioned. The amounts in the prescriptions are very carefully given, also the times per day when they are to be taken or applied by rubbing or poultice.

It is not surprising that at an early age my father decided to study medicine as many other Garstangs at that time did. He was apprenticed, as the custom was, to a well-known doctor who practised in Bradford. After this practical experience he enjoyed studying for higher and ever higher degrees, always wanting to know more. There is a very long letter (another Victorian custom) written before his 21st birthday, from Glasgow to his father (Thomas) describing the town and university where he was studying, and this letter soon followed:

Saturday, April 12, 1853.

Dear Father,

The second half of the £5 Bank note arrived in due course. I propose to go up for the M.D. examination and hope to be successful. The examination extends over four days, commencing on the first Monday in May; so that I may be expected home the following Saturday, or early the week after. My intention was to spend a day or two at the sea-side or in some romantic locality, after I shall have got over that examination; but as you are not very well just now, and as I feel best when I am busily employed at some kind of work, I think I shall come home as soon as I can.

Regarding the money matters which you say I had better leave to you, I shall merely observe that, while I feel much pleasure in leaving the arrangement to you, *yet in reality I myself am the sole person on whom I would have the responsibility of their payment to rest, and feel proud to say that I myself am the man who expects to have ere long every farthing repaid.* On this account therefore it behoves me that I spend as little money as possible, and that, more importantly, I get into active employment as soon as I can. This I find to be all the more necessary for my own health's sake; for the constitution of man's frail body is such, that it must be supplied with an abundance of good food; then it must have plenty of honest work to do, together with exercise in the open air, to the end that the food may do it good, or in other words, may nourish it. And this leads me to remark that I consider neither the constitution of your own, nor mine, nor John's, nor James' nor Alice's, nor Eliza's, nor Luke's body to be of the very best material; so that we all have need, separately, and for one another, to practise, and so far as common sense teaches, the best means of procuring our bodily health. And, lo! this is the very thing which *God* has appointed us to do! And how remarkable it is, that God, in his good providence, has raised up one of us a doctor! and has implanted in his mind an uncontrollable thirst for knowledge, has given him skill to apply that knowledge, to the intent that he may lay a soothing and comforting hand on his brethren in their afflictions: and, above all, has so ordered it, that he feels a pleasure inexpressible whenever he has that solemn portion of his duties to perform! What say you to this?

I should like to know by what means you have come to the conclusion that you 'would interrupt me in my studies' by telling me that you were ill. This has puzzled me not a little. And when I recall to my memory the fact that I have again and again urged upon you a request that you would mention your ailments to me, whenever they should assail; and that the almost last word I addressed to you before I left home was to the effect that if you should happen to be unwell at any time, on writing to me, I would advise immediately on receipt of the letter. I say, when I think of such things, I cry out alas! for my anxiety for others' welfare! How is it my words take so little effect. Herein, I think I may say, I am altogether blameless. Before leaving home I well remember I dwelt particularly upon the fact that, however busy I might make myself here, I said *I would always find time to write home, and that immediately, should circumstances demand.* How then could you with any show of reason be afraid of 'interrupting me in my studies'? I may state this grave truth—and I trust it may leave an everlasting impression—that I have been more interrupted and annoyed by suspense of news from home, and consequently by suspicions of ill, than by any other circumstance or event within the range of my recollection: and that very suspense was one of those evils which last winter conspired to throw me into a fever.

But it will all blow over, and be entirely done away with in the course of two or three weeks and it will be a long time ere I shall wish to pass three such winters as the last!

I need say nothing more on this point, as I am sure you know my mind concerning it as well as I do myself, and it is to be hoped that, if you need advice, you will take the earliest opportunity to inform me. Who have you in all the world in whom you can implicitly confide as in your own son?

Word arrived to a student from England—a person for whom I have great respect—that his mother has died, after a very short illness on Saturday last; a circumstance which for the present has upset that young man entirely. I believe he comes to Glasgow in much the same position as I did; the present is his second winter, and from what he has told me I learn that his mother was the only person that had an heartfelt desire to see her son a member of the profession. And yet she died without being permitted to wish her son Godspeed!

I say to myself, well, surely I am not going to stand, in regard to my father, in the same predicament as he, in regard to his departed mother. NO! Let me assure my father that he is yet only just turned the prime of life, and only 56 years of age; *that he has yet to live retired in his own house in the country;* and that his sons, in flourishing businesses in their native town, will come a-visiting him on the fine evenings of summer, when the hedges are bedecked with lily-white blooms, and the roses are in flower, and the pinks are in flower, and when many a little peggy, and linnet, and thrush, are sending up their sweet wood-notes in harmony to heaven, but my eyes are brim full of tears, and I cannot see to write.

Yours most affectionately,
W. Garstang.

My father had written in red ink all the words now in italics in that letter. I was particularly interested to see that my grandfather used to send money by post in the form of Bank of England notes which he had cut into two halves, as my father used to do the same if he was sending money to my eldest brother when he was an undergraduate in Oxford. I always wondered why I was so often given half a note to enclose with my letters to Walter when I was a child, but I suppose it must have been the only safe way in the early days of the Post Office, and before the invention of cheques to represent money.

Father's references to the flowers and birds at the end of his letter show how the love of nature must have been inherited from him in all of us; for gardening and bird watching have given most of us more pleasure than any other pastime, even taming the wild birds to take food from our hands has been possible.

When my father writes of going home after his examination, it would be to the house at Lane End where a steep road from Blackburn, known as Duke's Brow, entered the ridge way, known as Revidge. Beyond the Revidge Road on the crest of the hill stretched pastures and woodlands towards the village of Mellor.

In some of his letters Father chaffs his father for thinking the walks to Mellor and Billinge Hill from the Lane End Barn were too long. Father was a great walker and the distance of the few miles mentioned was just a stroll to any of us as children.

While he was studying in Glasgow Father wrote frequently to his brothers and sisters, the following was his first letter to Alice on arriving there for a new term:

When the train arrived at Carlisle I was greatly disappointed with the place. It seemed somewhat larger than our Darwen, the shops and inns seemed fitted up in an inferior way, approaching to what I should call a rather low scale of elegance. The Carlisle prison or gaol is an extensive one, and it is built of a reddish sort of stone. A very plain structure, but grim looking and disheartening.

I had an hour's stay here, and had the misfortune to need two cups of coffee. (I told them I had something to eat, but they brought some bread and butter for all that) for which I was to pay 1/-, and I was insane enough to pay it; but the coffee didn't agree well because it was too expensive! I found the bread and meat that you had put up for me exceedingly useful. However I shall never require any more coffee in Carlisle at 6d. a cup.

The country at this stage of my journey was eminently beautiful and verdant, being in a high state of cultivation and naturally fruitful; it contrasted strangely with the recently seen moors and hills of Cumberland, and the dark shadowy clouds above them. Then came Gretna Green, or rather we came to it—a really lovely spot. No wonder the runaway brides and bridegrooms are attracted thither—green velvety grass and foliage under their feet, and a smokeless sky over their heads! The song of birds—the bliss and quiet of Paradise—the breath of the Garden of Eden or indeed of any garden—and the dance of their own lightsome hearts, too often, alas! of a momentary character. These, these are the charms, the one grand characteristic of the climate in Gretna Green! The wedding place or Registry is a plain stone house, without the least attraction about it itself, which circumstance will a little astonish the expectation of the curious.

A little distance farther on brought us to a narrow puny stream, which is said to divide England from Scotland. I need scarcely say that I passed over it without feeling any decided shock of impression. So farewell old England!

A very fine country for many miles is Scotland, and then I beheld the looming of the distant hills. Here and there a house struck the sight, only one storey high, thatched roof. It would be after seven o'clock when the train arrived at the junction where the line branches off for Edinburgh. I did not here much notice the country as I was getting weary, and there was nothing worth looking at. Bye the bye I smelt the breath, not of an Englishman, but of the furnaces of two or three Iron Works, else, so far as I could see, there had been a total absence of factory chimneys etc. from Lancaster to within 20 miles of Glasgow, perhaps here and there one, and a few about Carlisle.

At length the train arrived at a place something like but longer than Yates' foundry yard. A little farther and it was Glasgow itself, and the time 8½ p.m. However I walked in some of the principal streets, and to the General Post Office, where two letters were awaiting my arrival, but which were not to my purpose. I now began to revolve in my noodle the question of a night's lodging. I inspected several beds (not very clean and welcome ones) in several localities in the space of an hour. At last I got into one, not because I selected it, but because I was forced to it as it was after 10 p.m. I awoke, or was awakened at 5½ next morning, and looking out of the window, found myself on a level with the house tops, that is to say, I was 4 or 5 storeys from the ground floor! In a room 3½ yds. by 3 which might not have been cleaned for 6 months! O Sweet Glasgow!!

Next day I hunted suitable lodgings, and inspected again several rooms in different localities; of course I durst not ask about any below the third storey on account of expense.

I now unexpectedly slipped into or rather up to a room immediately below the room of the house in which I now am, but that room had just been taken, and I was directed to the ground floor. Here was a room which a medical student was at that moment leaving. That room was 58 Weaver Street in which I now write and reside. But such descriptions would be endless, so I shall bring this letter to a close.

This letter has an attractive wood-cut of the port of Glasgow, etched on the top of the first page, a bridge in the distance, and dozens of tall masted sailing ships in the foreground. The second page shows a view of the city from the north-west corner of Blythswood Square: two men in top hats, light grey trousers, frock coats, two women in light long dresses and mantles with dark hats, and a small boy in long trousers, belted long coat and large hat standing in the foreground with a dog; a hill on the left, trees and a few long important-looking buildings with trees and grass to the right, no other people, no carriages or carts. The next page has a wood-cut of the University building, solidly built in stone, four storeys high, pillars by the imposing front-door, a church spire in the distance, a carriage and pair, a horse and cart, and six people in the wide straight street. My father continues:

I have already seen everything of importance in the city, and am on the eve of fixing my course of study, to which I am anxious to apply myself as soon as possible. The session commences next Tuesday. Glasgow is a fine city—finer than Liverpool, but its harbour is not nearly so capacious. From what I recollect of Liverpool, Manchester, Bradford, Leeds, Sheffield, Birmingham, Wolverhampton, Preston, etc. etc., the city of Glasgow is larger and superior to any of these places. Indeed it has exceeded my most sanguine expectations. It is built of stone, quite a Londonized Manchester. The wealthier classes walk the streets in great numbers, and are richly dressed—males and females or both Ladies and Gentlemen I ought to say!

There is nothing peculiarly Scottish in the features of the Upper Classes, the majority are well made and well found, and look exceedingly healthy. I never before have seen such an array of shops as are here. The shop windows are crammed full of things, no matter what or how costly—Books, draperies, gold and silver watches, clothes, hats, bonnets, groceries, loaves, chinaware, etc. etc., quite past my enumeration. I consider things are much cheaper here than in any other place with which I am acquainted —a cap like our James has is 2/6, a pair of shoes like mine from Brindles 8/-, Cloth trousers 15/-, Stays 1/6 to 2/-, collars 3 ply like those you made for me 6d. each, a Duplex watch with *true* seconds, although not centre, movement same as the one I was about to exchange £5 17s. 6d., etc. etc. etc. etc.

There is a grand cemetery (or Necropolis, as it is called) here; it overlooks a considerable portion of the city, which, seen from the cemetery, has rather an oriental aspect. It is behind the venerable Cathedral, in a southerly direction. In the middle of the Necropolis, which is the highest part, is a vast fluted column and statue to the memory of the celebrated John Knox the Reformer. A little below to the west is a sculptured figured mass of masonry among a great number of others bearing the following inscription:

"To John Henry Alexander.
Fallen is the curtain the last scene is o'er.
The favourite actor treads life's stage no more,
Oft lavish plaudits from the crowd he drew,
And laughing eyes confess'd his humour true,
Here proud affection rears this sculptured stone
For virtues not enacted, but his own—
A constancy unshaken unto death,
A true unswerving and a Christian's faith,
Who knew him best have cause to mourn him most.
Oh weep the man, more than the actor lost,
Unnumbered parts he played, yet to the end,
His best were those of husband, father, friend."

But I must bring my scribbling to a close; at all events I have no more pictured paper, although more could be had for money—but what I have sent will perhaps suffice for the present.

If you cannot make out some of the words, our John will, I have had no time for pre-composition, or pre-meditation. I cannot say exactly if it is colder here than in Blackburn. Perhaps it is a little, but not much felt in the streets, although the wind has been north or north-east. But there is no need for a fire in my room, especially as on Tuesday I shall have something else to do.

The motto of the tradespeople here seems to be to sell at *some* price, and the motto of the people generally, to get money any how; how far I am right, experience has not yet informed me.

Perhaps James will keep an eye on Mason's watch for a little time, to see whether he will dispose of it elsewhere.

Trusting your health will severally remain good,
     I remain,
                    Yours affectionately,
                    W. Garstang.

This letter was written in 1856 and at the end of the summer term in that year Father received a small prize for the best work of the year. In the previous year when working as an assistant in Bradford he asked his brother James to send him "once a week, or once in ten days, the *sides* of four or five of the Times Newspapers containing the Leading Articles neatly folded as you would a Newspaper. It would afford me an exceeding rich supply of intellectual variation if now and again you enclosed an article from the Morning Chronicle, Daily News. This is a good work, and it deserves to be carried on by you!"

From Bradford on Oct. 14th, 1854 he had written also to Alice:

I have no need to tell you that we lately were greatly deluded by a false telegraphic despatch reporting the fall of Sepastopol, which censored though it was, caused much hilarity among us here, as was manifested by a general relaxation of all kinds of labour (except physic), the pealing of bells

Matilda Mary Garstang

Dr. Walter Garstang

In the churches, the booming of cannon, a multitude of flags and colours waving on the roofs of warehouses, factories etc.!

For about ten years after he had taken his degrees Father worked in hospitals and under the Poor Law Authority gaining experience, and riding long distance on horse-back to visit patients in outlying districts. I remember my sister Florence telling me that, after his reputation had been established, he had been called to Valemont, Over Darwen, the home of James Wardley who was the owner of one of the new steam-driven cotton mills, and there his son was suffering great pain from an accident on the hunting field.

When Father arrived at the drive gate on his horse as usual, a young lady ran from the house to open the gate and then she held it open for him to pass through to the house. She was wearing a sunbonnet, and expressed her pleasure and relief at his arrival so charmingly that he thereupon decided that she must be the wife he would choose. She was the second daughter of James Wardley, Matilda Mary, and it was her most beloved brother who was in the house suffering great pain from a fall while riding to hounds.

Father's hope was realised, and he married her within a few months of this meeting. I remember her as a gentle-faced Mother, her brown hair parted down the middle, and with smiling large brown eyes. In the photograph at the time of her wedding her hair is dressed in ringlets reaching to her shoulders, and she is wearing a long silk gown with the skirt draped over a crinoline (see facing plate).

The following announcement of the marriage is taken from the *Blackburn Standard* of 21 February 1866:

> The marriage was solemnised on the 14th instant at Over Darwen, by the Rev. Professor Harley, F.R.S., and the Rev. Chas. Stovel, of Walter Garstang, Esq., F.R.C.S.E., L.R.C.P.L., of Blackburn, to Matilda Mary. second daughter of James Wardley, Esq., of Valemont, Over Darwen.

After the ceremony the wedding guests were invited to Grandfather's house in Darwen where the refreshments had been prepared for them.

Menu

The wedding breakfast at Valemont, Wednesday, February 14th, 1866.

Soups

Jardiniere   Oyster

Fish

Salmon à la mayonnaise

Entrées

Sweetbreads   Mushrooms   Ragout of Venison

Cullotes of Lamb with Asparagus

Braised Salmon

Relevés

Roast Lamb   Spiced Hump of Beef

Galantine of Veal

Game Pies   Savoury Pies   Hams   Tongues

Turkey with Truffles   Capons Roast Pheasants

Fowls à la Béchamel   Aspic Soles

Lobster Salads   Lobster Patties

Aspic Beef

Aspic of Lobster

Aspic Veal

Shrimp Patties

Entremêts

Orange Jelly   Charlotte Russe

Wine Jelly

Dessert

Pines, Grapes, Pears, etc.

Ices

Strawberry à la Nesselrode   Strawberry Cream

Orange Water

The work-people assembled at the mill of Grandfather and his brother to celebrate the occasion on the following Saturday. Their festivities are described in the following extract taken from the *Blackburn Standard* of February 23rd, 1866:

On Saturday last the work-people employed by Messrs C. and James Wardley, calico printers, Spring Vale, Over Darwen, assembled in one of the rooms of the works, which had been tastefully decorated for the occasion, and partook of an excellent tea from tables well supplied by a variety of eatables, in celebration of the marriage on the previous Thursday, February 14th, 1866, between Walter Garstang, Esq., M.D., of Blackburn, and Matilda Mary, second daughter of James Wardley, Esq., of Valemont, Over Darwen, when the service was conducted by the Rev. Professor Harley, F.R.S., and the Rev. Charles Stovel.

After tea when the tables were removed, Charles Wardley, Esq., of Manchester, was called to the chair, and opened the proceedings with a neat and suitable speech. The usual toasts were given with "The health and prosperity to the newly wedded pair."

The company afterwards engaged in dancing and amusing games, interspersed with recitations and songs until eleven o'clock.

The table of close relationships in Pedigree V will explain who were the parents of the different cousins and half-cousins whose names occur throughout the narrative.

My parents at first lived in a large Georgian house in the centre of Blackburn, which was then one of the newly developed towns where the industrial revolution in the manufacture of textiles had transformed pastoral Lancashire.

King Street, where the house stood, had been the residential area of the old market town, but it was becoming commercialized; by 1870 shops and warehouses lined the pavements, and in the smaller streets leading off from the main thoroughfare, cotton mills with huge chimneys belching smoke broke the monotony of small terraced houses opening straight on to the flagged side-walks, with back yards (but no gardens) to which access was gained through a covered passage-way between every dozen houses to a narrow cobbled lane. This was known as an 'entry' and it ran straight along the backs of the yards to enable the men to carry away the refuse bins and tubs which were the only forms of sanitation. These houses were inhabited by the operatives who had flocked to the town from the countryside to work in the cotton and a few woollen mills. Except on Sundays their clogs clacked along the roughly cobbled streets or flagged pavements of the side-walks each morning around six o'clock, the men wearing cloth caps, a red spotted handkerchief tied round their necks; the women and girls protected their heads and shoulders from the cold or rain by large brown or grey patterned woven shawls.

On turning to the right from the house one came to a crossing of four roads, straight forward led to the Railway Station, that to the left opened into the Market Square, and to the right a wider road provided a tramway to the neighbouring town of Darwen. Down the middle of this road tram lines were laid with double lines at intervals for crossing. The noisy tram was drawn by two strong horses with an extra one plying backwards and forwards to help up a hill, and this was the way to reach our grandfather Wardley's house, Valemont.

If one turned to the left from the house a side road led to Saint Peter's Church which was attended by the family, and opposite to it was a tiny Grammar School with small diamond paned windows to light the two main rooms. This establishment had provided education since the time of Queen Elizabeth I for the sons of such parents as thought it was either necessary or desirable.

Beyond St. Peter Street the thoroughfare gradually became narrower and eventually led to a country lane, surrounded by the colourful hills of Lancashire, from the near heather-covered slopes of Billinge Hill to the region of distant Pendle, the reputed home of witches, to the right; and on the left the well-known moors round Tockholes.

On December 15th 1866 there was great rejoicing in my parents' home when their first baby was born. She was christened Ida Wardley, then after about two year intervals in each case appeared Walter, Florence, and Alice who, though christened Alice after Father's only sister, was usually called 'Daisy', because she always looked so bright and cheerful when she smiled up at Mother from the cradle.

During this period my mother was able to make friends with her new neighbours and with Father's relations in other towns and villages. Instead of riding to his patients he was able to drive with her to visit his patients' houses. In 1868 he had evidently been trying to make up a party to visit an exhibition in Darwen. They had missed the opening ceremonies and on 25th of May he received a disappointing letter from Dr. James Garstang whose medical practice was centred in Clitheroe:

> I am very much obliged by your kind offer to accompany me to the Darwen Exhibition—I have not been yet, but I think I shall try to get over there before it closes—somehow one loses the relish of sight seeing as one gets older. I shall be in Blackburn before long, and I will call to see you at your fresh residence.
> Accept my thanks. With kind regards to your good lady and yourself, believe me sincerely yours,
>
>   J. Garstang.

The 'fresh residence' of which Dr. James speaks would be the house in King Street where Father had established a thriving practice at the time of his marriage. This James Garstang must have been a generation older than Father as he, like my own grandfather Thomas, could claim as his Garstang great-grandfather the James of Whittle who had departed to Blackburn and lived in Beardwood Fold. From the following table it can be seen that a contemporary would be Dr. Thomas Blacklidge Garstang, the nephew of Dr. James of Clitheroe. From him in the same year 1868 Father received a more favourable reply about the suggested visit to the Darwen Exhibition:

>   Bolton.
> My wife and I have arranged to visit the Darwen Exhibition tomorrow. We shall be there about noon and should be glad if it be quite convenient and if the weather be congenial, to meet you and Mrs. G. there.
>   In haste, yours very truly,
>   T. B. Garstang.

Dr. Thomas's second wife who is mentioned in this letter was Miss Jane Pohlman, whose family had come originally from the Harz Mountains in Germany, but she was probably half English and she became very friendly with my mother. Her father owned a pianoforte factory in Halifax, and her two sons were Arthur Harold of Southport and Samuel Kay who continued to live in Bolton-le-Moor, a thriving and important town in the cotton industry, and before the reign of James I, in the woollen trade. My father often visited Bolton but Dr. Thomas died before I was born. Even in those days the uncle in his letter spoke of my mother in the respectful way as 'your good lady', and the nephew with the more friendly 'Mrs. G.', and in the following note of the same year even as 'your better half'!

16th July, 1868

You will perceive on reading the accompanying documents that Dr. Synnott who is a Med. man in Halifax—is anxious to become F.R.C.S.E. and wants your recommendation—a form which I suppose is necessary. I believe he is a very respectable man and that you may venture to recommend him without fear. If you see your way to doing this will you be good enough to forward the accompanying documents to his address in Halifax.

Pedigree III.

The Garstangs of Lower Darwen.
William
Husbandman of Lower Darwen
Will proved 16 May 1775

Thomas 1750-1809 of
Moss Bridge Farm, Moss Fold, Lower Darwen
m. Betty Croft 1756-1840

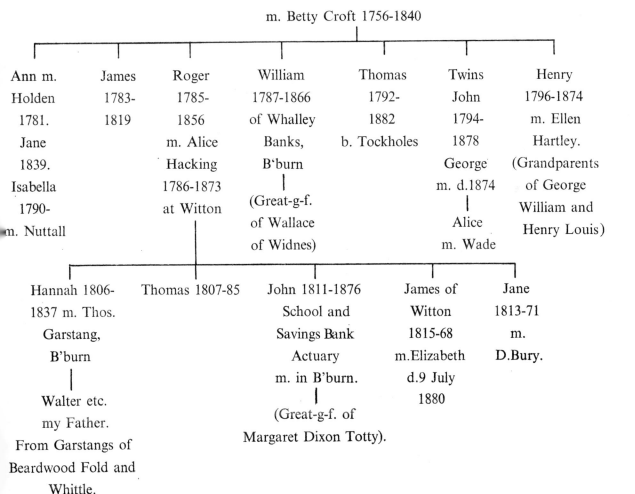

Ann m.	James	Roger	William	Thomas	Twins	Henry
Holden	1783-	1785-	1787-1866	1792-	John	1796-1874
1781.	1819	1856	of Whalley	1882	1794-	m. Ellen
Jane		m. Alice	Banks,	b. Tockholes	1878	Hartley.
1839.		Hacking	B'burn		George	(Grandparents
Isabella		1786-1873			m. d.1874	of George
1790-		at Witton	(Great-g-f.			William and
m. Nuttall			of Wallace		Alice	Henry Louis)
			of Widnes)		m. Wade	

Hannah 1806-	Thomas 1807-85	John 1811-1876	James of	Jane
1837 m. Thos.		School and	Witton	1813-71
Garstang,		Savings Bank	1815-68	m.
B'burn		Actuary	m.Elizabeth	D.Bury.
		m. in B'burn.	d.9 July	
Walter etc.			1880	
my Father.		(Great-g-f. of		
From Garstangs of		Margaret Dixon Totty).		
Beardwood Fold and				
Whittle.				

c

I hope you, your wife, and son are well. Accept my sincere thanks for your kind inquiries after my health—I am a little better than I have been, but still far from well—I need not say how glad we should be to see you and your better half over here. We were sorry we missed you when you were over in Bolton recently.

The 'son' mentioned in this letter would be my eldest brother Walter, who would be the only boy at that time. Father had been thinking of taking the practice in Bradford where he had formerly acted as the assistant of an old physician and where he had been very happy; but after he married my mother he had remembered that in 1865 he had received from Dr. James Garstang the name of an assistant of his own whom he then recommended as a suitable person to help my father: he was a "good midwife and knew what he was about." Now that Father had decided not to go to Bradford he had evidently written again about this assistant as on July 11th, 1871 Dr. James wrote again:

I was surprised some time ago when told by John Walsh at Bank Top that you were thinking of leaving Blackburn. I always looked upon you as a settled resident in your native town. . . .
In reply to your enquiry about my late assistant, I shall be glad if I can help him for the sake of his wife and family of three children. . . . He is not without talent and I have no doubt would earn a livelihood if he attended properly to his duties—His conduct has not been good, but I have received such earnest promises of amendment that I have consented again to help

Pedigree IV.

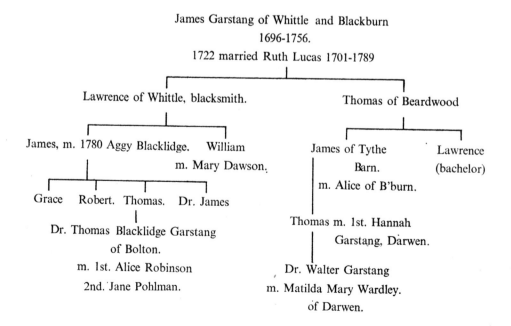

James Garstang of Whittle and Blackburn
1696-1756.
1722 married Ruth Lucas 1701-1789

Lawrence of Whittle, blacksmith.   Thomas of Beardwood

James, m. 1780 Aggy Blacklidge.   William   James of Tythe   Lawrence
                        m. Mary Dawson.   Barn.   (bachelor)
                                        m. Alice of B'burn.

Grace   Robert. Thomas.   Dr. James
            Dr. Thomas Blacklidge Garstang   Thomas m. 1st. Hannah
                of Bolton.   Garstang, Darwen.
            m. 1st. Alice Robinson
                2nd. Jane Pohlman.   Dr. Walter Garstang
                                    m. Matilda Mary Wardley.
                                        of Darwen.

him altho' my confidence in him is wavering—This is my opinion of this unfortunate man.

With kind regards and good wishes to you and yours, I am

Yours truly,

J. Garstang.

Father had taken his L.R.C.P. in 1859 and the Medical Register for February 1871 announced his success in gaining his M.R.C.P. This higher degree made a great difference to his position as a doctor; for now instead of attending vast numbers of patients in his surgery, he was entitled to become a consultant physician, so in the spring of 1874 he decided to move the family to another district of the town, away from the smoking mill chimneys. The only house available, and in a suitable position for his work, was at the corner where a steep paved street joined the new highway to Preston. It was known as Strawberry Bank Villa, but there were no strawberries and it seemed too small after the many-roomed King Street house. Mother needed a holiday, so to avoid the extra fatigue of a removal, she went away with Ida who was then seven years old, to stay in Mitcham with her sister Sarah McMaster, leaving Emma Biddulph and her sister Mary to manage the removal with Lavinia the cook.

Aunt Sarah's daughters were taught by a governess at home, so Ida, who was about the same age as Mary, learned her lessons with them, and was very happy indeed. In July Mother's second son was born while she was away from home, and he was christened Thomas James, the first name after Grandfather Garstang, and the second, James, after Grandfather Wardley. Mother stayed away nearly a year while Father tried to find a larger house in the right position, but there seemed to be no other houses empty, so he took Strawberry Bank on a lease and also Bridge Cottage in the charming nearby village of Whalley for the summer months. So Mother came home in June, 1875, and received a tumultuous welcome from Father, Walter, Florrie and Daisy, who were all longing to see the new baby boy. Ida had been left behind to continue her lessons with her cousins.

Another year dawned and on May 5th a third son was born, this time uncle John Garstang became his godfather, and so John, the new baby, was christened after him. When he was a month old, Mother took the children to Whalley with the exception of Walter; he stayed behind with Father as he was a pupil at the school for young boys known as 'Lower Bank Academy'. Ida had come home because Aunt Sarah became very ill and was taken to hospital; on June 13th 1876 she died of smallpox. It was lucky that Father had insisted on all the babies being vaccinated, so Ida was safe.

The day Mother heard about the death of Aunt Sarah she received a little note from Walter forwarded by Father from Strawberry Bank. Walter was only eight years old and he must have been very strictly instructed in polite letter writing to have composed such a very prim note, not even mentioning the new baby John who was little more than a month old.

June 12, 1876.

My dear Parents,

I now take the pleasure of writing a few lines to you. We are breaking up on Saturday next and on Thursday the drawings finished during the half-year will be laid out for inspection of Parents and Friends, and the result of the examination will then be known.

With kind love I remain
Your effectionate son,
W. Garstang.

The distribution of prizes took place at the Academy on the Thursday morning and an account of the exhibition of drawings was printed in the Blackburn Times for December 23rd 1876. The landscapes and mechanical drawings, both in water colours, and architectural designs were highly praised.

After a short visit with the family in Whalley Father thought that Walter should go to Clitheroe for a few days to stay with Aunt Alice and Uncle Whewell, and he posted a letter from Whalley on the Saturday to tell them to expect Walter on the Sunday, as letters were then delivered on Sundays and Clitheroe is quite near Whalley, so Father expected Walter to be met at the station. However on July 8th Walter wrote:

Dear Papa,

I wish to tell you I got to Aunt Alice's house all safe on Sunday morning. Aunt and Uncle were glad to see me. I am very well and comfortable. I have been in the printing office today. Tell sisters and brothers I am just at home, and will tell them all the news when I return. My love to Mama and all,

Your loving son,
Walter.

The next morning Father received another letter from Clitheroe, this time from Uncle Whewell,* dated 17th July 1876:

Dear Brother,

Your son Walter is here and appears as happy as a king. He reached our house yesterday morning before we received your letter, and he says on arriving at Clitheroe station he made straight for our house.

After breakfast your son had a walk to the Ribble and stayed until near Dinner time. In the afternoon we all remained in the house. After tea Alice, myself, and Walter to the Ribble again and all roamed in the fields.

We have strictly followed your advice with respect to his medicine. Thanks on behalf of Alice for the bandage and medicine sent to her. We will report to you every other day how we get on while Walter is here. Our respects to all,

Yours very truly,
Bro. Whewell.

Walter would thoroughly enjoy roaming along the banks of the Ribble, looking under the stones and watching the fish as well as all the wild life in the meadows. Clitheroe lay on the upper reaches of the Ribble near the rising

* See photograph of Uncle Whewell as a Freemason, facing p. 159.

ground at the foot of Pendle Hill. The inhabitants were proud of the Royal Charter granted to them by King Stephen in the year 1146 which had raised their little country town to the status of 'Borough', and it became famous as a centre for the weaving and printing of cotton fabrics, and also for a high level of scholarship attained by the grammar school founded in 1554. As Walter was already interested in everything he saw, Uncle Whewell took him over his cotton printing works and the ancient castle; they called upon Dr. James Garstang and his wife Anne (née Eccles), whose parents also lived in Clitheroe; for Walter liked talking to people of an older generation who knew stories about the days of Nelson, Sir John Moore, Napoleon and Waterloo.

When the time came for Walter to return home he joined Mother in Whalley again. The small river Calder flowed through the garden to meet the Ribble at Mitton. A steep tree-topped hill, known as the Nab, rose abruptly from the village, covered with bilberries and blackberries free to be gathered. 1877 slipped by and July 1878 found Mother again in Whalley with Florrie and Daisy, James and John, eagerly expecting Ida home for the holidays once more from boarding school. Walter was in Blackburn with Father and now he attended the grammar school going to Whalley only on Saturdays.

On this sunny summer day the two little boys were out with the young maid Mary, so their old nurse Emma called in Florrie and Daisy from the garden to make them tidy for their elder sister's homecoming. Florrie was then seven years old and Daisy two years younger but much more adventurous than her sisters. They were duly washed and dressed in clean frocks and pinafores and warned to behave well "as their elder sister," said Emma, "was accustomed to good little ladies at the boarding school, and," she added very solemnly, "she has just passed her examination for the College of Preceptors, so she is clever as well as polite. Now do remember, both of you, to keep yourselves clean, and when she arrives, come and welcome her nicely."

The two little girls, thoroughly awed and frightened by these unusual instructions, were then sent into the garden to watch for the arrival of Mama's brougham bringing this apparently terrifying paragon of all the virtues. Even Florrie did not very well remember their gentle blue-eyed sister who had been at home for only a few weeks the previous year. They walked along the path with their arms around each other chanting a plaintive ditty characteristically invented for the occasion by Florrie.

"Two little saddy girls," she whispered with a sigh, "that's what we are, isn't it?"

"Come on, let's sing it," rejoined Daisy, "sing up!"

"Two little saddy girls! Two little saddy girls!" They chanted their doleful song over and over again until they reached a low stone wall overlooking the road. Having worked themselves into a thoroughly miserable and apprehensive frame of mind, they suddenly stopped, and with horror-stricken faces gazed at each other.

"What shall we do?" Daisy questioned, her hazel eyes wide with anxiety.

"Run," gasped Florrie; for when they had reached the low stone wall they saw Mama's chestnut horse turn the corner into the gateway. They completely forgot all nurse's instructions and rushed helter skelter towards the river Calder hoping to find there a suitable hiding place under the bank, and so postpone if not avoid the unwelcome tryst. Some way along the path they came upon a shed from the roof of which rain could drain into a water butt beneath a pipe from the gutter. "Let us hide," said Florrie breathlessly, and standing on tip-toe she peeped into this heaven-sent retreat, and Daisy the adventurous placed her hands above her head and grasping the top of the barrel, levered herself over the edge, and snuggled down in security upon the muddy bottom. Florrie was soon beside her, but she looked doubtfully at the treacly smelly mire left behind when the water had been drained off to 'deg' the garden.

"Never mind the mud," urged the happy Daisy from her safe retreat, but Florrie viewed their once shiny shoes with some misgiving; what, she wondered would happen to their blue gingham frocks and white pinafores! However at that moment she heard their mother and sister approaching and calling their names, so Florrie too cowered lower and pressed against the muddy sides of the barrel.

At last they were found, and history does not relate what happened when their beautifully tidy curly-haired sister confronted the two bedraggled little culprits. We can but imagine how ashamed their surprised little Mama must have felt, and with what reproaches the two were greeted by the disappointed Emma; but Ida would have brought back a present for everyone, and soon Florrie and Daisy, cleaned and chastened, would be called to Ida's bedroom to help her unpack the colossal trunk and seek the unknown treasures. Soon scampering feet would be heard rushing down the passage, and the two little boys would enter the exciting room, Jamie to shake hands with a winning smile, and Johnny to fall into Ida's outstretched arms with welcoming kisses. He had been only a baby at Ida's last visit, but now he was two years old, and Mama's stories had filled him with loving anticipations.

One morning in August when life had resumed its more normal pattern, Mary had taken Johnny to meet James coming from the little school to which he had been invited to play games, as Saturday was a half-holiday, and the small boys were breaking up at noon. Emma, with Florrie and Daisy, had been to the village shop for groceries and they were on their way to take flowers to the church for Sunday. As they walked through the churchyard Florrie pointed out three huge stone crosses which Mama had told her had been put there hundreds of years ago when the first preachers had come to tell the people here about Jesus. The crosses were of old British workmanship, decorated with interlaced knot design, but Daisy was impatient and said:

"Never mind the crosses, come inside and see if that man in long robes is still lying on his stones."

"Of course he is," replied Florrie, "Mama told me he lived here to preach, and though he died in Blackburn, he wanted to have his tomb here."

"We must be quick," urged Emma, "because I told Mary we would meet her and the little boys." They left the flowers in the church and coming out Daisy whispered: "Emma, do you know what the boys call your sister?"

"No, dear, what do they?" Emma answered casually.

"Fat Mary," Daisy announced with a mischievous grin.

Meanwhile Mother was busy preparing a huge joint of beef for the mid-day meal, for Walter would be returning from Blackburn with Father for the week-end. Into the kitchen came Ida, quickly adapting herself to become Mother's helper. "Let me make the Yorkshire pudding, Mama," she said, "I learned in the Mitcham Cookery School with Mary."

Gratefully Mama passed her the basin and spoon while she began to peel the potatoes to roast with the joint. That done she poked the oven flue and piled on more of the rich glistening coal. Then she sat down and closed her eyes. Her face flushed and suddenly turned white.

Ida ran to her and knelt down: "Mama, what is the matter? Are you feeling ill?"

"Oh Ida, my dear, I am always so tired," she replied.

"Why do you work so hard? Where is Cook?"

"I left her with Papa and Walter," Mother replied, "since Papa took his last degree he has become a consultant and he does not make so large an income. We could not afford two cooks this year, but I am very proud of his success. There is no other consultant nearer than Manchester."

"Darling Mama, it is too much for you," murmured Ida stroking Mother's thin hand, "but little Johnny has grown a lot, and Mary will soon have more time to help you."

"I know, dear," came the hesitating reply as Mother's eyes filled with tears even as she smiled at her worried eldest daughter. "I know it will be easier in that way, but he is very troublesome now, and I am sorry to say I am expecting another little one in November."

"Oh Mama," cried Ida, enchanted at the prospect of another little baby. "Will it be a little girl this time? I could look after her then, could not I?"

"We cannot choose, dear, God will send us the child He wills, and we must do our best to make the little stranger welcome, whichever it may be, but— I am so tired. I had hoped Johnny would be the last."

"But Mama," murmured Ida, "I am here now. I will not go back to school and I can help you all the time. You were not many years older than I am now when you married Papa, so I really can help, and I love my little sister already."

This ready sympathy proved too much for the weary mother. Her great brown eyes again filled with tears, and dropping her head upon her arms stretched out upon the table, she sobbed as if her heart would break. Ida knelt beside her pouring comforting words into Mother's ear, and that day a lasting bond of understanding, love and friendship was forged between them.

The sunny days of August 1878 melted into September. Ida turned her skilled fingers to the making of a rich cake for Florrie's birthday on the second of the month. She had a light hand for cooking and could even make delicious bread with yeast, better even than Mary. All families then had to bake their own loaves, so there was plenty of cooking for both of them. The children gathered bilberries and blackberries, so with apples from the orchard and cream from the farm, everyone agreed that they had never enjoyed so many delicious pies and puddings. Then came Daisy's sixth birthday on September 24th and a wonderful sponge cake was produced covered with powdery sugar. The school which Ida had attended with her cousin Mary certainly had not neglected the art of cooking and homemaking. She proved a tower of strength, young as she was, and Mother began to look less tired; but she decided to send the little girls back to Blackburn to attend school, and Emma could take Johnny too, then Ida and Jamie could return later with Mother herself as they were so used to being together.

Daisy could fold clothes surprisingly well, and Florrie tried to pack, but she was in such a hurry that Ida had to take most of the things out again when Florrie was out of the room in order to pack them more evenly. After they had been gone for a week or two Mother received the following note from Walter:

Strawberry Bank Villa,
Blackburn.

My dear Mama,

I write these few lines to you hoping to find you and James and Ida very well. I was so bothered about my lessons on Sunday that I could not find my writing desk any 'ware' until Lavinia went to look for it. I hope you have enjoyed yourself, but it has been just like the North Pole here. I thought I was in the Arctic regions.

Daisy has not murmured a bit about going to school and has been the most 'excellent" little girl, and she was nearly blown away this morning as she was going to school. I remain,

Your loving son,
Walter.

At the end of October Mother brought the other two children back to Strawberry Bank, and Florrie always remembered the specially comforting feeling of the nursery the night Mother returned. The fire was blazing on the hearth, the candles were shining all over the room, and as she knelt down to say her prayers by Mother's knee, her bare toes felt the fur of the skin rug all warm and comfy.

The middle of November drew near. Mother began to dread the complications that the birth of a seventh child would bring in so small a house. On Saturday, the sixteenth, I appeared, small enough, Ida said. to be dressed in her discarded doll's clothes. For six months I was kept in the house, but when the sun shone with spring splendour the whole family moved to a more suitable house, which had not been for sale until then. It was known as Spring Well House, although no one had seen a well or a spring at first. The house stood at the bottom of an even steeper hill than that above Strawberry Bank, and below the front garden there was a lamp-post where our road widened out to join the new road to Preston. When twilight was approaching we could see a lamp-lighter hurrying along with a tall wand, he seemed just to touch the lower part of the glass shade and suddenly as if by magic a bright flame appeared and a steady glow brightened the whole area where the two roads joined.

To see the lamp-lighter we looked down the hill to the left; on the right side the whole garden, back and front, was contained by a high wall, or rather two eight foot walls one above the other, built in order to hold the earth dug away from the far side of the slope, and so to form level ground for a huge bowling green just above our garden. It was beautifully green and smooth; we could watch from a bedroom window the excited men dancing with joy when they were winning a match. So the 'Green Room' as we called it was particularly attractive.

At first I had not been allowed to go out of doors even in the old family 'pram', but when the spring and warm weather came, I could sleep in the mornings in it or watch the trees waving against the blue sky. One day Mother had just tucked me in the pram to sleep when Father came along and she said: "I would like to call the baby 'Sarah' in memory of my poor sister".

Father agreed of course and then remembered that Mother had just received a letter from Uncle McMaster, the heartbroken husband, and asked Mother how he was bearing her death. So as they walked into the house she took it out of her pocket and offered to read the letter to Father.

"I cannot get Sarah out of my mind," she said, "how awful it must have been for her to know that she must leave all her little children."

"How awful for Brother McMaster!" Father murmured. "Read what he says, Matilda dear."

"He wrote it on April 2nd, 1879 from their house in Mitcham:

My dear Matilda,
I have just a few minutes before breakfast to drop you a line. Nearly all days are alike to me, my darling one ever coming up before me, whether it be something to get for the children, or to advise what is best to be done, or numerous other things where her wise counsel settled little difficulties, I have *no lack of reasons for not forgetting her,* if that were possible, *which never can be under my circumstances*—I gave my two best photos to Miss C. who is now teaching the three little ones, to see if she could make a drawing to catch the expression of my loved Sallie's face. She has not yet returned them and I miss them very much. In them I could see her as I cannot in any of the others. If I get a good picture I might get photographs from it.

The Monument is now up, and when the inscription is cut I shall have it all photographed and will send you a copy. In the front of the base I have: 'In memory of Sarah, the beloved wife of (then my name) 1876.' On the side next the grave: 'Sarah McMaster, died 13th June, 1876, aged 33 years.'

The Monument is a light grey dove-coloured granite, a copy of an old Irish Cross in Sligo, rather like the Iona Crosses only a better shape, 9 feet 6 inches high. The coping is red granite, all from Aberdeen.

I hope your children are all well. When you write give me a little home news. All are very well here. Miss C. has gone for the afternoon to see

her god-child of whom she is very proud. It has hair about four inches long
—which cannot be kept tidy for long at a time.

C. is growing a very fine boy, my pet and comfort now, I hope he will
always be so. H. will go to school with W. at Easter. N. is nearly as tall
as A. and Mary keeps creeping up. Fenny is doing well in every way.

Now I must close, with much love from *all*.

I remain your affectionate brother,

J. S. McMaster.

P.S.   How is the doctor? I hope he keeps well, and has an increased
practice, and how are you yourself?   J. McM."

"Poor man! Poor man!" Father sighed. Mother's eyes filled with tears.
"Yes," he continued, "we must call our little girl 'Sarah', and as soon as she
seems strong enough we will take her to be christened at St. Peter's." "Yes,"
Mother answered, "she is quite all right now the weather has improved. I will
look out the christening robes worn by the older children."

Father had been very much interested the last few years in teaching himself
Hebrew, and while Mother was putting the letter away, he had been quietly
thinking out a plan for my name which has turned out to be rather a joke.
He said: "As we have three boys and three girls already, I will choose a
Hebrew name for the baby as well as Sarah. We'll call her 'Gamzu' which
means 'Also This' or better, 'This Also'. So, as 'This Also' was easier for
Johnny to say and remember than the Hebrew 'Gamzu', he tried to say it but
our friends thought he said 'Thistle', and after my christening in June, Thistle
became my nickname.

The weeks and years sped by. With seven children of such different ages
and characters the days were never dull. Most of the older children went to
a dame's school. I spent most mornings in the garden, or at first being pushed
in the pram to feed the ducks in the nearby park. I spent much of the time
alone and found plenty to do and wonder about in my own way.

By 1880 after Jamie had celebrated his sixth birthday in July my parents
used to take me with them sometimes to see their friends or relations. One of
the most enjoyable visits was to our Great-aunt Elizabeth Garstang who lived
in a cottage at Witton, then just a country village. Her husband, Grandmother's younger brother James had taken their own widowed mother to live
at Witton too, but now Great-uncle James and his mother were both dead.
As a rule Great-aunt had taken me into the garden and she would show me
how to pick a lovely bunch of flowers with long stalks to take home to
Ida. This time I was told to gather them by myself, for Great-aunt was very
ill and that was the last visit for me. The next week Mother took only Ida,
and they were going to Great-aunt's funeral in the new Witton church. Ida
was very sad as Great-aunt Elizabeth had loved us as much as if she had been
really our grandmother.

These expeditions always took place in the summer, and another I remember enjoying two years later (1882). Father took me for a drive to Tockholes,
away over the hills and moors beyond Witton. The skylarks used to sing
there just as they did in the Mellor fields, away up in the blue sky. We were

Pedigree V.

The Garstangs of Blackburn, Lane End.

Thomas of Whittle to Beardwood Fold 1735-1822
m. Ann Ellison 1738-1825 (2 sons, 7 daughters)
James of Lane End   1764-1853
m. Alice   1763-1828
Thomas of Lane End   1803-1864
m. 1st. Hannah Garstang   m. 2nd. Susanna Pilkington
of Darwen, 1806-1837   d.1865

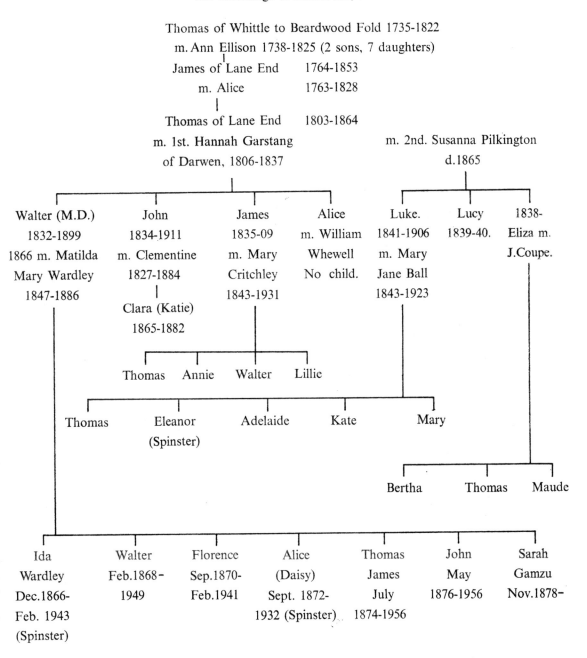

Walter (M.D.)	John	James	Alice	Luke.	Lucy	1838-
1832-1899	1834-1911	1835-09	m. William	1841-1906	1839-40.	Eliza m.
1866 m. Matilda	m. Clementine	m. Mary	Whewell	m. Mary		J.Coupe.
Mary Wardley	1827-1884	Critchley	No child.	Jane Ball		
1847-1886		1843-1931		1843-1923		

Clara (Katie)
1865-1882

Thomas   Annie   Walter   Lillie

Thomas   Eleanor   Adelaide   Kate   Mary
         (Spinster)

Bertha   Thomas   Maude

Ida	Walter	Florence	Alice	Thomas	John	Sarah
Wardley	Feb.1868-	Sep.1870-	(Daisy)	James	May	Gamzu
Dec.1866-	1949	Feb.1941	Sept. 1872-	July	1876-1956	Nov.1878-
Feb. 1943			1932 (Spinster)	1874-1956		
(Spinster)						

driving along a road towards Darwen, and I hoped I should see the flames shooting out from the iron works, because on Revidge we could see only the glow made by them in the sky. We did not drive far enough as Father was going to visit his Great-uncle Thomas Garstang who was not only very old, but ill as well (Ped. III).

When we arrived at the house Father left me in the garden to amuse myself and went in to see his old uncle. There were flowers everywhere, a hive of bees like a basket turned upside down was placed on a low table and bees kept flying or creeping in and out. There was also a low stone wall round a well with a wooden bucket suspended over it by a chain fixed to an arch. A path led out of the garden gate to a rough lane where there was a stone trough with water pouring into it from a high grassy bank. The water cascaded out again on the other side and splashed into a stream by the side of the lane. Now I find that the old uncle died soon after our visit when he was 90 years old.

During the spring of 1883, Ida bought me a new trowel all for myself, and some wallflower seedlings because we each had a little plot of land for ourselves in the garden at the back of the house, and I loved gardening better than anything I could do. After I had planted and watered them I went to show my trowel to Mother. She said she could see that I had been gardening as I was covered in mud. After she had tidied me she told me about a little book which cousin Thomas of Leyland had shewn her as he had heard that I was very fond of hearing stories about animals. The book had belonged to his mother Ann Holden (Pedigree IV. 24), and she had given it to him when he was a little boy. Mother had looked through it so that she could describe the story to me. There was a picture as frontispiece of a lamb by a waterfall and a dove resting on a tree by the stream. Below the picture his mother's name 'Ann Holden' was written in childish writing, and at the back: 'Thomas Garstang from his mother, 1859'.

When Mother came home she told me the story. It was about a Good Shepherd visiting his fold to see two lambs called Peace and Inexperience. One is happy and the other jumps over the wall of the fold because he wants to be free. When he meets with danger and disaster he calls out for the Good Shepherd to take him back to the Fold. Of course I had a number of questions to ask, especially about their names, but Mother explained it all to me and promised to take me some day to see Cousin Thomas and the little book.

That visit never took place because the December of that year turned out to be very frosty with quantities of frozen snow on the roads. Mother took Daisy to do some Christmas shopping; they had to walk very carefully, and coming home with their baskets piled up with parcels Mother slipped on a piece of orange peel just covering a patch of ice. She happened to put her foot right on it and fell down, all her parcels scattering around her basket as it jerked out of her hand. Daisy helped her up but at first she could not move her leg and she was obliged to lean against a wall while Daisy gathered up the parcels. After she had rested she was able to limp home, but father had gone to Manchester for the day, and when he arrived home she did not tell him for a few days. Some days her hip became very painful after the New Year festivities were over, so she had to tell Father about the accident and she often had to stay in bed all day.

Meanwhile Father had arranged for Walter to reside in Jesus College Oxford to get coaching for the Oxford entrance examination, as the Blackburn Grammar School, then still in a little one room building near St. Peter's Church, could not give him any individual teaching above the heads of other boys. There are some interesting letters from him to Mother, and on November 10th 1884 Mother began her letter in this way:

My darling Walter,
   No doubt you find this term very different from the beautiful Spring term when you went first to Oxford, but from your letter, I judge that they try to make each term as enjoyable as possible. I hope you keep well, take care of yourself, and God helping you, do nothing that in after years you may regret.
   I was very pleased indeed to receive a letter from you, and in reply to your kind enquiries, I am glad to say that I am getting nicely better, altho' it was a very sharp attack of illness I had.
   After reading your letter I looked out for another train for your Papa to leave London by, as I said you would be disappointed if he did not have dinner with you. So all being well he will leave London at 3 o'clock, arriving at Oxford at 5.50. If you could comfortably meet him that would be nice, only he says that you need not order anything very extra for dinner. So we shall think of you two having dinner at 6.30 in your pleasant sitting room.

Mother's letter continued with the little affairs at home. She was bitterly disappointed that she had not been able to go with Father to Oxford. She ended her next letter in this way:

   Ida, Florrie, and John are gone to church, and I am not yet well enough. I only went out yesterday for the first time, and today I feel very tired. It is really delightful weather, and it is quite amusing to look through Ida's bedroom window at the passers by on Sundays.

After Walter came home he joined us in long walks with Father, but although she rested a good deal, Mother could no longer walk even down to St. Peter's church, but on the Monday she felt strong enough to go with Walter to a French soirée to meet the pupils of M. Merchier, who was the French master at the Grammar school, and his pupils were to act L'Avare in the Lecture hall of the former Exchange. She must have felt too tired to enjoy it because the next day she said that she would not go out again to any evening entertainment.

Gradually we became used to Ida looking after everything; although she was young she seemed grown up to me. Mother was nearly always in bed and Father brought her bed downstairs so that she could be with us all. He took her to Manchester to see a specialist, but as X-rays had not been invented, even the specialist did not know what was the matter with her leg.

The day after my birthday in 1885 I wrote to Walter, no one ever thought of sending me to school, but Florrie had shewn me how to read and write. My letter began:

> When are you coming home for I am very lonely? Smut is very ill and Ida has made it some arrowroot which the doctor ordered when we took it there. That has done it a bit of good, and now it can bite like fun.

In 1886 Mother was not able to get out of bed at all. Ida looked after her and a nice cook from Welshpool looked after the cooking and house-keeping.

In the early summer of 1886 another specialist came from Manchester to see Mother as her leg was more swollen and painful; then we were all told that she would not be able to get up any more, and a very kind Amelia Owen came to help and she took me down to the market to buy primrose roots for my garden. Then I was sent in the guard's van to Lytham to stay with Aunt Alice.

Father finished his next letter to Walter on July 13th 1886 with these words:

> Go on doing your best, for none can do more, keeping a cheerful mind as is your wont, under whatever sorrow may betide. Only get all things whatsoever in order, so that you can leave your pleasant abode at a day's notice; i.e. on the day following the warning receipt of a note from me, or of a telegram.

Aunt Martha and Aunt Annie, Mother's sisters, both came to see her again, and the vicar came up as usual to administer the Eucharist, and just before my birthday in November Mother died.

Nothing was ever quite the same again. Of course the bed and my toys disappeared from the dining room. Ida was given a canary which Father tamed and taught to run through the toast racks so that we could all laugh and forget. But not Ida. She was never quite the same either. Father took us walks on Sunday afternoons, and kept natural history books in the cupboards of his book-case to show us after the walks.

That little book about the two lambs which Mother had explained to me is now here in the Garstang archives as Cousin Thomas's daughter Alice gave it to our collection. When I was looking at it just now in order to describe it properly I found with it two similar treasures of mine belonging to the period of Mother's death. These three books are only about 3″ by 2″ and all bound in brown cloth with beautiful wood cuts; they are probably representative of the period in children's books. The first was a New Testament with delicately coloured maps given to me by Mother on September 6 1886 just two months before she died. The second is inscribed "Sarah Gamzu Garstang a wee gift from her father 5th June 1888", the title is *The Little Picture Testament,* and the alternate pages are wood-cut illustrations of Bible characters in real oriental clothing of the right period.

On November 5th in 1886 Father had found in Mother's Prayer Book after she died a letter written in pencil to us seven children and ending with the words:

Lastly, if you love Jesus, and you all say you do, I have only to put you in mind of his own words: 'If you love me keep my commandments', and 'Little children love one another.'

From a note-book of my father's 1883.

Teach thy son Obedience, and she shall bless him;
Teach him Diligence, and his wealth shall increase;
Teach him Science, and his life shall be useful:
Teach him Religion, and his death shall be happy.

CHAPTER II

THE GARSTANGS OF CIRENCESTER, TOCKHOLES, AND DARWEN

One morning in 1890 a reporter from the *Blackburn Standard* weekly newspaper called to see my father about writing an article concerning the Garstangs as a Clan. He had been talking to Jane Garstang's granddaughter, a Miss Wilson, who knew the story of the ancestors at Beardwood Fold and had given to Mother the beautiful old china teacup. She had told the reporter that as a Clan the Garstangs had been very long lived, and he wanted some more details which Father could supply. (See pp. 20, 21.)

When John and I returned home from school the reporter had gone, but Father told us some more about the landing of Gair on the Wyre with Agmund and Orme which had resulted in the founding of Garstang and Ormskirk, and the name Amounderness with other Scandinavian names nearby. Then he advised us to look out for the article in the *Standard* in about a week's time; it would be called 'A long-lived Blackburn Clan, the Garstangs.'

We both rushed for the paper on the next Saturday morning, but the article was not there and we had to wait until June 21st. There it was with the title in large type just as we had expected. It was all most exciting, giving the names of any of our ancestors who had lived to an unusual age: five lived to be in the sixties, nine to the seventies, eighteen to the eighties, and five had actually lived to be over ninety, nearly as old as the China teacup that had now been cherished for a hundred years!

The reporter had added:

> The reader of what follows will allow that the Garstangs of the present generation, if they have retained the ancestral stamina and tendency, and as they lead sober and godly virtuous lives, have as good a chance as any persons in this community of attaining unto length of days.

That was very encouraging, and as I had always been very curious about what the end of the world would be like, there seemed to be some chance that I might actually live to see it!

The reporter had referred to Gair's landing and then mentioned Tockholes, Lower Darwen, and Whittle as some of the places where Garstangs had settled after they had moved away southwards from the Wyre valley, and also Leyland where I could remember going with Father although Mother could not take me.

For a long time I had been wanting to ride to Garstang and after we all

49

possessed bicycles in 1898, I was very curious to see if there really was an old stone house with the rhyme of fate carved on the beam across the fire place in the hall:

> When Garstang shall with Garstang mate,
> The curse will fall however late.

I knew that my grandparents had both been Garstangs, and I hoped that the death of my Mother had been the curse and so all the rest of us would be freed.

My sister Florence had just become engaged to the curate at Whalley, Ernest Elliot, and when his great friend, Dr. Hillyer, came to stay with him, we all bicycled to our old friends at Hurst Green, a village on the other side of the Ribble from our favourite picnic place, Dinckley. Dr. Hillyer agreed to bicycle with me to Garstang, but we could not find the 'Grange', because I had not then read A. Trollope's novel, *The Garstangs of Garstang Grange,* so I did not know that the house was situated on the top of the cliffs by the sea-shore to the west of Garstang. Of course the book was only a novel and the Grange probably never existed, certainly the Garstangs described in it were not characteristic of the Clan, judging by the letters written by recent Garstangs now living in Lancashire.

James Rowland Garstang and his wife (Pedigree III. 19) went later to see Garstang and the Vicar of St. Helen's Church gave him a copy of the Latin inscription beginning 'Santa Maria ora pro nobis', dated A.D. MDXXII. They called to look at the Penwortham Parish Records now in the Preston Public Record Office and found that Garstangs used the name of the town as a surname in the seventeenth century:

> Thomas Garstang de Chorley September 1633
> Thomas Garstang de Longton July 1702

Our interest in the Clan had been further increased by a recent discovery of John's while he was an undergraduate at Oxford. After a long bicycle ride which had by chance taken him to Cirencester he wrote to Father about it on January 8th 1898:

Jesus College
Oxford.

Dear Father,
    Thank you very sincerely for your very welcome parcel, and much more for the spirit that prompted the sending.
    In the course of some researches I came across the following information about the 'Garstangs of Garstang'. You noticed that they have now disappeared from Garstang, and that this had occurred just before our first record of the name in Blackburn. I found that the name had lingered in their original parish until about two centuries before that. My last discovery is that in 1464 a Henry Garstang died in Cirencester and left £10 to be distributed to his kinsfolk in Garstang!
    Henry had desired to be buried in Cirencester Church in the wall near the altar of St. Edmund the Confessor. His widow Margaret carried out his wishes, and an arched recess in the wall of the South aisle with two shields,

Henry Garstang's Arms and Wool-mark on his Chantry Screen, Cirencester

(by kind permission of the Vicar, the Revd. Rowland E. Hill)

photograph by Wm. Barrett of Silver St., Cirencester

photograph by Wm. Barrett of Silver St., Cirencester

Henry Garstang's tomb in his Chantry, Cirencester Church
(*by kind permission of the Vicar, the Revd. Rowland E. Hill*)

one at each end, marking his resting place, can still be seen. One of these shields bears his Merchant Mark and the other his Coat of Arms. The painting of this is modern, it reads: 'Azure three mascles, or, a Chief argent, and bordure engrailed gules.'

An oak screen round the whole corner of the south aisle bears his Arms and Mark; these are also found in the Lady Chapel to which in 1457 he gave a suit of vestments.

Henry G. is supposed to have been engaged in the wool trade which was prosperous around there then. He seems to have left no family.

This was so inspiring that I immediately drew and painted a copy of a Coat-of-Arms that the Heraldry Office had once sent to Father, but it turned out to be a form of the Garston arms (see p. 65). Four days later John wrote to me on the subject:

> I found Henry Garstang's Coat of Arms (about which I wrote to Father) was described in the Bodleian Library. Subsequently I drew them after much patient labour and research in the Camera (under the eye of Johannes Radcliffe M.D., to say nothing of various Ajax's, Achilles's, Venus's, and others). The *Chief*, which I mentioned to Father, is a strip of the field one third of the whole height along the top; it is almost a parallelogram in silver.
>
> Do you feel inclined to paint a specimen of this?

Later, Bessie, the daughter of our cousin Adelaide, made some drawings of the Cirencester tomb and of a ceiling boss in which an angel is holding a shield with Henry's Coat-of-Arms. In Somerset House she and her husband, George Squibb, discovered that in his will Henry had left to this church (of St. John the Baptist) a Primer to be chained to the Chantry Chapel of St. Edmund, Archbishop and Confessor, and provision for a priest during his wife's lifetime to say a thousand masses after his death; Henry also gave a pall of gold and red to serve for funerals, together with all the timber lying in a meadow near the church for the general use of the parish where the need was greatest. A beautifully bound Bible with four silver markers was to be placed in the Lady Chapel and kept covered with a red and gold cloth, also 'two white copeyes and chisypl, two tunicys with purtenances on sute for festivals, a peyr vestments for week days, and for Sundays a peyr of cloth of gold.

All this had happened in 1464 and twenty years earlier a Henry Gairstang in Lancashire had given to Agnes, wife of Henry Staumford, a messuage with 100 acres of land, 12 of meadow, 200 of pasture, 6 of wood, and 100 of turbary in Claughton, and she was to render each year one rose to Henry and his heirs.

Now here was a picture for the young Garstangs! Henry makes his will, receives his rose from his sister in Claughton, two and a half miles to the south-east of Garstang, packs his strong horses with bales of the year's wool, and rides off to the prosperous wool merchants of Stroud and Cirencester.

Henry's Arms (three mascles and a chief) appear also in the upper part of the centre light in the east window at Cirencester. He must have been a citizen of no little importance and have done some service for the King (probably Henry VI) as he left in his will 'a liberature dni Regis de SS', which was a livery collar embellished with SS, and worn to denote loyalty to the House of Lancaster.

Figs. 1-6.

1. Garstang Coat of Arms, in East window.
2. Garstang Merchants Mark, in East window.
3. Garstang Coat of Arms, on corbel.
4. Garstang Merchants Mark, on corbel.
5. Trade Mark of wool merchants, in St. John's Chapel
6. Crowned shuttle, in window tracery on South side.

The drawings of Garstang Arms and Merchant Marks of Henry in Cirencester Church, Figs. 1-6, were taken from the *Transactions of the Bristol and Gloucestershire Archaeological Society* for 1892-93 by Diane Gurney. The relevant passages (condensed) from these *Transactions* follow.

p.39.   In the eastern part of the south wall with the two windows, there is work of the middle of the 15th century, having been reconstructed as the Chantry Chapel of a family named Garstang, the tomb in the corner being that of Henry Garstang, who died in 1464, desiring to be buried in the wall nearest the altar of St. Edmund the Confessor. (His will is at Somerset House.)

p.275-6.   The glass at present in the East window was collected from various parts at the beginning of this century. The shield towards the top, az., 3 mascles or, and a chief arg. (Fig. 1) with the adjacent Merchant's Mark (2) are the cognizances of the family of Garstang. This is a some-what rare example of a merchant bearing his Coat of Arms and his Merchant's Mark. These shields came from the windows in the eastern part of the South aisle of the nave.

p.274.   Merchants' Marks were used in the same manner as Armorial bearings. Besides stamping their bales of merchandise, they are found set up over the doors of their houses, upon their seals, carved on the bench ends of the seats they occupied in Churches. The marks for the most part consisted of a shaft with a spreading foot and a cross at the top; near this, especially in the wool districts, is a small banner flying, very similar to that of the *Agnus Dei*, from which it is supposed to have been adopted, and the shaft is intersected by one or more horizontal lines or beams, which are also usually terminated by crosses. Sometimes the Marks are distinguished by the addition of the *initials of their owners' names,* and this is commonly the case in the Cirencester Marks, and the shaft sur-mounted by a triangular device resembling the figure 4, which is supposed by some to indicate that the Mark is that of a wool-stapler, it being very common in wool districts. (The 4 is made with crossed Shepherd's crooks. S.G.G.)

p.281.   On some shields in an upper range of corbels at the East end of the South aisle, are the Arms of Garstang with their Merchants Mark (Figs. 3 and 4). The two shields occur together again in the recessed tomb at the south-east corner of the aisle, which the added initials *H.G.* identify as the tomb of Henry Garstang who died in 1464 and desired to be buried there. It is noticeable that the Garstang shield appears in glass, and carved on stone and wood, in three forms:
1)   a plain shield bearing *three mascles,* among these upper shields,
2)   the same coat *with a chief* in ancient glass in the East window (Fig. 1),
3)   all this within *an engrailed bordure* in sundry carved shields (Fig. 3).

So also the Merchant's Mark varies, compare Figs. 2 and 4.

p.287. In the Lady Chapel on shields below the principals of the roof are coats already figured of Garstang, Chedworth, and Prelatte, and a shield with a Merchant's Mark consisting of *two somewhat tapering beams saltirewise, in the upper space two chevronels braced, in the lower a brush, on either side the letters d.i.*

pp.288-89.   Henry Garstang's body is buried in the wall near the altar of St. Edmund, Archbishop and Confessor. Henry was a wealthy merchant, gave timber from his meadow to the church, directed his widow to provide a priest to say a thousand masses. The Chantry was due to the widow's devotion, possibly some of his own timber was used. The Chapel was 12 feet by 9 feet and screened off from the aisle by a carved screen carrying in the panels the armorial bearings within a bordure and the Merchant's Mark of the Garstang family. See figures 3 and 4. The floor was raised 8 inches above the level of the aisle.

This was later known as the Jesus Chapel; in 1803 the oak panels were removed and stored in the disused Chapel of John the Baptist. In 1867 the floor of the Chapel was levelled when the Church was restored, and the screen was used to cut off part of the Lady Chapel for use as a Choir vestry.

The shields along the upper portion of the screen, according to Mr. Carles, were originally charged with the *Arms of Christ's Passion*. These were apparently *painted over in* 1698 *to carry the Coats* of those who had been benefactors of the Church and especially of those who had contributed to the fund for the augmentation of the value of the Benefice of Cirencester in that year. (Mr. Carles was Perpetual Curator of the parish in 1673.)

pp.317-18. In the Chancel on the 15*th Stall* is the *Coat of Garstang*: 3 lozenges pced . . . in chief. (Appendix by Mr. Carles.)

p.293.   In St. John the Baptist's Chapel on the northern wall are two wooden shields carved with a *large pair of shears* representing the woollen trade of the town. See Fig. 5.

p.280.   When standing in the North Aisle one can see in the tracery of the easternmost clerestory window on the South side of the nave in ancient glass some *crowned shuttles or,* a reminiscence of the old clothing trade of the town, Fig. 6.

Later Walter received a letter from Miss Edith Blundell of Cirencester about the Garstang chapel and Henry's gifts. She wrote:

Henry's widow continued to support the Chapel Service, but later the Chapel was used for other dedications. It is now altarless and used for extra seating accommodation. The arched recess within the screen contains the tomb of Henry. His name is seventh in our bidding prayer. The Oak Screen, which has been somewhat altered and restored, bears small shields with the Garstang Arms and Merchant's mark as well as the painted ones on the upper part. The same arms can be seen above the pillars of the S. E. aisle, part of which he rebuilt. The glass from the Garstang chapel now incorporated in the East Chapel window shows the same arms.

When I read this letter after I began to write the story of the Garstangs, Sylvia, Walter's second daughter, and I motored to Cirencester to see what had happened. All the ancient glass had been collected in 1800 and re-arranged under Mr. S. Lysons, the well-known antiquary, in the East window, the figures of St. John of Beverly, Archbishop of York, and St. William, Archbishop of York, had been taken from the Garstang Chapel.

The stipend reserved for the organist by Henry had been confiscated in 1548.

About the time when the glass had been taken from Henry's Chapel the oak screen itself had been taken away and in 1867 it had been erected elsewhere to serve as a choir vestry, but when John and I had seen it there was a printed notice inside it stating that its origin was 'The Garstang Chapel'. When Sylvia and I went the screen was back in its proper place by the tomb but it was called by the verger 'The Jesus Chapel'. So we went to see the Vicar, Archdeacon Sutch, about it, and in letters which followed he explained away all our troubles:

> The Garstang screen is the original one. It was moved into the Lady Chapel to make a vestry when the church was restored in 1876. Archdeacon Sinclair put it back in its original position in 1908. The painted shield of Garstang arms and wool merchants mark were touched up two or three years ago when several of the other shields were repaired. At the moment an artist is working on six panels which are to go under the tower. They are quite beautifully painted, with the interesting history of the church in writing and illustration, and it may be that some reference to the chapel may be made in them. If not we may consider putting some label in the chapel itself.

The next time I went with my niece Joan, about 1960, we found everything perfectly restored in the right place; there was a clear label identifying the tomb and chapel as that of Henry Garstang, also it is described on the beautiful and interesting panels now fixed on the wall under the tower.

Henry's connexion with Merton College

After we came to live in Oxford, Dr. Roger Highfield, the Librarian of Merton College, took my son Oliver and me to see another very interesting gift of Henry's which came into the College Library after the year 1410. As Henry's name is spelt 'Gairstang' I take it that it was presented by the Henry who gave his property to his sister Agnes before he left Garstang for his trek to the south.

It is a book of 'distinctiones', a kind of Biblical concordance, given in memory of Richard le Scroop, Archbishop of York, who was executed in 1405 for taking part in a rebellion against Henry IV, and was afterwards looked upon by many as a Saint.

The book belonged originally to Thomas Burstal, who gave it to John Brockholes, and from him it passed to Henry Gairstang. He presented it to Merton College 'ad orandum pro anima magistri Ricardi le Schrop nuper Ebor Archiepiscopi et animabus supra-dictorum.' Dr. Roger Highfield said that the words presumably refer to Henry and the Archbishop.

There is a possible link between Henry in Garstang and Merton College in the fact that Archbishop Kemp retained the See of York from 1425 until 1454, and for part of that period he was also a Fellow of Merton College.[1]

---

[1] See F. M. Powicke, *Mediaeval Books of Merton College* No. 705 p.192 (1928). Emden. *Biographical Register of the Members of the University of Oxford to 1540.*

Before Henry's death in 1464 he had presented to the Cirencester Church the window of beautiful coloured glass depicting St. John of Beverly, Archbishop of York until 721, St. William, another Archbishop of York who died in 1154 still in office, and St. Osmund, Bishop of Salisbury. All were at first placed in his chantry.

The Garstang connexion with Cirencester had been established before the middle of the fifteenth century when Elizabeth Garstang, the widow of another Henry, lord of the Manor of Barton Hundred in Northamptonshire, had married Peter Humphrey in Cirencester. It is clear that the Clan was no longer confined to Lancashire, but in whatever direction they travelled they seemed to have been interested in public affairs, particularly in the local churches as in Cirencester, so that my grandfather's entries in his diaries about the laying of foundation stones for new churches in his neighbourhood kept to an old tradition.

From Garstang to Tockholes

In the years 1195-1198 William de Gairstang with his brothers Robert and Paulinus had acted as sureties for the Chaplain of St. Michael's on Wyre in agreement with the Abbot of Wyresdale during the reign of Richard I. William was a clerk in the Manorial Court, and Richard de Gairstang had been appointed the 'parson' of Garstang itself. The second 'parson' in 1199 after King John came to the throne, was Robert de Gairstange, and in the present restored church of St. Helen the old carved oak stalls of his day have been preserved in the chancel, also a piscina, and the carved oak screen with a part of the stairway leading to the rood.

In 1228 a Charter of Water Rights connects Paulinus de Gerstan with Amounderness when he witnessed the transferring of the right to make ponds and ditches for the purpose of draining the Moss (or marsh) in Carlton and stretching as far as Poulton-le-Fylde.

When I was staying with Nell Howard after my father died, we bicycled along a raised causeway to Carlton across the marsh, but we found no trace of Agmund except a lane called 'Dane's Way', and the name Amounderness, the west part of the moss is called the Fylde from an Old English word meaning flat land, a plain. Also we learned that Poulton had once been a port in connexion with the river Wyre, but drainage prevented the passage of shipping. The market place dates far back and contains a Market Cross raised on steps, with stocks and rogues' post near by. The Church is dedicated to St. Chad and follows the style of Norman architecture being built on the site of an eleventh century chapel. Pedigrees II.1 and 2 show Garstangs in Chorley, Leyland, and Blackburn and other villages in their neighbourhoods.

On September 11th, 1937, George Squibb wrote to Walter about the visit he and Bessie had paid to Whittle, and then they moved on to Heapey where they found two of the old Garstang houses:

The house known as 'Higher Garstang House' is empty, so we were able

Pedigree II.1

GARSTANG OF BRINDLE

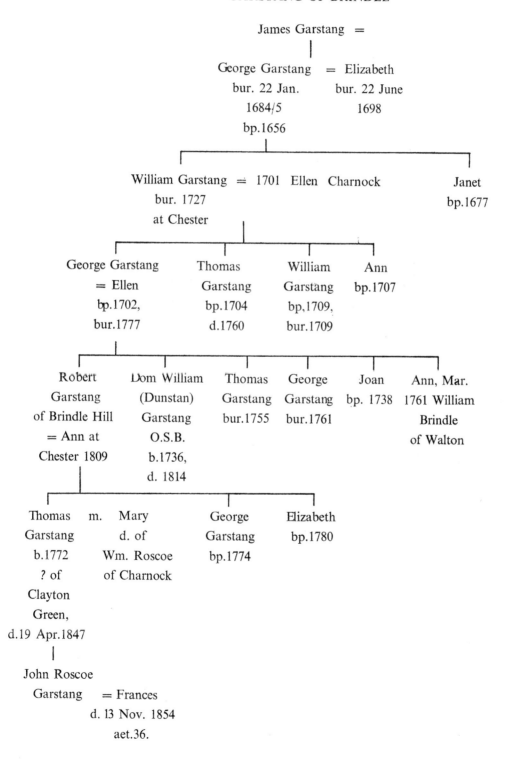

James Garstang =

George Garstang = Elizabeth
bur. 22 Jan.   bur. 22 June
1684/5   1698
bp.1656

William Garstang = 1701 Ellen Charnock   Janet
bur. 1727   bp.1677
at Chester

George Garstang   Thomas   William   Ann
= Ellen   Garstang   Garstang   bp.1707
bp.1702,   bp.1704   bp,1709,
bur.1777   d.1760   bur.1709

Robert   Dom William   Thomas   George   Joan   Ann, Mar.
Garstang   (Dunstan)   Garstang   Garstang   bp. 1738   1761 William
of Brindle Hill   Garstang   bur.1755   bur.1761   Brindle
= Ann at   O.S.B.   of Walton
Chester 1809   b.1736,
                      d. 1814

Thomas   m.   Mary   George   Elizabeth
Garstang   d. of   Garstang   bp.1780
b.1772   Wm. Roscoe   bp.1774
? of   of Charnock
Clayton
Green,
d.19 Apr.1847

John Roscoe
Garstang   = Frances
d. 13 Nov. 1854
aet.36.

Pedigree II.2

Some Garstangs of Heapey.
With connexions in Brindle etc.

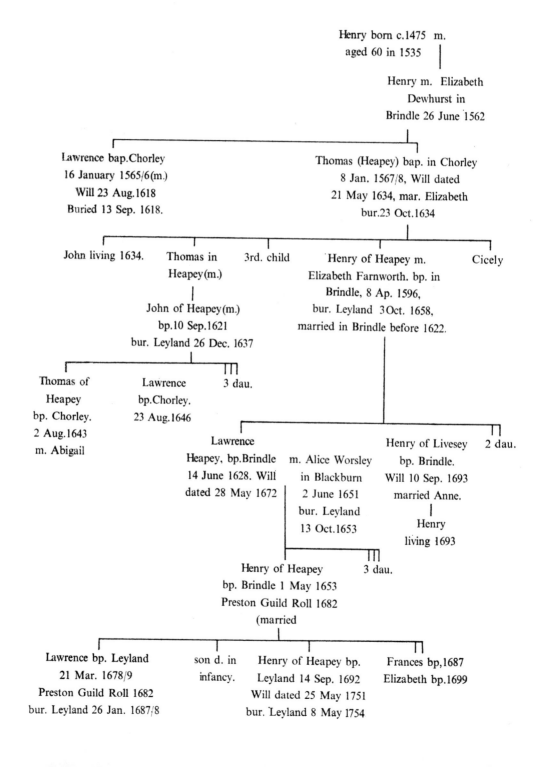

Henry born c.1475 m.
aged 60 in 1535

Henry m. Elizabeth
Dewhurst in
Brindle 26 June 1562

Lawrence bap.Chorley
16 January 1565/6(m.)
Will 23 Aug.1618
Buried 13 Sep. 1618.

Thomas (Heapey) bap. in Chorley
8 Jan. 1567/8, Will dated
21 May 1634, mar. Elizabeth
bur.23 Oct.1634

John living 1634.   Thomas in   3rd. child   Henry of Heapey m.   Cicely
Heapey(m.)   Elizabeth Farnworth. bp. in
Brindle, 8 Ap. 1596,
bur. Leyland 3 Oct. 1658,
John of Heapey(m.)   married in Brindle before 1622.
bp.10 Sep.1621
bur. Leyland 26 Dec. 1637

Thomas of   Lawrence   3 dau.
Heapey   bp.Chorley.
bp. Chorley.   23 Aug.1646
2 Aug.1643
m. Abigail

Lawrence   Henry of Livesey   2 dau.
Heapey, bp.Brindle   m. Alice Worsley   bp. Brindle.
14 June 1628. Will   in Blackburn   Will 10 Sep. 1693
dated 28 May 1672   2 June 1651   married Anne.
                     bur. Leyland
                     13 Oct.1653   Henry
                                         living 1693

Henry of Heapey   3 dau.
bp. Brindle 1 May 1653
Preston Guild Roll 1682
(married

Lawrence bp. Leyland   son d. in   Henry of Heapey bp.   Frances bp,1687
21 Mar. 1678/9   infancy.   Leyland 14 Sep. 1692   Elizabeth bp.1699
Preston Guild Roll 1682   Will dated 25 May 1751
bur. Leyland 26 Jan. 1687/8   bur. Leyland 8 May 1754

to explore the precincts. We found over the door of the barn a stone inscribed—

G

I   A

1730

The Parish Register reveals the existence of a John and Alice Garstang living at Heapey at that time.

Although a great many Garstangs had moved southwards, even as far as Cirencester and Northampton, there were still some living between Preston and Garstang: in 1592 Anthony Garstang of Eccleston in Amounderness, yeoman, who had been appointed Surveyor of the highways, on July 10th charged three labourers and a husbandman at the Preston Quarter Sessions with refusing to perform their statutory duties of highway repair.

There were two Ecclestons in Amounderness, Great and Little Eccleston, and in 1589 'Anthony Garstang of Much Eccleston, yeoman, conveyed some property there to Thomas Eccleston', therefore he was living only six miles to the south of Garstang, but Little Eccleston is in the parish of Kirkham, seven miles to the north-west of Preston.

When we had all settled down in homes of our own, Walter was a Professor in Leeds and John in Liverpool, both near the Garstang country, Ida and Daisy too were often in Blackburn, so they all took part with Bessie and George Squibb in a great quest for Garstang history and pedigrees, writing to any members of the Clan they were unable to interview, and copying tombstones or notes in various registers. Robert and I were in Norfolk and out of the Quest there.

Cecil Garstang (Pedigree IV.30) gave me the actual date of A.D. 832 for the landing of Gair and his oarsmen by the Wyre, but it was not the first time that the Vikings had taken the western route round Scotland, for the Christian buildings on the island of Iona had been destroyed already by them, the Isle of Man was entirely in their hands, and a great many had settled in Ireland. After the departure of the Roman soldiers from Britain there was only a very scattered population of British people in the neighbourhood of Lancaster. They had been newly converted to Christianity by the monks and nuns living in the nearby abbeys and monasteries, and they trusted in the power of St. Michael with his holy angels to protect his church. Therefore no armies opposed the landing of the Vikings, who, having chosen the three sites for their settlements, would at once begin the building of their wooden dwellings. The most suitable trees in the surrounding forests fell before their heavy axes and Gair-stang was born.

From time to time out of various newspapers Walter had collected references in Lancashire and Yorkshire to an old custom known as 'stanging'. Four men would carry round a chair perched upon two strong poles, force some of the villagers to mount in turn, and carry them to the Garstang Arms where they were expected to pay for a round of drinks.

When the task of writing the story of the Clan fell upon me I wrote to Mr. W. W. Yeates for any references to the Vikings or early settlements that he could find in the Blackburn Free Library. He sent me three quotations from books he found in the shelves about the Scandinavian invaders:

Worsare tells of the Orm family as settled citizens by A.D. 925, one of them being a supporter of King Athelstan, and another in 1033 added his signature to a document in Canute's reign.

Collingwood mentions Orm also as one of the Scandinavian invaders, all the landowners of North Lancashire at that time were listed in Domesday Book with Scandinavian names.

Baines gives a list of Scandinavian landowners killed at the battle of Wednesfield, then known as Woden's field, and gives the name of Agmund as one of the opponents of Edward the Elder, son of King Alfred, who from 910 to 919 was attempting to stop the advance of the Vikings round Wulfrane's Hanton, now Wolverhampton in Staffordshire.

James Iddon Garstang (see Longton section p.94) in his researches through documents of the next period found that Paulinus de 'Gairstang' held office in the reign of Henry III c.1216.

During the reigns of Richard I and John the frequent quarrels of the kings and archbishops of Canterbury with the Pope had left North Lancashire undisturbed, while the signing of Magna Carta in 1215 had brought security to all inhabitants on an equality. The men 'of Garstang' then were found supporting law and order beyond their home town: Gilbert and Paulinus de Gairstang (sometimes de Gerstang) were witnesses to many documents dealing with grants of land, rights of grazing, or the cutting of peat, and they had stood surety for the Chaplain of St. Michael's on Wyre in 1195.

The western part of Amounderness near the Wyre estuary was a useless bog until 1228 when John de Carlton with Paulinus de Gerstan obtained a licence (as we have said) to make ponds and ditches for drainage between Poulton and Little Carlton, thus enlarging the healthy area for dwellings and corn-growing, but river traffic which formerly reached Poulton then must enter the estuary along a channel.

In 1325 William de Gairstang should have been present at the Preston Wapentake, the Scandinavian word for the old British Hundred Moot.

The next year 1326 William and his brother Roger are described as 'Sons of Henry de Gayrestang' when they appeared in person at the Lancashire Assizes.

In 1347 the name is used in a more complicated sense when Ralph de Gayrestang of Cockersand was accused of taking cattle from the highway and impounding them in company with the Abbot of Cockersand; later that year he was summoned to the court of Edward III at Westminster.

George Squibb explains the use of the name 'Garstang' in this way:

In early documents about the Clan we meet with men described as 'of Garstang' because that was where they lived. Some of them were probably related to each other, but the designation would be equally apt for men who had nothing in common but their place of residence. It was when they were

Pedigree II.3.

Garstangs of Tockholes

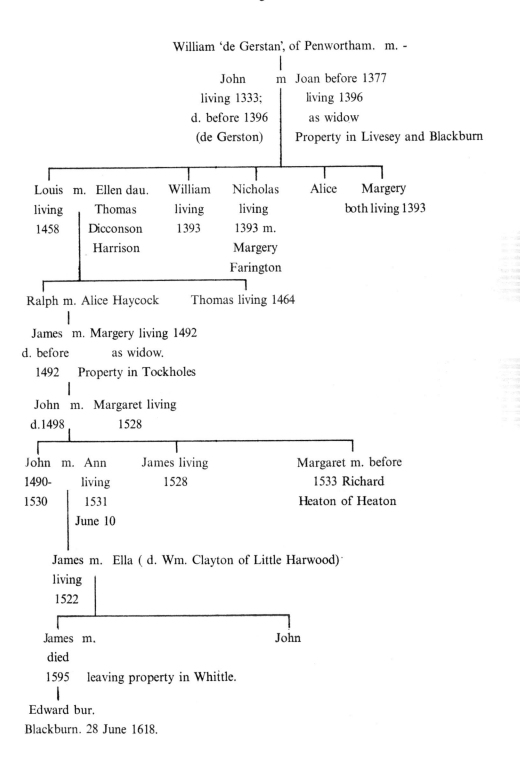

William 'de Gerstan', of Penwortham. m. -

John   m   Joan before 1377

living 1333;   living 1396

d. before 1396   as widow

(de Gerston)   Property in Livesey and Blackburn

Louis m. Ellen dau.   William   Nicholas   Alice   Margery

living   Thomas   living   living   both living 1393

1458   Dicconson   1393   1393 m.

             Harrison   Margery

                                      Farington

Ralph m. Alice Haycock   Thomas living 1464

James m. Margery living 1492

d. before   as widow.

1492   Property in Tockholes

John   m. Margaret living

d.1498   1528

John   m. Ann   James living   Margaret m. before

1490-   living   1528   1533 Richard

1530   1531   Heaton of Heaton

            June 10

James m. Ella (d. Wm. Clayton of Little Harwood)

living

1522

James m.   John

died

1595   leaving property in Whittle.

Edward bur.

Blackburn. 28 June 1618.

described as 'of Garstang' because that was where they came from that the name became a family name. Thus in 1377 we find 'William Gerstan of Penwortham', and in 1401 Thomas Gayrstang of Faryngton. Of the latter we know little, but the descendants of the former settled in the parish of Blackburn, where successive generations continued to be described by the name of the place whence their ancestors had sprung.

It is reasonable to suppose that all the oarsmen who came south with Gair, Agmund, and Orme, were clansmen but not necessarily of the same family, and, as the Wyre loch was their landing ground, most of them settled there; but in fact we hear of Orme and Agmund fighting in distant places at an early date.

William de Gerstan of Penwortham near Preston mentioned above appears at the head of Pedigree II.3 because George Squibb was able to trace his descendants from 1377. His son, John, with his wife, Joan, had mortgaged two messuages and land in Livesey, the greater part of which formed the south-west part of the borough of Blackburn, and had settled them on their son Louis. This seems to be the first time that Garstangs were connected with Blackburn and Tockholes, as the grandson James apparently married Margery Shaw whose family had been Lords of the Manor in Green Tock-holes since the time of Edward II.

Our attention had been called to the fact that Garstangs had lived in Tockholes before the time of great-uncle Thomas by a paragraph printed in the *Blackburn Standard* on June 21st 1890:

> We meet with the Garstang clan in Tockholes and there is a tenement in Tockholes bearing their name. This belonged to the family long ago, and somewhat later more members of the clan were living about Whittle on the farther side of the fells of Anglesark and Wheelton Moor.

Later my brother John with Marie (his wife), and Jamie's son Tom motored there to make investigations. John wrote:

> We went to Wheelton in Leyland Hundred, the church is said to be of Saxon origin and has curious unknown writing painted on the windows. We took a photograph of 'Higher Garstang' house; and 'Garstang House' was lower down across the railway.
>
> In Tockholes we found that 'Garstang Hall' had been near a mill. An old resident told us that two areas in Tockholes beyond the vicarage were known as 'The Gerstangs', but the Hall had been demolished and many of the stones carried off to the church and vicarage. Houses known as Garstang Terrace' had been built on some of the land, and the rest had been converted into gardens.
>
> Among the stones taken to the vicarage was an old pulpit and a large stone like a cheese-press built into the wall, and on a round stone arch the words: 'The Norman arch over this well was removed from Garstang Hall, Tockholes, and placed here in 1910 by the Rev. A. T. Corfield, Vicar.' Above was a Coat of Arms carved in stone with the motto 'Serva Fidem' on a ribbon below. This visit took place on August 3rd 1934.

When my cousins Bessie and George Squibb were exploring the neighbourhood of Tockholes they found that the Congregational Chapel had been built on part of the Garstang estate and that most of the land had been acquired by the Liverpool corporation for a new reservoir and gathering ground. Between 1710 and 1720 the Nonconformists had bought a site for their first chapel from a *James Garsden* of Tockholes. The site was about 20 yards square and they completed a suitable hall with a thatched roof; before this they had used the Anglican chapelry on alternate Sundays, made possible by the fact that the chapels of Tockholes and Darwen were served by the same Curate under the vicar of Blackburn.

The next information about Tockholes was sent by James Rowland Garstang who visited the district with his wife a few years ago in 1963 and said:

> The Coat of Arms which you told us about was not carved in one of the stones of the Garstang arch, but on a separate piece of stone work above the arch. I think they are the arms of the vicar. We saw the vicar afterwards, he told us that he had not been the incumbent for very long. He had heard that a history of Tockholes had been written, but he had not seen it. I will try to get a copy.

While I was searching through the Garstang notes left by my Father and Walter, I found a paragraph cut from an old newspaper with 'Tockholes' written on it, it was not dated, but 1948 and 1951 are mentioned in a law case on the other side:

Family Motto found by Clerk.

The motto 'Serva Fidem'—Keep faith—was that of the Gerstone family of Tockholes and was found by the Clerk (Mr. F. A. Clifford) on a wall by the roadside at Tockholes.

The writer then explains that the Blackburn Rural District Council had accepted a new design for the Council's Coat of Arms which included this motto 'Serva Fidem'.

This had puzzled Walter as *Gerstone* had been considered as a variant spelling of Garstang, and the arms depicted at Tockholes above the motto were not those seen at Henry Garstang's tomb in Cirencester church. He describes them in this way:

> The arms said to come from Gerstone Hall show two upper lozenges separated from one lower lozenge by a narrow chevron, and do not lie below a clear bare chief, and all three have the shape of five-sided shields each enclosing a heart; they are neither solid lozenges nor hollow mascles, but inescutcheons. Also there is no engrailed border.

There Walter's notes ended, so I asked James Rowland to repeat what impression he felt when he went to Tockholes, and he replied that he did not think the arms were meant to be a part of the arch brought from Gerstone Hall. They seemed to be above and behind the wall which had been built with the old stones, and he repeated that the arms might be those of a vicar who had placed them on the vicarage wall behind the old stone arch.

Although the Garstang arms have been already fully described I will report what George Squibb and Dr. Maclaren replied when I asked them about the Tockholes arms.

In writing to me about the Garstang arms George Squibb said:

The Garstang arms appear in three forms in Cirencester church:
1. Three mascles on corbels in the south aisle.
2. Three mascles and a chief in the upper part of the centre light in the east window.
3. Three mascles and a chief within a bordure engrailed on Henry's tomb, and on the screen round St. Edmund's chapel. The field is always azure, the mascles or, the chief argent, and the bordure gules.

Mr. F. W. Yeates, F.L.A., the Librarian and Curator of the Blackburn Museum, kindly sent this information:

No reference to the Garstang arms is given in W. A. Abram's *Lancashire Armoury,* but Gregson's *Portfolio of Fragments* quotes the Garstang arms as: 'Azure, 3 mascles within a border, gules, and includes a small illustration, of which I enclose a copy.

I sent this sketch of the Garstang arms with a copy of the Tockholes arms to Mr. Michael Maclagan in Oxford, and he replied that the Tockholes arms is of three inescutcheons, and therefore quite different from the Garstang arms.

None of these descriptions mentioned the motto, so my son, Oliver, looked up 'Serva Fidem' in the Bodleian Library, he found as James Rowland G. had thought, that it was the motto below the arms of the Corfield family, Chatwell Hall, Shropshire, and must have been placed there by the Rev. A. T. Corfield in 1910 when he was the vicar. In the 1952 edition of *Burke's Landed Gentry* there is an illustration of the arms, motto, and crest.

The crest, which my brother John could not decipher, is a hand grasping two palm branches.

Except for the Corfield Coat of Arms above the wall, the rest of the stones were indeed brought from Gerston Hall, and in the list of vicars which James Rowland also examined, the names appear of

Ludovic de Gerston 1486
James Gerstane   1552

Mr. Henry Whittaker of Blackburn told Walter that he had seen the name 'Walter de Gerstang' carved on a stone from Garstang Hall and built into a wall by the side of the road to the vicarage.

The mystery about the motto 'Serva Fidem' was solved, the book in the Bodleian, *The General Armory,* by Sir Edmund Burke, describes the Coat of Arms but does not illustrate it.

I was still worried about the cutting from the old Blackburn paper and so wrote to the Town Clerk about it, and he replied:

15 January 1969.
I have read with great interest of your searches into the Garstang family history, and the little story about the motto found by Mr. F. A. Clifford. The

Council referred to is not the Blackburn County Borough Council, but the Blackburn Rural District Council, which administers a section of the rural area surrounding the town of Blackburn. This Council has, in fact, adopted the motto "Serva Fidem" and uses it to this day.

I am glad to say that the Garstang lectures are going extremely well. At the Public Lecture, we always have a very enthusiastic audience of up to 800, and the Schools' Lectures are very much appreciated. We always make a point of mentioning the great debt we owe to the Garstang family for the provision of these facilities. (See below pp. 81-82.)

The Grammar School continues as a Direct Grant School, but the High School has been combined with the Witton Park School to form a large comprehensive school, and is called Witton Park School.

Yours sincerely,
Brian Scholes.   Chief Executive Officer /
Town Clerk.

I am sorry about that motto not belonging to the Garstangs, but I was also not surprised as we used to have a Coat of Arms with a motto hanging up in our dining room before John had been to Cirencester in his undergraduate days. This motto read 'Approbemus nos Deo'. I had drawn and copied in colour this Coat of Arms when a child, and when John wrote to tell Father about Henry Garstang's tomb and the real Garstang Arms, we asked Father about it and he said it had been sent to him as Garstang Arms. Now my son Oliver has searched in the *General Armory,* and finds that it is almost identical with the old Garston Arms: Ar. on a fesse az. between two Cornish choughs ppr. in chief, and in base a lion passant gu. crowned or, a fort of the first. *Crest*: out of a mural coronet ar. a wivern or, charged on the breast with a fireball sa.

There is no motto for Garston. There is also a Garstin Coat: Ar. on a pale sa. a pike's head couped or. *Crest*: a dexter hand holding a broken hammer.

Among Walter's notes I have found the following references to Garsdens in Tockholes:

James Garsden born 1677 m. Elizabeth Thompson of Eccleshill 1708, Thomas Garsden of Tockholes had a brother born in 1697, and his son was born in 1709. The old messuage that belonged to this family is now known as 'Garstanes'.

During the seventeenth and eighteenth centuries there were other William, James, and John Garstangs, Garstins, and Garsdens, as well as Gerstones living in that neighbourhood, and in 1697 the will of William Garsden, yeoman of Tockholes, was proved at Chester. It was given to my brother, and we have it now in the Garstang archives. See p. 68.

This reminds me that there were at my school in Blackburn two sisters, Sybil and May Garsden, who had said to me that long ago their family had been related to mine. Instead of asking them to explain I had replied: "I don't see how we could be related as our name is spelt like the town 'Garstang'."

Also at my school were two more sisters, Amy and Lilian Clayton, who lived at Little Harwood where their brother or his descendants may still be

E

living. They too have a connexion with Garstangs in the past. Returning to Pedigree II.3 above of William Gerstan of Penwortham, we see that between the two dates when Garstangs were serving as Vicars of the Tockholes church, in 1492 when James Garstang was dead, his widow Margery was living in one of the Tockholes houses while probably her son John with his wife Ann was living in the other. When their son James had reached the age of marriage, their choice fell upon Ella, the daughter of William Clayton of Little Harwood.

In 1590 the son of James and Ella, also baptised James, was appointed a governor of the Blackburn Grammar School; he died in 1595. His son Edward was buried in Blackburn.

The mystery of the Garsden relationship was solved this morning, February 3rd 1969, when Alec sent me this information:

> Found by me Alec Garstang, January 30th 1969 on an old piece of paper, written by my father Henry Louis Garstang:
> 'John Garston of Tockholes.
> James Garston 1552.
> Some of the family were settled in Whittle.
> Oliver and Lawrence Gerstone (or Garstane) 1574.
> William Garston of Tockholes died 1703.
> Then they changed to Garsdens 1708.
> The old family Messuage yet called Garstanes.'

Although the above mentioned names are difficult to identify and the date of William Garston's death does not tally with the date 1697 when the will of William Garsden was proved in Chester, we do find that after c.1708 there are no variant spellings of the names, but only Garstangs and Garsdens.

On January 22nd, 1964, James Rowland succeeded in his efforts to send me a copy of the *Tockholes Centenary Souvenir Handbook,* borrowed from Mr. T. Mares, Greenthorn Farm, Livesey, near Darwen.

I am sorry to have to record the death of Mr. Mares suddenly on 28 November 1967. I had written to ask him about a new church to be built at Tockholes, and received a letter from Miss Leach on 11 June 1969. She is the Chief Superintendent of the Women Police Force for the new amalgamated Police of Lancashire, and was answering for her sister, Mrs. Eveline Mares, with whom she was staying. "We were talking only yesterday," she wrote, "to people having connexions with the Moss family of Garstangs. I would be very interested in the book you have written if you can tell me how to get it."

The following is an extract from the Handbook:

> The centenary observed in 1933 was that of the present church dedicated to St. Stephen by the Bishop of Chester in 1833. It replaced a small low structure, dedicated to St. Michael, restored 200 years previously from an earlier building which was 50ft. long by 20ft. wide and 18ft. high and without a chancel. Initials in the east end wall, above the south porch, the bell, and a piece of stained glass hanging in the window facing the porch, bear the date 1620. A font stood in the north-west corner opposite the main door.

The Rev. Gilmour Robinson was the Incumbent at the time, tall with military bearing having taken part in the battle of Waterloo, a Freemason, a Constable, and possessing considerable medical skill.

The vicarage then stood upon a site within the present graveyard. The first school was erected in 1834 near the present Lych Gate. John Morley was baptised in Tockholes Church on March 9th 1839, and in 1848 when the Diocese of Manchester was formed out of that of Chester the Church came under the jurisdiction of Manchester. Blackburn was then a small town with only four churches, and Darwen was merely an overgrown village.

While the Rev. A. T. Corfield was Incumbent the Liverpool Corporation bought up the southern end of the parish as a gathering ground for their water supply, and among the farmsteads demolished were Garstane Hall and Hollinshead Hall. Masonry from these was brought, and built into a stone pulpit in the churchyard, the well casing in the Vicarage wall in Rock Lane, and the cornice over the Vicarage door near by the above.

By 1933 the Episcopal jurisdiction was transferred to the Bishop of Blackburn, and the income of the Incumbent raised to £400 a year. A French horn in the vestry once supplied the music.

A cannon-ball which stands on a pedestal near the Sanctuary rails was discovered in the neighbourhood.

The font is reputed to be of Saxon origin.

Some crests in the lancet windows may be of families connected at one time with Tockholes and its Church.

There is an embossed figure in chains over the old Vestry door—its origin and significance are lost.

The cannon ball would be left in the neighbourhood after the battle fought there during Cromwell's civil war.

Although I had visited Tockholes as described in Chapter 1, to see great-uncle Thomas just before he died, I do not remember ever being taken to see the house Moss Fold where he and my grandmother Hannah had been born and had spent their childhood. The reason must have been that she died when my father was only a little boy of five or six, and grandfather's second wife soon must have taken the place of Hannah in the lives of Father and his sister and two brothers. Therefore Tockholes, being so near Moss Fold on the outskirts of Darwen, has always been of special interest to us, and now that I have got to know Alec, a descendant of Henry, old Thomas Garstang's brother, I find that Tockholes has the same mysterious attraction for him. Just as I remember my visit there when about four years old, so Alec remembers his father telling of his visits as a child to see the old relations, and take them little presents of home-made pies and similar delights. They always insisted that young Henry Louis enjoy a piece of whatever he had taken before he set out for home.

The writing of this book has brought into closer friendship Thomas Garstang of Southport, whose father, George William, had sent to Walter the old will of William Garsden, the Yeoman of Tockholes, which, as I have already mentioned, was proved in the year 1697. It had been in the keeping of George William's sister Mrs. Ellen Eastham Carnson, who very kindly said that Walter could keep it in the family archives. So while dealing with Tockholes here it is:

In the name of God Amen the twentieth day of December in the year of our Lord one thousand and six hundred ninety three I William Garsden of Tockholes in the county of Lancaster yeoman being seventy four years or thereabouts yet of sound and perfect mind and memory praise bee given therefore to Almighty God doe make and ordaine this my present last will and Testament in manner and form following. First and principally

I commende my soule into the hands of Almighty God my Creator and of his Son Jesus Christ my Redeemer hoping through merits death and passion to have full and free pardon and forgiveness of all my sins and to inherit everlasting life and to be made partaker with his holy elect in his heavenly Kingdom and my body I commit to the earth to bee decently buried att the discrition of my Executrix hereinafter named and as touching the disposition of all such temporall as it hath pleased Almighty God to bestowe upon mee I give and dispose thereof as followeth. First it is my will and mind that my debts funeral expenses and the charge of the Probate of this my last Will and Testament be first paid and discharged out of my whole personall estate then I give and bequeath to my loving Wife Ellen Garsden the one halfe of all my goods chatels utensills and household stuffe and personall estate of what nature kind or quality soever the same bee after the payment of my debts funeral expences probate of this my Will and the legacies herein and hereby now by me given and bequeathed. Then I give and bequeath to my eldest Son Richard Garsden one shilling. Then I give and bequeath to my Son Nathanial Garsden the sum of five shillings in full of all claims and demands hereafter to bee made by him of in or unto any part of my personall estate hee having had from mee much more than his proportion thereof. And whereas my Master John Warren Esqr. now stands indebted to mee for sixteen years service as his Bailiffe within his Lordshipps of Darwen and Tockholes my Sallary in the life of his Father and Father-in-Lawe Edward Warren and Hugh Cooper Esqrs. being six pounds p.annum and is to bee the same from him whereof I have only received the sum of ten shillings in all that time and noe more I doe therefore give devise and bequeath the same as following the one half share to my said loving Wife and the other half to my daughters Jane Garsden and Margaret Garsden equally betwixt them. Then I give and bequeath to my said two daughters Jane and Margaret Garsden the other half of all my personal estate goods chattells and household stuffe after the payment of my debts funerall charges and Probate of my Will and legacies hereby bequeathed equally to be divided betwixt them. And lastly I doe hereby nominate and appoint my said loving wife Ellen Garsden to be my sole executrix of this my present last Will and Testament and I doe hereby revoke disannull and make void all former Wills and Testaments by mee heretofor made. In witness whereof I hereunto putt my hand and seal the day and year first above written—

William Garsden   X   his mark (seal)

Signed sealed published and declared to bee the last Will and Testament of the said Testator in the presence of us
                John Whitehead — Robert Whitle — Chris Roby
Proved in the Consistory Court of Chester on the 5th day of May 1697 by Ellen Garsden the sole Executrix.
                                                    Seal of Chester Registry.

On December 20th 1968 Alec Garstang of Sheffield, who was helping to collect the final information, received the following letter from Thomas, the son of George William:

Firstly, I thank you for your letter and am so glad to hear that the history of the Clan is nearing completion.

My father gave all the information he knew to Professor Garstang in 1936. Later in 1946 I met the Professor personally when I became a member of Formby Golf Club and we had several talks about our family and kindred subjects.

(This would be Professor John G. who lived at Formby, was devoted to golf and attached to Liverpool University.)

The earliest ancestor I know is my grandfather Thomas who married Margaret Eastham, they resided in Darwen and had four children, three sons and one daughter, Ellen (Nellie) Eastham who married A. T. Carnson and lived in Longridge. They have one surviving spinster daughter aged 83 who still resides there. Her younger brother was my father, George William (born 13.1.1875 died 2.10.1938), and when their parents both died before my father was 12 years old, the Carnsons brought him up. He later entered the old Manchester and County bank in Clitheroe and married Elizabeth Leeming Parkinson, whose father was a quarry owner and founder of Horrocksford, Lane Co. Ltd. later taken over by T. W. Ward Ltd. of Sheffield. Their elder son George Parkinson born 7.12.1912 died 15.9.1918, and self born 16.1.1905. I have no children.

My grandfather's two eldest children, Harry and Thomas, both went to U.S.A. Thomas was not very successful, but he did correspond with my father and once came over to see us in 1920 when we lived in Clitheroe.

Harry went to California after working at the original Ford factory at Detroit. He did very well. He was a born craftsman and made unusual toys, bric-à-brac, fancy shoes etc., and sold them to the original film stars. He became a large property owner 100% American, but we heard little from him until a few years ago.

He had one daughter, Dorothy, about my age. She married Walter Robinson, an Englishman who had done well in oil. In 1958 Dorothy came to England with a Bowling Team, and we had a pleasant meeting, and again in the next year 1959 when they stayed in these parts for a few days. Harry now 93 had sent a message for us to visit him in Los Angeles as he wanted to see some of his own 'stock' as he put it. I'm afraid he had left it a bit too late and it could not be arranged.

Now they are both dead. Dorothy leaves only one son as far as I know. He is with the U.S.A. Atom Energy group, and he was born in Seattle.

Please advise me when the book is ready. Best wishes for Christmas and the New Year.
                        Yours sincerely,
                        Thomas Garstang.

It is clear that Thomas, whose aunt Nellie had married T. A. Carnson as his second wife, did not realise that he was writing to the nephew (Alec) of T. A. Carnson's first wife, Henrietta, and Alec had just been telling Miss Carnson at Longridge by telephone about the story of the Clan to be published.

When Alec saw how closely he and Thomas were related to each other he arranged to go and see Thomas the following week when he would have to visit Lancashire for business reasons. This morning January 13th 1969 I received a letter saying that he had been to see Tom and "had a really jolly time with him and his wife Elizabeth." He had no information about the Garsden will sent to Walter by his father, but was delighted to hear more news about the Clan.

Most of the interviews when Walter had visited unknown Garstangs had resulted in his notes, or in letters, giving the names of the ancestors and descendants of various Garstangs living in Lancashire, and I have tried to make genealogical tables from the information. The result shows that Garstangs unknown to each other share many of the same ancestors. When this is the case I have placed them in a group although all of them do not mention all the ancestors. I began with the families descended from the same forefather as my grandmother Hannah in Darwen.

Pedigrees II.4 and II.5.
George William and Thomas of Middleton and Southport.
Henry Louis Garstang of Manchester.

One of the first letters Walter received after an appeal he had made was from George William Garstang then residing in Middleton. He was the father of Thomas whose letter to Alec I have just quoted.

Kingsway,
Middleton.
7 January 1930.

Dear Sir,
I am obliged and interested by your letter and enclosure. Being the youngest of our family and my parents dying when I was quite young, I know very little of our history except from hearing my father (Thomas) say that we descended from the Garstangs of Tockholes. I am writing to my sister for some information and will write further in a few days.

I am the manager of the Manchester and county Bank branch here in Middleton.

Yours faithfully,
G. W. Garstang.

On January 18 he wrote again:

The particulars I have gathered are as follows:
My grandparent was Henry of Moss Farm, Darwen. Three brothers of his, Thomas, George, and John, were all buried at Tockholes church.

My father was Thomas, he had three sons, Thomas, Harry, and myself; and a daughter, Ellen Eastham, my mother being an Eastham of Mytton near Clitheroe and a sister of John Eastham the late Town Clerk of that place.

My father used to get a book out of the Blackburn Library all about the family, no doubt you probably know about it. I enclose an old will for your perusal and return, it is of one of our ancestors and is the only relic we possess.

Walter was interested in the will and had evidently asked if he might keep it in the Garstang archives as he had been studying the question of Garsdens in Tockholes. On January 23rd George William replied:

In reply to your letter my sister is quite willing to give up the old will referred to, so that it can be added to your collection. I was under the impression that we were related but did not know how.

Our family are as follows:

Henry Garstang, grandparent, 1796-1874, was interred at Over Darwen on May 20th. His four children were— James 1836-1837, Thomas -1888, Henry -1889, Ellen.

My father Thomas also had four children: Thomas born in 1865 was married but had no family, he was my eldest brother, but he went to Washington State U.S.A. to some post in a school.

The second son Henry was born 1868, also went to Washington State U.S.A. He was a farmer, married, and has one son and one daughter, I believe both of them are married.

Self, George William, born 1875, married Elizabeth Parkinson of Rockmount, Clitheroe, we have had two boys, the one now living is Thomas born 1905.

My grandfather's youngest son, James, married Jane Ellen Place, and their fifth child is Henry Louis Garstang of Garstang and Galloway, Manchester. His sister Henrietta Jane was the first wife of T. A. Carnson and she died in 1883 (without children). My sister Ellen Carnson is his second wife.

I enclose the funeral cards of my grandfather Henry and his three brothers interred in St. Stephens Church, Tockholes.

When Alec, the son of Henry Louis mentioned above, told me that he had seen in Middleton church a stained glass window connected with a Garstang, I wrote to the vicar to ask if he could tell me anything about it. On November 23rd 1968 Mr. F. E. North, the Clerk and verger, very kindly wrote:

There is a window in Middleton Parish church of St. Leonard to James Garstang who died on January 9th 1866 aged 71 years and Martha his wife who died December 16th 1847 aged 53 years. The window was erected by their daughter Anne and her husband Alex Brogden.

The window is that of the central east window, the subject being the Crucifixion, the Last supper, and six incidents in the life of Christ.

Mr. North added that he was unable to give any information about the Garstang family from the church register; so far I have not been able to discover if the window was in any way connected with George William and other Garstangs who have also lived in Middleton.

Pedigree II 4.

Garstangs of Moss Fold, Lower Darwen.
1697 May 5, Will was proved of ancestor William of Tockholes.

William
Husbandman of Lower Darwen

Thomas 1750-1809 of
Moss Bridge Farm, Moss Fold, Lower Darwen.
m. Betty Croft 1756-1840

1. Ann m.
Holden
1781.
2. Jane
-1839.
3. Isabella
1790- m.
Nuttall.

James
1783-1819

Roger
1785-1856
m. Alice Hacking.
1786-1873 d. at
Witton.

William
1787-1866
of
Whalley
Banks
Blackburn
Gt. grandfather
of Wallace

Thomas
1792-1882
of Tockholes

Twins
John
1794-
1878
George m.
d. 1874

Alice
m. Wade

Henry
1796-1874
m. Ellen
Hartley
g-f. of
George
William
and Henry
Louis

Hannah
1806-1837
m. Thomas
Garstang of
Blackburn
| | | |
Walter, my
father.
also John
James
Alice

Thomas 1807-85

John
1811-76
School and
Actuary
m. in
Blackburn.
Gt. G-father
of Margaret
Dixon Totty.

James of
Witton
1815-68 m.
Elizabeth
July
1880.

Jane
1813-1871
m.Bury

John

Thomas
1840-79.

Mary
Alice
1847-79

Henry Louis himself also wrote to Walter on November 27th, 1929 :

> Fern Lea, Bracklay Rd.
> Manton Eccles, Nr. Manchester.

My dear Dr. Garstang,

It was quite a surprise and pleasure to receive your letter and papers re the Garstang family. I am the son of James and Grandson of Henry and Great-grandson of Thomas. I was at the Blackburn Grammar School during 1878 and 1880. I remember you perfectly well, curly hair and good teeth, both of which you took good care; I only wish I had done likewise. Willie Haworth used to point you out to me as an example, as my hair was not always so nice! My sister May was a nurse in London for many years, I had no sister an actress in Musical Comedy. My name in full is Henry Louis, but the name I am known by is just Louis. My brother John Place died when 6 years of age. I don't remember my Grandfather having a brother called Roger, but I remember three brothers of his called John, Thomas, and George, who were at Moss Fold, Lower Darwen. I believe there is a book in existence entitled 'The Garstangs of Garstang Grange' i.e. Moss Fold.

I am sorry I cannot furnish you with any further information as I have never taken any great interest in the Garstang genealogy, but you certainly have revived it, and I should greatly esteem it if you would kindly send me a copy of what you have done so far. I sincerely hope you are in good health, and that you will have good fortune in your researches. Believe me,

> Yours faithfully,
> H. L. Garstang.

P.S.   My son was born on June 20th 1902, and my daughter on June 6th 1906. She married A. Robinson on September 14th 1927. My father, James Garstang, was a Cotton Manufacturer at Lower Wood and Cotton Hall Mills in Darwen in partnership with his two brothers Henry and Thomas. Henry lived at Holly Cottage, Darwen, and died in 1889; Thomas lived in Hollins Grove, Darwen, and died on November 3rd 1888. My father moved from Lower Wood, Darwen, in later years, to Snowdon Road in Eccles.

So all these letters together gave us clear proof of the identity of George William and Henry Louis, and of their relationship to our grandmother Hannah of Moss Fold, Darwen. See Ped. III (p.33).

Alec Garstang of Dronfield.
Son of Henry Louis.

On October 18 1968 I received a letter from Alec Garstang of Dronfield near Sheffield as follows :

> Calling today at the church in Cirencester I found a photographer busy taking shots of the Garstang chapel. He gave me your address and told me that you have been writing a book about our Clan. I am looking forward to seeing it, and would like to have a copy.

I was very interested to find that the Garstang who had gone so long ago to Cirencester had the same name as my father, Henry.

After I had answered this letter Alec sent me a pedigree which had more recent names than that sent by his father to my brother Walter. I then realised that Alec was the son mentioned in Henry Louis's letter as born on June 20th, 1902, and Alec knew of the many discoveries made by George Squibb as well as by Walter.

"My father told me," he continued, "that he had understood a quarrel had arisen between two Garstang brothers and that one had gone sheep-farming to the south of Lancashire. Also that a family with a name something like Garstang had changed their own family name by deed-poll." (See above p.66).

After receiving this letter I suggested that Alec could call to see me and the book before it goes finally to the publishers.

When he came I asked him to write something about his experiences, and he sent the following:

It seemed that I was destined to be concerned with engineering; my great grandfather was engaged in the hand weaving of cotton goods. At the beginning of the eighteenth century he built a cotton mill, Lower Wood Mill, in Darwen, and installed in it a steam engine to power his looms.

My maternal grandfather and his father before him were both engineers, actively engaged in chemical engineering and engine design, and I was brought up closely in touch with their works.

During nearly 50 years I have worked as an engineer, specialising in the glass industry, and in particular on furnace engineering. My work has provided experience in many countries, and brought me into contact with people curiously interested in my name. On one of my visits to Israel, I was accompanied by a companion on a journey to Jerusalem from Haifa, and as we approached Caesarea I asked him to guide me to an excavation which I had not seen on previous visits. I found that he was interested in archaeology and then asked me to repeat my name which had not been given very clearly. When I had explained he at once asked if I was related to Professor John Garstang. When I told him that we were kinsmen he changed his programme and took me to see where John had been excavating near Ramla and Lod. Then I saw excavations near Ramat Rahel and was shewn the Dead Sea Scrolls just newly exhibited in the University of Jerusalem. I found this most interesting and so did my friend.

Again this year when I was acting as chairman at one of the meetings of the International Congress on Glass, Dr. D. B. Harden in a similar way informed me that he knew John Garstang well.

On a number of other occasions when I have been travelling I have been mistaken for another Garstang connected with travel and sea-port investigations whom I did not know, but now I understand that he may have been Cecil Garstang pre-eminently a travel organiser. The putting together of these pieces of information about our Clan has become to me an absorbing interest.

In May 1969 I received another letter from Alec Garstang pointing out that there was a mistake in Pedigree II.5 about his sister Kathleen's birthday. The date is given correctly in the postscript to their father's letter p.73 as 6 June 1906. He enclosed a Newspaper paragraph about the death of his grandfather James (1836-1897): James was the youngest son of Henry (1796-1874) of Moss Fold near Tockholes, who had acted as agent for the purchasers of cotton materials in Blackburn and Darwen neighbourhoods. Henry used to give out 'beams' of spun cotton yarn wound round a wooden cylinder by the various spinners in their own homes; he took the beams to farms and cottages in the neighbourhood, also supplying the 'cops' for the shuttle as weft, the beams supplying the warp. At the same time he took away the finished 'pieces' of cloth to pass on to the merchants in Manchester, and took in exchange food to the distant homesteads. "The timing of the introduction of steam power weaving at St. Louis (see p.140) fits with the building of Lower Wood Mill by my grandfather and that was steam driven," he added.

In May Alec was elected President of the Society of Glass Technology at a meeting held at Turnberry in Scotland, where a symposium attended by members from all parts of the world was brought to a close with the Annual Dinner. To this he invited his daughter Sandra, as well as Professor Gunther of Germany. This year Alec is also President of the Furnace Builders' Society. He wrote on June 6th, 1969: "I have now located and seen Moss Bridge Fold in Lower Darwen about a mile from Tockholes. It consists of a group of buildings, very aged, forming Upper, Middle and Lower Moss Bridge. The farms and cottages seem to be occupied, all the buildings nearly touching each other with some in a decayed state though standing. I removed layer after layer of whitewash from a door lintel and found a date, 1687, clearly written, and the initials T and H not so clear, printed on a ruined building adjacent to the main house, which was in the middle of the built up area."

On June 27th he found the following description of the district in the *Blackburn Times*: "Tockholes village, remote and isolated among the hills, has retained much of its ancient character. Change and innovations are for the valley folk; here in this land of waving heath and purpling heather, time has no meaning, all things are eternal.

"Typical of this continuity are its farmsteads, still retaining their picturesque Tudor or Jacobean features unmarred. . . .

"There is still one link with the past in a small outhouse carefully rebuilt at the cost of the Liverpool Corporation.

"Here" (writes the chronicler) "no less than five different springs of water, after uniting and passing through a very old carved stone representing a lion's head, flow into a well. To this well pilgrimages were formerly made.

"When last I visited this lonely spot a number of coins, the oblations of modern pilgrims, could be seen below the limpid water.

"Higher Hill is a fine 17th century house formerly the residence of the Walmsleys, and others include Crowtrees (1671), Bradley (1704), and Lower Garstangs (1748). Altogether here is a great deal of antiquity packed into a very small compass. The unfettered power of the elements has moulded the lives and destinies of these moorland folk as a potter moulds his clay, making them what they are, sturdy and resolute. They and their forebears have

Pedigree II.5.

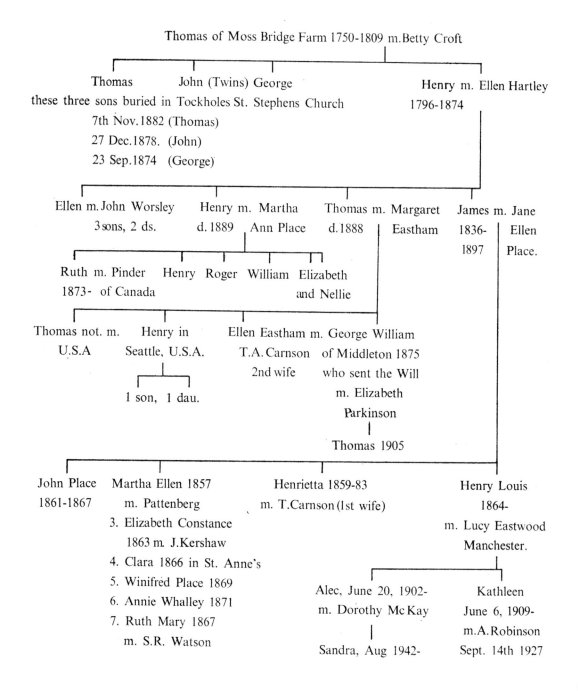

Thomas of Moss Bridge Farm 1750-1809 m.Betty Croft

Thomas   John (Twins) George
these three sons buried in Tockholes St. Stephens Church
7th Nov.1882 (Thomas)
27 Dec.1878. (John)
23 Sep.1874 (George)

Henry m. Ellen Hartley
1796-1874

Ellen m.John Worsley   Henry m. Martha   Thomas m. Margaret   James m. Jane
3 sons, 2 ds.   d.1889 Ann Place   d.1888 Eastham   1836-   Ellen
1897   Place.

Ruth m. Pinder   Henry Roger William Elizabeth
1873- of Canada   and Nellie

Thomas not. m.   Henry in   Ellen Eastham m. George William
U.S.A   Seattle, U.S.A.   T.A.Carnson   of Middleton 1875
2nd wife   who sent the Will
1 son, 1 dau.   m. Elizabeth
Parkinson
Thomas 1905

John Place   Martha Ellen 1857   Henrietta 1859-83   Henry Louis
1861-1867   m. Pattenberg   m. T.Carnson (1st wife)   1864-
3. Elizabeth Constance   m. Lucy Eastwood
1863 m. J.Kershaw   Manchester.
4. Clara 1866 in St. Anne's
5. Winifred Place 1869   Alec, June 20, 1902-   Kathleen
6. Annie Whalley 1871   m. Dorothy McKay   June 6, 1909-
7. Ruth Mary 1867   m.A.Robinson
m. S.R. Watson   Sandra, Aug 1942-   Sept. 14th 1927

wrestled with nature for more than a thousand years--what have they to fear from man?"

In Pedigrees III.15 and 16 mention is made of Moody's Farm in Heapey, and in Alec's next letter he described how he explored the neighbourhood and made friends with the farmers. They were all interested in the Garstang history; at Moody's the farmer actually brought out his deeds but found they did not go far enough back to mention the Henry Garstang living 1833-1897. This farm is only half a mile from Higher and Lower Garstang, and lies in the direction of Anglezarke Moor, not far from Chorley. The people now farming the Garstang lands, he said, all use still the pronunciation 'Gairstang' for that name. See pp.105, 108, 111.

Alec said that the house still stands with the initials and date on the wall as described by George Squibb years ago. See p.59.

Pedigree II.6
Wallace Garstang, Great-grandson of William

In 1922 my sister Daisy's nursing adventures were practically over, but working in Cairo and Rangoon hospitals as Matron, and in Serbia for the 'Save the Children' fund, had all left their mark, and she was content to live with Nell Howard in the house in Blackburn where I had been made welcome in 1900, and she worked for the Town Council. She wrote to Walter:

> Please send any letters for me to Ingham Old Hall as Thistle says that my luggage has arrived there from Serbia. I am returning your note-book before I go there, and you will see many entries I have copied from grave-stones, among them a Giggleswick Garstang, James, the brother of Dr. Thomas Blacklidge G. and only 20 years old, he was buried in St. John's, Blackburn.
>
> I shall see Aunt James again this afternoon, she wants Ida to call before Lily goes back to Halifax. Aunt and Uncle James were at the reading of the Will at Moss Farm, also Mrs. Walter James G., as Walter was the Grandson of our Grandmother's Uncle, *William of Moss Fold*. There were some spade guineas distributed, so it is a pity you could not be there as Aunt James does not know where she has put hers. The sisters of that Walter live in Bury, both married, one of them is very keen on our family history. Alice Wade used to know all about the family but of course it was she who had kept George's Will, and it was after her death that it was read.
>
> The Rev. Corfield, who married Arthur Pughe's sister, was Vicar of Tockholes, and is writing a history of the place, he used to ask this Walter James G. for details.

Daisy also went to see the widow of Mr. John Thomas Garstang, the son of the schoolmaster and actuary. She had one son, a motor engineer called Harry Garstang.

The next year on October 7th, 1923, Ida wrote to Walter with more details about the family, and adds:

I saw our cousin Walter's widow yesterday whose daughter Marjorie married Wallace, the son of the other Walter James Garstang. He is going to copy out for you the Family Tree which connects him with the Darwen Garstangs of Grandmama Hannah—both Garstangs again!

Wallace kept his promise on February 4th 1924, writing from Widnes, 6 miles W.S.W. of Warrington which is 18 miles west of Manchester:

> The genealogical table and newspaper cutting about the longevity of the Garstangs were the property of my father, Walter James Garstang of Blackburn. He was a very proud man — extremely so concerning the Garstangs, and he set himself very high ideals in life. He died in 1919 and his rather early demise upsets me somewhat, affecting as it does, our high average of longevity.
>
> Like a young fool I joined the R.F.A. as a combatant instead of the R.A.M.C.—like a bigger fool I stayed in the mud etc. of Flanders when I could have come home to qualify L.R.C.P. After four years of it the Bosche sent me to Blighty with a 'small packet'. After this I felt I could not go through with the Medical Conjoint Board—I just took the L.D.S. in Manchester.
>
> You will find the name of my wife on the Pedigree—Marjorie Lillian Garstang, 2nd daughter of the late Walter James Garstang of Blackburn. She is a nearer relative to you than myself. Our wedding announcement was rather singular:

> Garstang—Garstang
> Wallace, son of Mrs. and the late Mr. Walter James Garstang to Marjorie Lillian, second daughter of Mr. and Mrs. Walter James Garstang.

> Another peculiar point was, that my mother's name was Ellen, and my wife's mother's name was Eleanor!
>
> I believe the Pedigree table was made in conjunction with the Moss Farm Estate, Darwen.

The next two Pedigrees 6 and 7 show how Wallace and Marjorie were related to us as well as to each other.

So Wallace's great grandfather William was another brother of Great Grandfather Roger, and Marjorie's father was my first cousin, and yet Daisy and Ida were the only members of our family who had met them. How easily therefore do families lose their connexions!

We have the funeral card of Great Grandmother Alice, wife of Roger, dated December 30th 1873, she had lived at Witton until she was 87 years old, also the funeral card of her grand-daughter Mary Alice, wife of Henry Thompson; she was buried in Whalley Parish churchyard on May 2nd 1879, but although we often visited Whalley I do not remember ever seeing the gravestone. (See her brother John of Witton's letter below.)

A letter to Uncle John giving the correct dates concerning Grandmother Hannah's family, not dated, written before 1899:

Dear Cousin,

In answer to your letter of the 1st inst. I wish to give you the best information I can with regard to our family.

1st. My Father James, born July 8th 1815, died August 28th 1868 aged 53 years.

2nd. My Grandfather, Roger, as near as I can tell, born in 1784, (actually on January 23rd 1785) died in the year 1856 (October 24th). If you will kindly look in Chapel Street Chapel Graveyard you will find the exact date on the gravestone of Uncle David Bury in whose vault Grandfather and Grandmother Alice were buried.

My brother Thomas born Dec. 31st 1840, died 1879 aged 39 years.

My sister Mary Alice born March 1847 died April 28th 1879 aged 32. I am sorry I cannot oblige you with the funeral cards as I have looked and cannot find one amongst what I have here, they must have got mislaid with removing or something.

You will please excuse me not replying to your former letter with regard to the Whittle Garstangs as I sent one gardener to ask him to come up and he brought word back that the old man died about July, but the son said he would come and see me, but he has not been yet. I own in due courtesy that I ought to have written you earlier, but constantly expecting him coming up, it was put off. (About that time I was unable to go out of the grounds).

I am now doing very nicely, but I require to take care, the weather is so open and changeable. I will call according to your former invitation as soon as convenient. If there is any other information which I can render, I shall be glad to give it you.

With the compliments of the season, I remain yours,

Jno. Garstang.

This interesting old letter is written on note-paper bearing a wood-cut of a gabled building standing in a park with a pavilion among trees and shrubs, and with a hill at the back where men appear to be hay-making, and inscribed:

Whittle Springs Hotel and Bath near Chorley.

Pedigree II.6.

James Garstang 10 May 1835-2 Feb.1909
m. Mary Critchley, 12 May 1843-6 Oct. 1931.

| Thomas Critchley 1862-1921 m. Anne Martin | Walter James. m. Eleanor Lewis 1864-1922 | Annie Eliza m. Edward Hill b. Sept.1866 | Alice Lilian m. James Lord. b.Nov.1868. |

| Dorothy | Marjorie m. Wallace Garstang, L.D.S. of Widnes. | Kathleen. |

Pedigree II.7.

Wallace Garstang's Family Tree. (The Darwen Branch).

Thomas Garstang of Moss Farm. 1750-1809
m. Betty Croft 1756-1840

William (6 brothers, 3 sisters)
1787-1866 of Whalley Banks, Blackburn.

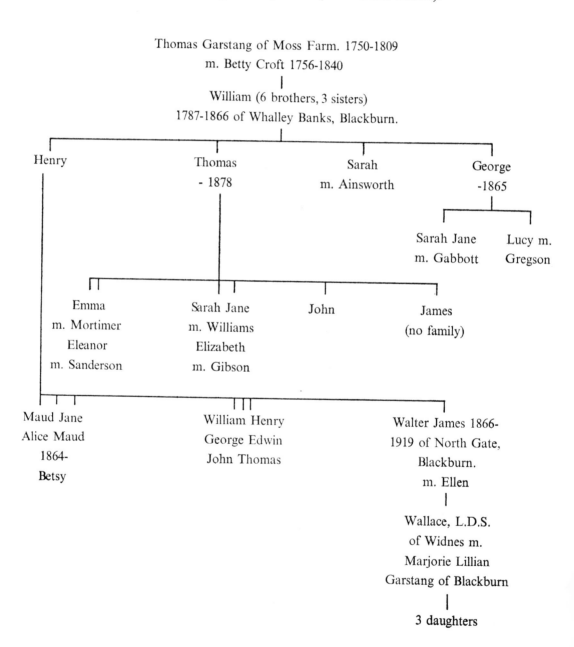

Henry

Thomas
- 1878

Sarah
m. Ainsworth

George
-1865

Sarah Jane
m. Gabbott

Lucy m.
Gregson

Emma
m. Mortimer
Eleanor
m. Sanderson

Sarah Jane
m. Williams
Elizabeth
m. Gibson

John

James
(no family)

Maud Jane
Alice Maud
1864-
Betsy

William Henry
George Edwin
John Thomas

Walter James 1866-
1919 of North Gate,
Blackburn.
m. Ellen

Wallace, L.D.S.
of Widnes m.
Marjorie Lillian
Garstang of Blackburn

3 daughters

Pedigree II. 8
Margaret Dixon Totty.

In one of Daisy's letters to Walter she told him that she had been to see the widow of John Thomas Garstang, the son of the schoolmaster and actuary, and so the nephew of Grandmother Hannah. The son Harry married Margaret Dixon, and their daughter, Margaret Dixon Totty married Harold Totty in 1936. Walter had not been able to get into touch with her, but in 1945, July 1st, she wrote to him:

Dear Mr. Garstang,
    I have just read the account in the *Blackburn Times* of your interesting proposal to form a Lecture Trust. Although I never attended a Gilchrist Lecture I often heard Mother speak of them. What a happy way to keep one's parents' memory green! I'm sure the Blackburn youngsters will much appreciate your generosity.

Here I will interrupt Margaret's letter to copy the account about the Trust which she had read in the *Times*; the Trust was one of Walter's ideas after the death of our three sisters. The same report appeared in the *Northern Daily Telegraph* 29 June 1945.

BEQUEST FOR LECTURE TRUST
Family's gratitude to Blackburn

An offer of a combined bequest by the three Garstang brothers and their sister, all Blackburnians of scientific and scholastic repute, to establish a Lecture Trust in the town has been provisionally accepted after negotiations in which the Mayor (Councillor E. Holden) has taken part.
The first move was made by Dr. Walter Garstang, M.A., D.Sc., of Oxford, who wrote to the Town Clerk asking whether the Council would be willing to accept certain legacies which were intended partly as a memorial to the zeal of their father, Dr. Walter Garstang, a native of Blackburn, for their education, and partly as a token of their gratitude for the early education they received in Blackburn, without which, and the financial assistance given by the schools—the Grammar School and the Girls' High School—a University career for all of them would have been impossible.

ANNUAL LECTURES

The donors propose to provide for a total bequest . . . for the endowment of annual lectures on the sciences and arts and their bearings on citizenship, industry, and education. . . .

The donors of the trust are:

Dr. Walter Garstang, M.A., D.Sc., Emeritus Professor of Zoology at Leeds University, ex-fellow of Lincoln College, Oxford, head boy at Blackburn Grammar School in 1883-4, and first exhibitioner.

Mr. Thomas James Garstang, M.A., a retired Schoolmaster, open Scholar of Corpus Christi College, Oxford, head boy at Blackburn Grammar School 1889-90, Langworthy and Foundation Scholar, and Head boy at the Manchester Grammar School, 1892-3.

Dr. John Garstang, M.A., D.Sc., B. Litt., Emeritus Professor of Archaeology at Liverpool University, open Scholar at Jesus College, Oxford, captain of Blackburn Grammar School in 1891-3, and Tattersall Exhibitioner.

Mrs. S. G. Gurney, M.B.E., authoress of Bible Studies, open Exhibitioner of Somerville College, Oxford, the first Eccles Scholar at Blackburn High School.

It has been agreed that the four trustees should be the Mayor of Blackburn, the Director of Education, the Head Master of the Grammar School, and the Head Mistress of the Girls' High School.

Margaret then suggests that Walter might have attended her grandfather's academy. (Here was an exclamation mark put in pencil by Walter, as it was Father who attended under his uncle John, and Walter under a successor.) Margaret's letter continues:

I remember some years ago Professor Walter Garstang wrote to my Father and made some date enquiries, and I wonder if the Family Tree was ever completed, if it is possible I should be extremely grateful if I might become possessed of a copy. Particularly as last week I produced my second lusty son and would like them to be proud of their ancestry as I am myself. Naturally I should be tremendously pleased if you could spare a moment to answer my note.

I had the good fortune to attend the Blackburn High School from 1922-28, and my brother the Grammar School for some eight years.

On October 27th of the same year Margaret wrote again:

My Father came over here and I tackled him about our Family Tree! He laboured under the delusion that he had answered my old enquiry—but now says he may have meant to, but was very busy working with the F.A. at that time.

He confirms your definition of John Garstang, my Great-grandfather, and has his (J.G.'s) gold watch to prove his point! He knew that John G. was Actuary to Blackburn Savings Bank and apparently a very able one if accounts are true. So I have enclosed our Pedigree Table, but I can't give you even approximate dates of my cousins' births, they are so very scattered; but if you should need these dates I will write to my various Aunts and Uncles. One or two of them are married, but again I have no details.

Could you please tell me if my Grandmother on the distaff side, Margaret Dixon of Back Commons, Clitheroe, Lancs., who married Robinson Dixon —(hence my Mother was Margaret Dixon)—occurs in any of your tangled threads. I can give dates from my Mother if these names ring any bell in your memory.

My eldest son—aged seven—is intensely interested, and wants to know why I changed my name when I was married, as my old name was so much nicer??! Fortunately he didn't ask in his Daddy's hearing. My husband's family is an old Shropshire one. My brother Robin lives in Blackburn.

Pedigree II 8

Margaret Dixon Garstang Pedigree

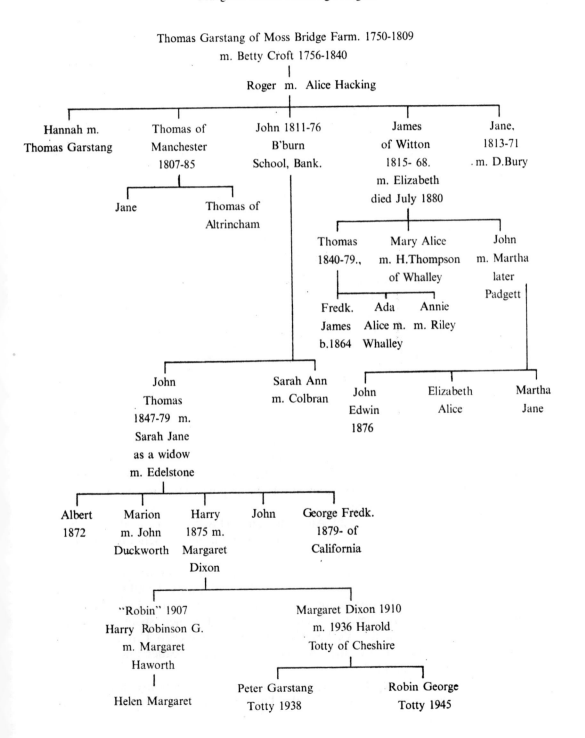

Thomas Garstang of Moss Bridge Farm. 1750-1809
m. Betty Croft 1756-1840

Roger m. Alice Hacking

Hannah m.
Thomas Garstang

Thomas of
Manchester
1807-85

John 1811-76
B'burn
School, Bank.

James
of Witton
1815- 68.
m. Elizabeth
died July 1880

Jane,
1813-71
. m. D.Bury

Jane

Thomas of
Altrincham

Thomas
1840-79.,

Mary Alice
m. H.Thompson
of Whalley

John
m. Martha
later
Padgett

Fredk.
James
b.1864

Ada
Alice m.
Whalley

Annie
m. Riley

John
Thomas
1847-79 m.
Sarah Jane
as a widow
m. Edelstone

Sarah Ann
m. Colbran

John
Edwin
1876

Elizabeth
Alice

Martha
Jane

Albert
1872

Marion
m. John
Duckworth

Harry
1875 m.
Margaret
Dixon

John

George Fredk.
1879- of
California

"Robin" 1907
Harry Robinson G.
m. Margaret
Haworth

Margaret Dixon 1910
m. 1936 Harold
Totty of Cheshire

Helen Margaret

Peter Garstang
Totty 1938

Robin George
Totty 1945

Pedigree II.10
Roy Henry Garstang
Royal Astronomical Society, London N.W.4.

Having received R. H. Garstang's address from Cecil Garstang of London, I wrote to him in June 1963 and received the following reply:

> I was interested to receive your letter and I am sending you some details of the family.
>
> My father, Percy Brocklehurst Garstang was born and lived in Lancashire, for most of his working life in Southport, where I was born. I am his only child. My mother, Eunice Garstang née Gledhill, came from Rochdale, and moved to Southport as a girl. She still lives there, where you could write. She can tell you much more than I about my father (who died when I was a boy) and about other relatives in the family. I suggest you write to her yourself. Many years ago, it may have been Walter Garstang, visited my father and gave him a copy of the results in research into Church records and the like relating to the Garstang family in Lancashire. My mother may still have it.
>
> If you write to my mother and get some details from her I can confine myself in my present letter to myself.

I looked in Walter's rough notebook in which he had recorded his various visits, and found the Brocklehurst pedigree. I wrote to R.H.G's mother all the same as he had asked me to do so, and in a few days I received a letter from her agreeing that Walter had called to see them in 1929 or thereabouts, and they had helped in the researches of the family records. "I am sorry," she continued, "that I cannot give you any more particulars of our Branch as my late husband's father died when he was 12, and my husband died in 1938 when he was 56; so you see time has overtaken me and I never met many relations. I have not been in touch with any for many years now. I wish you every success with the story."

While I was waiting for this reply I looked through the Pedigrees again, and found that the Brocklehurst connexion dated back to Thomas Henry Garstang 1844-1895; and there were letters and a pedigree from Henry Edward Garstang then of Heaton Moor, Stockport, who proved to be the brother of Roy Henry's father.

Roy Henry married in 1959 Ann Clemence Hawk of Cornwall who had been teaching Mathematics at various London Grammar Schools for Girls since she took her degree in Cambridge.

Roy himself was born on September 18th 1925, and after winning scholarships in 1942 and 1943, he went to Gonville and Caius, Cambridge, from which college he gained distinction in the Mathematical Tripos Part III, afterwards becoming Isaac Newton Student in 1950. He then spent a year as Research Associate in the Yerkes Observatory of Chicago University, and returned to London as Lecturer in Astronomy, then Reader and Assistant Director of the London Observatory.

Although Roy Henry has filled various posts in Astronomy and Physics in London, he is still attracted by the United States of America after his experiences in 1951-2, and returned there more recently as Guest Worker in the National Bureau of Standards. He was looking forward to returning there in September 1964 as Professor of Astrophysics in the University of Colorado. I have not heard from him since he went there, but Alec wrote to his mother in Southport for further information in December 1968: "No further change has taken place," she replied, "except that my son, Roy Henry, has been awarded his Ph.D. at Cambridge. He was a Reader at University College in London until 1964 and is now in the Joint Institute of Laboratory Astro-Physics at Colorado University where he has just completed two years as the Chairman. He lives near the University and has two daughters Jennifer Katherine and Susan Veronica, four years and two years old respectively. I hope this information will help in your difficult task."

Pedigree II. 9.
Henry Edward Garstang, Heaton Moor, Nr. Stockport, Lancs.

In the summer of 1929 Walter had a letter from Henry Edward Garstang who claimed that his ancestors had lived in Darwen. Our Darwen family pedigree was fairly well defined by that time, and I think Walter must have sent a copy of it to H.E.G. as on December 9th 1929 he received a second letter:

> I have now had an opportunity of looking into the question of the ancestry of my family and I return herewith the table you sent to me. I commenced to alter this in red ink, but found the alterations too numerous and therefore made out a new table. I think John and Ellen were the parents of my Grandfather Henry who was a Cotton Finisher, and he migrated early in life to Manchester and lived in Broughton two miles to the north-west of it in the Hundred of Salford. There was also a Thomas Garstang who was killed at the Paper Works in Over Darwen on February 5th 1830; he was buried in New Church, Over Darwen, I have no idea who he was, but perhaps he was the brother of my ancestor John.
>
> My Grandfather Henry was born at Over Darwen January 11 1818, went to live in Manchester, and was buried in Rushulme Cemetery. I do not know where the burial ground is, but I should imagine it is somewhere near Over Darwen.
>
> I do not know of any relationship with any other Garstang family. I fear I have added very little to your knowledge of the Clan, but should I come across any other information I will communicate it to you.

There is a township of Rushulme in the parish of Manchester in the Hundred of Salford, 2½ miles S.S.E. of Manchester, so probably Henry was buried there as he had left Darwen for Manchester.

Henry Edward was an Accountant by profession, and left two daughters, Amy Dorothy and Enid Mary, both born in Levershulme near Manchester, four miles to the south-east.

As Henry Edward was connected with Darwen, if Walter had sent him the pedigree table of Moss Fold Garstangs, it would have been useful to know

Pedigree II.9.

Sent by Henry Edward, with additions from cemeteries.

Garstang - Ancestor in Darwen m.

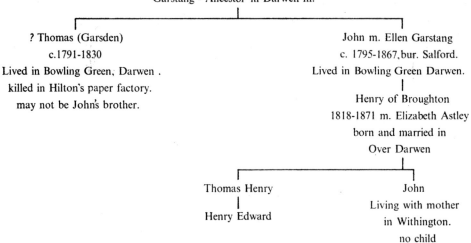

? Thomas (Garsden)
c.1791-1830
Lived in Bowling Green, Darwen .
killed in Hilton's paper factory.
may not be John's brother.

John m. Ellen Garstang
c. 1795-1867, bur. Salford.
Lived in Bowling Green Darwen.

Henry of Broughton
1818-1871 m. Elizabeth Astley
born and married in
Over Darwen

Thomas Henry

Henry Edward

John
Living with mother
in Withington.
no child

in what way the names and dates did agree with his own family if indeed he had found any connexion.

In November 1967 I wrote to the vicar of New Church, Darwen, to ask if he could tell me anything about the 'Thomas' who had been killed in the Darwen paper works in 1830.

The Rev. Hugh Williams, vicar of Holy Trinity Church, very kindly looked in the register of burials, and after searching back more than 100 years found that *Thomas Garsden* was buried there on February 2nd 1830, having been killed at Hilton's Paper Works. He had lived at 'Bowling Green', the Darwen suburb where John and Ellen, the ancestors of Henry Edward, had resided at that time.

Thomas was said to be 39 when he was killed; he was probably of the same family as the Thomas Garsden mentioned by Walter as living in Tockholes, and the James Garsden who had sold the plot of land for a chapel site.   (See above p.63.)

As Henry Edward had suggested that the Thomas who was killed might have been a brother of his ancestor John I wrote to the cemeteries of Rushulme and Cheetham Hill, in case the spelling 'Garsden' might appear again; I would like to clear up the mystery of the Garsden will, like the Tockholes Coat of Arms, which does not belong to a Garstang family.

My letter to Rushulme cemetery was forwarded to the Town Hall Manchester and the Town Clerk, G. C. Ogden, C.B.E., M.A. very kindly answered my questions:

Rushulme is a district of Manchester, and whilst there is no burial ground owned by the Corporation in that district, there are, of course, church burial grounds, but the Corporation have no information about burials in them.

Pedigree II. 9. with 10.

Percy Brocklehurst Garstang of Southport
Roy Henry Garstang of London
Pedigree from Henry Edward Garstang sent 1929 (Oct.9)

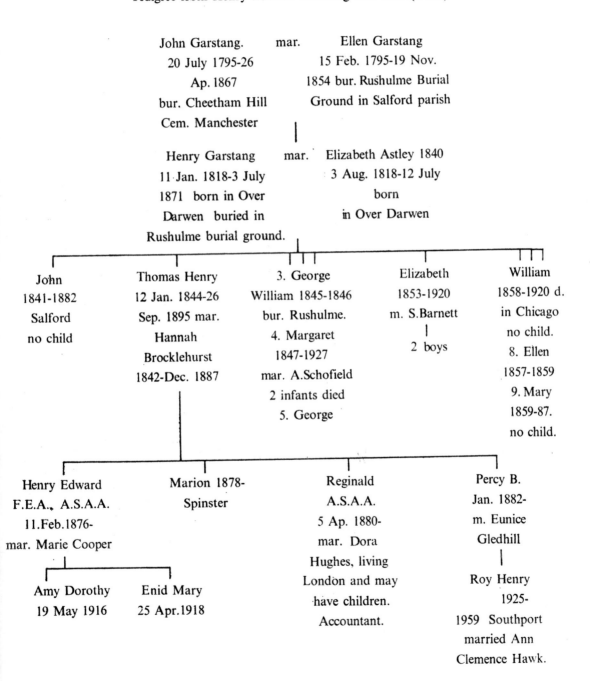

John Garstang.   mar.   Ellen Garstang
20 July 1795-26   15 Feb. 1795-19 Nov.
Ap. 1867   1854 bur. Rushulme Burial
bur. Cheetham Hill   Ground in Salford parish
Cem. Manchester

Henry Garstang   mar.   Elizabeth Astley 1840
11 Jan. 1818-3 July   3 Aug. 1818-12 July
1871 born in Over   born
Darwen buried in   in Over Darwen
Rushulme burial ground.

John   Thomas Henry   3. George   Elizabeth   William
1841-1882   12 Jan. 1844-26   William 1845-1846   1853-1920   1858-1920 d.
Salford   Sep. 1895 mar.   bur. Rushulme.   m. S.Barnett   in Chicago
no child   Hannah   4. Margaret   no child.
                    Brocklehurst   1847-1927   2 boys   8. Ellen
                    1842-Dec. 1887   mar. A.Schofield   1857-1859
                                         2 infants died   9. Mary
                                         5. George   1859-87.
                                                                                no child.

Henry Edward   Marion 1878-   Reginald   Percy B.
F.E.A., A.S.A.A.   Spinster   A.S.A.A.   Jan. 1882-
11.Feb.1876-   5 Ap. 1880-   m. Eunice
mar. Marie Cooper   mar. Dora   Gledhill
                                        Hughes, living
Amy Dorothy   Enid Mary   London and may   Roy Henry
19 May 1916   25 Apr.1918   have children.   1925-
                                        Accountant.   1959 Southport
                                                            married Ann
                                                            Clemence Hawk.

In 1436 Ludovic du Gerston was Vicar of Tockholes and James in 1552.

In 1590 James Garstang of Tockholes became governor of Blackburn Grammer School.

In 1775 will proved of William, Husbandman of Lower Darwen

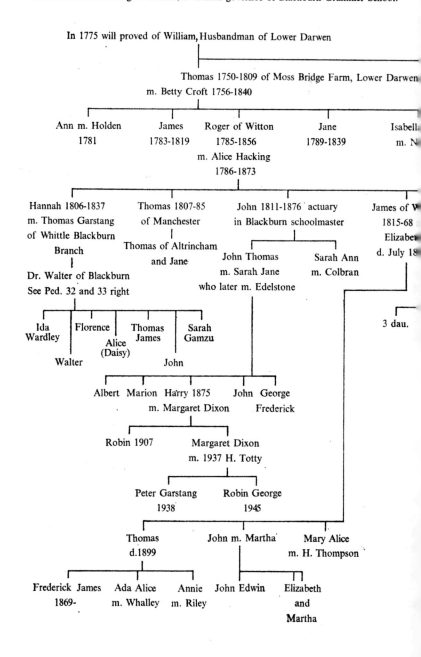

Thomas 1750-1809 of Moss Bridge Farm, Lower Darwen
m. Betty Croft 1756-1840

| Ann m. Holden 1781 | James 1783-1819 | Roger of Witton 1785-1856 m. Alice Hacking 1786-1873 | Jane 1789-1839 | Isabella m. N |

Hannah 1806-1837
m. Thomas Garstang
of Whittle Blackburn
Branch

Dr. Walter of Blackburn
See Ped. 32 and 33 right

Thomas 1807-85
of Manchester

Thomas of Altrincham
and Jane

John 1811-1876 actuary
in Blackburn schoolmaster

John Thomas
m. Sarah Jane
who later m. Edelstone

Sarah Ann
m. Colbran

James of W
1815-68
Elizabet
d. July 18

3 dau.

Ida
Wardley
Florence
Alice
(Daisy)
Thomas
James
Sarah
Gamzu

Walter
John

Albert   Marion   Harry 1875   John   George
m. Margaret Dixon   Frederick

Robin 1907   Margaret Dixon
m. 1937 H. Totty

Peter Garstang
1938
Robin George
1945

Thomas
d.1899

John m. Martha

Mary Alice
m. H. Thompson

Frederick James
1869-
Ada Alice
m. Whalley
Annie
m. Riley
John Edwin
Elizabeth
and
Martha

DARWEN BRANCH with TOCKHOLES

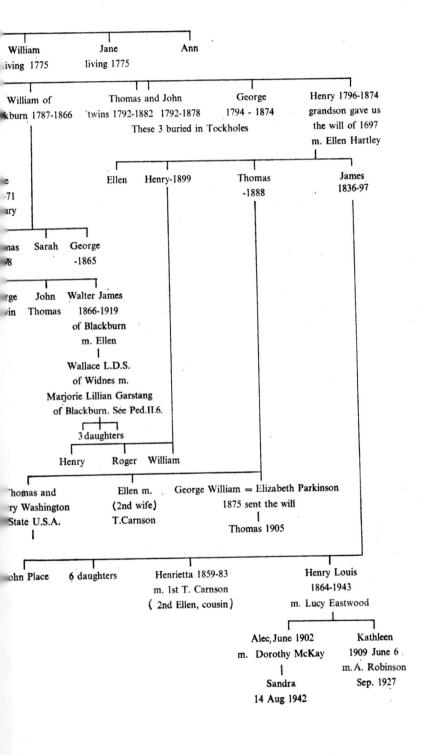

William
living 1775

Jane
living 1775

Ann

William of
kburn 1787-1866

Thomas and John
twins 1792-1882 1792-1878
These 3 buried in Tockholes

George
1794 - 1874

Henry 1796-1874
grandson gave us
the will of 1697
m. Ellen Hartley

e
71
ary

Ellen   Henry-1899

Thomas
-1888

James
1836-97

nas   Sarah   George
8   -1865

rge   John   Walter James
in   Thomas   1866-1919
of Blackburn
m. Ellen

Wallace L.D.S.
of Widnes m.
Marjorie Lillian Garstang
of Blackburn. See Ped.II.6.

3 daughters

Henry   Roger   William

homas and
ry Washington
State U.S.A.

Ellen m.
(2nd wife)
T.Carnson

George William = Elizabeth Parkinson
1875 sent the will

Thomas 1905

ohn Place   6 daughters

Henrietta 1859-83
m. 1st T. Carnson
(2nd Ellen, cousin)

Henry Louis
1864-1943
m. Lucy Eastwood

Alec, June 1902
m. Dorothy McKay

Sandra
14 Aug 1942

Kathleen
1909 June 6
m. A. Robinson
Sep. 1927

Pedigree II.11.

From the Will sent by George William. (See Ped.II.4. above).

William Garstang (spelt Garsden) m.Ellen

living in Tockholes near Darwen.

will proved 5 May 1697

Richard   Nathanael   Jane   Margaret.

There was formerly a commercial cemetery in Rushulme Road, which some years ago was taken over by the Corporation under Parliamentary powers, and was made into a public open space, 'Gartside Gardens'. The Burial and Graves Registers are now in the possession of the Corporation and a check has been made, but I regret to say that no trace of the burials you mention have been found. (Extract.)

Later I received another letter from the Town Clerk saying that Cheetham Hill cemetery has for the most part also been closed for burials, but he had sent my letter to the Methodist minister, the Rev. George Artingstall, the ground has not yet been transferred to the Corporation.

The Minister very kindly sent a list of Garstang burials of the period. John's name is there all right, buried in a grave belonging to Henry Garstang on April 29 1867 and said to have been living in Hulme, aged 72, so I suppose Ellen in 1854 must have been buried in an Anglican Church burial ground. In 1818 Henry himself, however, was buried in the Cheetham Hill cemetery, and had moved from Broughton to Bury New Rd. His son John, and his own wife, Elizabeth Astley, in July 1884, are both in the Cheetham Hill register, John was only 41 years old and had been living in Withington with his mother. Two Garstang babies of 10 weeks and of 11 months were also buried in Cheetham Hill Methodist Cemetery.

All the names are spelt in the modern way 'Garstang', so there is as yet no proof that Thomas Garsden was John's brother, or indeed that he was closely related to the Garsden whose will we have, but the name spelt as 'Garsden' has appeared so far in no other connexion with a *Garstang* pedigree.

CHAPTER III

THE QUEST FOR THE GARSTANG
PEDIGREES NEAR PRESTON

From Preston westward to the estuary of the Ribble at *Tarleton* the road stretches along low-lying land on the south of the river through *Penwortham, Hutton Bottoms, Longton Marsh,* Moor Side, Little Hoole and Much Hoole, then bends abruptly to the south in order to avoid the Moss and Hesketh Bank sands.

Freckleton is on the northern bank of the Ribble, almost opposite Tarleton across the estuary, and between Ashton Bank and Lytham, with Kirkham about three miles to the North. It is a township in the parish of Kirkham, in the Hundred of Amounderness, about seven miles to the west of Preston; it is surrounded by an open moor over which we used to bicycle between Blackburn and Lytham.

Tarleton was formerly a Chapel-of-Ease to Croston, six miles west of Chorley, and nine miles to the south-west of Preston. It became a separate parish in 1821 in the Archdeaconry of Chester. To the north of the village is a considerable morass known as Tarleton Moss, the name being derived from Old Norse. In Victorian days we used to bicycle along a raised causeway to reach the village, with the bog stretching far on either side. In the pedigree which follows, the wife, Betty Iddon, came from *Tarleton* when she married Thomas Garstang of *Longton* and *Preston.*

Longton is not far from Tarleton being 5 miles to the south-west of Preston. It is a chapelry in the Hundred of Leyland.

Until 1641 the parish of *Hoole* was included in the *Croston* area, a township which is a few miles to the south of Much Hoole; in these villages during the period of the Preston plague there are more funerals than births of Garstangs registered, which looks as if the low-lying land must have helped the plague to spread with devastating results.

The difficulties of communication, when few roads in the district were above flood level, may also account for the fact that, although brothers and close cousins may have settled in these villages at the same time, yet a few generations later among the families found by Walter to have similar Christian names and to have migrated originally from the Garstang area, no relationship was then recognised.

In a letter which James Iddon Garstang wrote to my brother on October 6th 1929 from Burnley, he expresses his enjoyment at delving into the Preston records even if it was only to find how the William baptised in Standish met his tragic death :

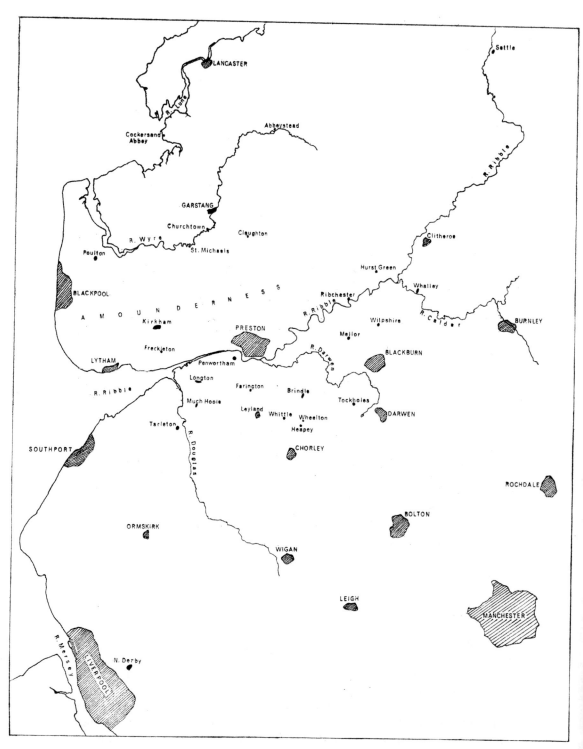

Map of Lancashire with Garstang settlements

I have now found time and opportunity to look further into the book of Preston Church annals which I mentioned when I wrote last, and hope I am not going over old ground for you in telling of it. The title is:

Records of the Parish Church of Preston in Amounderness,
by Tom C. Smith, Fellow Royal Historical Society.

It contains besides other matter a transcript of the registers from 1611 to 1631 and is indexed for all names mentioned. The entries of Garstang, even if they cannot now be linked into any pedigree, seem to me interesting; even hinting at a sad story. The first one is under date

March 1622-3

Burialls—Sep. Margreta uxor Willmi Garstang (3rd day of month).
The next—

August 1624

Marriages—Willmus Garstang et Agnes Bilsborow conjugate. (1st).
Later comes

July 1631

Burialls—Wm. Garstang and ux, and his searvant Sept. 29 *die.*
Further down

A searvant of Wm. Garstang *eod. die.*

Why! Whatever's this? I thought, then noticed the tremendous lists of burials, it must have been plague time! And sure enough I found the inscription under November 1630—"Heare begineth the Visitation of Allmighty God the Plague".

The number of burials rose from six or eight per month to 88 in June 1631, 317 in July, 282 in August, and 79 in September. The last Garstang entry is:

August 1631

A searvant of William Garstang Sept. *eod. die* (the 6th day).

So this William Garstang, whoever he may have been, would appear to have been a man of some substance, with at least three servants.

We see even in the modern world how scarcity of food in some countries is followed by an epidemic, and after 1595 a series of bad harvests had followed. Restrictions were imposed on exporting grain, and the numbers of licences to maltsters were reduced, a strict control was exercised on the sale of corn to dealers, and badgers had difficulty in obtaining licences for hawking grain. Even the owners of ale-houses who brewed their own beer were faced with restrictions.

All the same some of the Garstangs were among the favoured few: Roger Garstang in 1602 obtained a licence at Ormskirk as a badger in the Whittle district, while Ralph was granted one there as a malt-maker, and in the Preston records for 1601 Thomas Garstang of Great Hoole was licensed to keep an ale-house, and Thurston in Chorley to trade as a corn merchant.

While some families had moved to London, Cirencester, and Northampton, the greater number still lived in Lancashire, and judging by Walter's notes of baptisms, marriages, and funerals of Garstangs in the villages around Preston there must have been several families living in most of them to account for the fact that six baptisms of Thomas Garstangs, three Henrys, and perhaps four Johns, might appear in the register for the same village in one year.

When James Rowland Garstang was studying some of the pedigrees he said that he was convinced that all the great grandmothers and grandfathers must be linked up to connect most of the families, and so it has proved in many cases.

For an illustration of numbers of Garstangs in one small village refer to the Brindle pedigrees, pp.19 and 57.

The Garstangs of Longton
descended from Margaret of Heapey.

A number of families in Lancashire trace their descent from Margaret of Heapey, but the name of her husband varies in the different pedigrees sent to my brother Walter; he was probably baptised Thomas William as some give Thomas and some William as the name of her husband, living c.1736-1777 when her son Henry was born. The village of Heapey, 2½ miles N.E. of Chorley, was known in 1219 as Hepeie, derived from Old English words meaning *Hip hedge* or *enclosure*. Margaret's husband, whether William or Thomas, was born in Longton, a village near the south bank of the Ribble estuary 5 miles S.W. of Preston, and was known in 1153 as part of Penwortham.

The first family to be identified as descended from this connexion with Heapey and Longton was discovered by my brother Walter in a curious way: on April 17th 1929 he noticed in the *Yorkshire Post*:

Cat in Pit-shaft
Leigh Constable's Rescue at Great Risk.

A tabby cat was seen at the bottom of a disused pit-shaft, containing 60 feet of water and floating refuse, near the Sovereign Pits, Leigh, on Sunday, and an unsuccessful attempt at rescue was made.

Yesterday *P.C. Garstang* was again lowered down at great risk, and after 65 minutes' work succeeded in rescuing the cat alive. The constable said the fumes down the shaft were terrible.

Walter was always looking out for a Garstang hitherto not known to him and so wrote to Police H.Q. in Leigh asking for the letter to be passed on, and ten days later he received the following reply (Leigh is 4½ miles S.E. of Wigan):

Dear Sir,

In reply to your interesting letter of 19th inst. I have sent it on to my father, James I. Garstang, 25 Mizpah St., Burnley, who I have no doubt will take the matter up with pleasure. He is a native of Preston, where his antecedants on paternal side have lived, at least in the district around, for some considerable time. He knows more about them than I do.

I was born in Burnley, September 12th 1903, and I married on July 21st 1928 Jane E. Jones of Rhos near Wrexham, North Wales.

I knew of one other family of Garstangs in Burnley, but not their address now, and I never heard of any relationship existing between us. There was also a medical practitioner, Dr. Garstang, in Southport some years ago, but I cannot give any particulars about them.

Sincerely yours,
Ronald Garstang.

Pedigree III. 12.
The family of Ronald of Leigh, William Henry of Blackburn, and James Iddon Garstang of Burnley.

Burnley is not far from Blackburn being E.N.E. of Accrington, so Walter went to see Ronald's father, James Iddon Garstang, who promised to send his pedigree. He explained that he had inherited his name 'Iddon' from his grandmother, Betty Iddon of Tarleton, a village S.S.W. of Longton along the Ribble estuary. Her father, Thomas, had been the captain of a flat-boat on the Ribble, and being an 'overseer' as well, had been known as 'Praed Tommy Iddon, he wears two watches'! James Iddon then added, "My own father, Henry, married Betsy Holden from Bolton, and my brother, William Henry, married Lettice Smith of Oldham and lived in Blackburn. My wife, Sarah Holmes, came from Oldham too, and Ronald, the Constable who saved the cat in Leigh is our son."

When James Iddon sent his pedigree to Walter (III.12) he wrote:

Your letter describing the pedigree hunting is most interesting and should you work up an article on it as you suggest we might see a new popular pastime initiated. I cannot make out any connection with my family and any of the lines you have traced for me, and I am quite surprised at the number of members of the Clan. I think my ancestor Henry of 1777-1843 seems to be an only child according to my notes.

Thanks particularly for your kindly thought in looking up the Iddons. The two sisters whose grave you found would not, I think, be my grandmother's sisters, for I have the names of her brothers and sisters as James, John, William, Mary, and Jane. Perhaps they were cousins from the same grandfather, Thomas of Tarleton.

(In Walter's note-book I found that he went to St. Andrew's church in Longton, near Preston, and found the tombstones of Alice Iddon of Longton d. Oct. 27th 1893 aged 84; also her sister Isabella Bendworth d. March 2nd 1904 aged 84.)

The letter of James Iddon continues:

I have never found anything to connect the family name and the place name together, except that in the reign of Henry III Paulinus de Gairstang was a knight who took part in the 'perambulation of the forests' in Lancashire. That spelling interests me for when I was a boy in Preston few of the older people put any 'ah' sound into the name. It was more like *Gay-es-tin* or at best *Gairstun*. Old records spell the town's name *Gayrestang, Gierstang, Gerstang, Gresteng,* and *Geresteng.*

My wife joins me in kindest regards to yourself and to Mrs. Garstang,

yours very sincerely,
Jas. I. Garstang.

Pedigree III.12.

The Longton Garstangs
James Iddon Garstang from his father.

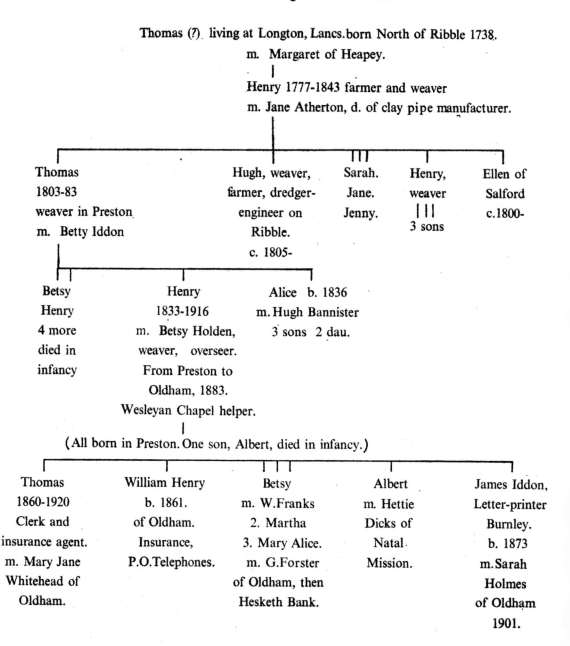

Thomas (?) living at Longton, Lancs.born North of Ribble 1738.
m. Margaret of Heapey.

Henry 1777-1843 farmer and weaver
m. Jane Atherton, d. of clay pipe manufacturer.

Thomas 1803-83 weaver in Preston m. Betty Iddon	Hugh, weaver, farmer, dredger-engineer on Ribble. c. 1805-	Sarah. Jane. Jenny.	Henry, weaver 3 sons	Ellen of Salford c.1800-

Betsy
Henry
4 more
died in
infancy

Henry
1833-1916
m. Betsy Holden,
weaver, overseer.
From Preston to
Oldham, 1883.
Wesleyan Chapel helper.

Alice b. 1836
m. Hugh Bannister
3 sons 2 dau.

(All born in Preston. One son, Albert, died in infancy.)

Thomas 1860-1920 Clerk and insurance agent. m. Mary Jane Whitehead of Oldham.	William Henry b. 1861. of Oldham. Insurance, P.O.Telephones.	Betsy m. W.Franks 2. Martha 3. Mary Alice. m. G.Forster of Oldham, then Hesketh Bank.	Albert m. Hettie Dicks of Natal Mission.	James Iddon, Letter-printer Burnley. b. 1873 m.Sarah Holmes of Oldham 1901.

William Henry Garstang
of Blackburn and Birkenhead.

When Walter had read in James Iddon's letter that his brother, William Henry, had lived in Blackburn, he remembered that Daisy had met a William Henry in the town, and that he had written to her after receiving the information about the discoveries in his Quest for Garstangs, and the Clan migrations. He looked up the letter and found that indeed he was James Iddon's brother.

In the letter he stated that his father was Henry who married Betsy Holden and had begun his working life as a hand-loom weaver in Preston where he himself, William Henry, was born. Then:

In 1883 the family moved to Oldham and my father became an overseer in a power-loom factory, and helped in the Wesleyan Chapel.

I was born in Preston in 1861, and married Lettice Smith in Oldham where I worked first with an Insurance Company, then in the retailing trade, and finally in Blackburn with the Post Office telephones.

We live in Manor Road in Blackburn now, and I am afraid that of my own knowledge I cannot be of much assistance as I can go back only to my grandfather who was a yeoman farmer and weaver. He was born at Longton Hall near Preston.

Some years ago I had a conversation with Dr. Garstang of Blackburn who told me that he had made some enquiries into the genealogy of the family, and he had a theory about the derivation of the name Garstang. I should say that he would have left some papers on the subject, and his sons may know something of the matter; they are both Professors, and your brother you mentioned as collecting information may already know them.

I should like to know if he has any knowledge of any branch of Garstangs springing from near or in Preston.

One could say more in a little chat, letter writing is too much trouble.

So William Henry who had made friends with my sister Daisy in Blackburn was James Iddon's elder brother, and the grandson of Henry who was born at Longton Hall and had married Betty Iddon. See Pedigree III.12 (the 'Ellen of Salford' mentioned as the youngest child of Jane (Atherton) and Henry Garstang, born c.1800 was probably the Ellen Garstang of Pedigrees II.9 and 9 with 10, the wife of John).

Pedigree III.13.
Longton and Heapey continued.
Frank of Birkenhead, Peter of Toronto, T. Maraschal, of London.

Among Walter's papers was a notice of lectures given in 1921-2 for the Workers' Educational Association in the Blackburn and District branch, and the Hon. Auditor was the William Henry Garstang who was the elder brother of James Iddon. Beside his name Walter had written "Now living with his son Frank in Birkenhead."

G

Walter went to Liverpool to see Frank who was well-known during the Second World War as the "Honorary Warden of the Services' Quiet Club" in Liverpool. They had not time to talk about Frank's career, but Walter was able to add Frank's name as the eldest son of William Henry in James Iddon's pedigree.

In April 1962 my nephew Eustace (son of my brother John) wrote to me from Canada (he was then Professor of Classics in McGill University in Montreal) saying that he had met a Peter Garstang in Toronto:

> He works in the Toronto Television studio, and is about 35 years old. He is the son of Tom the actor, who he thinks was born about 1892-5. His great grandfather was a weaver, born about 1833, and *his* father in turn was also a weaver born about 1803 of a Longton family of Garstangs.

In saying 'Tom the actor' Eustace seemed to imply that I knew something about him already, but I could not find any reference to an actor in any of Walter's notes. Luckily in July the same year 1962 his next letter began:

> Great excitement—yesterday in Toronto I met Peter Garstang's father, the actor, he has a distinctive beard and a small moustache. He was very friendly indeed and most interesting. I have given him your address and he says that he will get in touch with you when next he and his wife go to Oxford. He lives in St. John's Wood, London, and told me that he and his wife had acted with Irving.
> So we progress with the Quest.

Now that I knew the name of some one older than Peter I looked again at the pedigrees and found that Eustace had written the two names into one of the pedigrees while he was staying with me at my little house at Calthorpe Broad in Norfolk, and I had quite forgotten the fact, and that Peter had married Miss Gloria Luke in 1962. Now I knew that Tom was the younger brother of Frank in Birkenhead.

I had heard nothing more of this branch of Garstangs until the December of this year, 1968. Luckily Alec Garstang of Sheffield sent me the names and addresses of all the Garstangs in the Telephone Directories of each English county which he had in his office. The only two with Christian names were Frank and Sara with different addresses. So, as Frank was the very person who could help me to bring that family up to date, I wrote to him and on December 9 received the following reply:

> Your letter addressed to Frank Garstang at our previous address has been forwarded to him here. We have returned to our home town of Birkenhead nearly three months ago because of Frank's severe illness, and he has been ill ever since our return.
> I will try to help you with your enquiry; I am Sara Anne, the wife of Frank Garstang, O.B.E., M.A., J.P., an ex-Mayor and ex-Alderman of the town of Birkenhead. He is in his 78th year.
> We have one daughter, Claire Lettice; fourteen years ago she married Captain Michael Rawson Duke M.N., and they have three sons: Neill Rawson aged 11 years, Christopher Frank aged 8 years, and Patrick John aged 3 years.

Pedigree III 13
(Longton and Preston).
Sara and Frank Garstang of Birkenhead
with the Iddon connexion,
and Peter of Toronto.

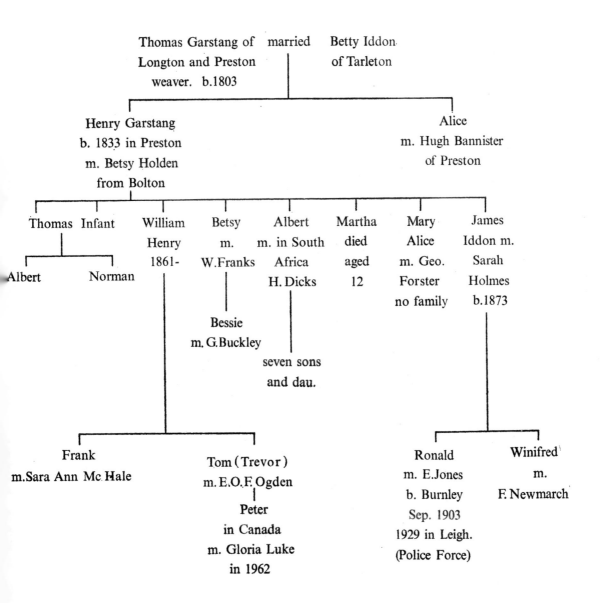

Thomas Garstang of married Betty Iddon
Longton and Preston   of Tarleton
weaver. b.1803

Henry Garstang   Alice
b. 1833 in Preston   m. Hugh Bannister
m. Betsy Holden   of Preston
from Bolton

Thomas Infant William Betsy   Albert   Martha Mary   James
                Henry   m.   m. in South died   Alice   Iddon m.
                1861-   W.Franks   Africa   aged   m. Geo. Sarah
Albert Norman   H. Dicks   12   Forster Holmes
                         Bessie   no family b.1873
                         m. G.Buckley
                                     seven sons
                                     and dau.

Frank   Tom (Trevor)   Ronald   Winifred
m.Sara Ann Mc.Hale   m. E.O.F.Ogden   m. E.Jones   m.
                         Peter   b. Burnley   F. Newmarch
                         in Canada   Sep. 1903
                         m. Gloria Luke   1929 in Leigh.
                         in 1962   (Police Force)

My husband was born in Blackburn, the eldest son of William Henry Garstang who married Lettice Smith, and they had one other son, Tom, who is now living in London. He is a retired actor and he adopted the name Maraschal. I understand his address is in the telephone directory.

My husband's grandfather was another Henry, born in Preston, Lancs. He and his wife had many children and I can remember some of the names: — Thomas the eldest, 2. Albert, 3. William Henry (Frank's father), 4. James, 5. Betsy, 6. Alice.

One of the daughters of Albert still writes to us from North Africa; she is staying with her daughter, Mrs. I. Bailey, in Rhodesia; her name is Olive Rhodes, and I will enclose the address.

Frank once met your brother, Professor W. Garstang, during his period in Liverpool, and we once saw part of the Family Tree. My daughter would certainly be delighted to have a copy of the book when it is ready if you would send details to us. She is a true Garstang and very proud of the fact. She lives in Pembrokeshire.

In answering this letter I mentioned that I had found a notice among the papers giving Lieut. Frank Garstang's name as a lecturer for the Royal Army Ordnance Corps during the Second War, and Sara replied that there must be two Franks as her husband was never in the army, but ran the 'Quiet Club' jointly with Liverpool University. He did provide educational facilities for the Forces in the Royal Institution in Liverpool, and lectured there sometimes, but was too busy organising to travel elsewhere.

After receiving Sara's letters I wrote to her brother-in-law, T. Maraschal Garstang in London and reminded him of how delighted Eustace had been to meet him in Toronto. On December 16th 1968 he replied:

Only just received your letter this a.m. been away all last week. I hasten to reply.

I don't think I can help you a great deal as I left my home to start my theatrical career at a very early age.

I don't see the connection between your branch of the clan and ours— my uncle Tom many years ago did a trace of our family and got to Oswald Thorald Alfreard Gar who came to STANG somewhere about 820 A.D. from Jarrow, I believe, where he landed.

However I was not interested and I think his 'book of the words' has been destroyed.

The name *Maraschal* is adopted from the Earl Marischals of Keith in Scotland somewhere in the 17th century.

Frank was never in the army—I was, but that doesn't matter. I never gave a lecture in my life—Shakespeare recitals in America yes—but no lectures.

My wife's name is Enid Olive Florence Maraschal Garstang, (Her maiden name was Ogden.)

Best of good wishes this Christmas Tide, your letter took five days to reach me, 1st class mail too—terrible!

Yours very truly,
T. Maraschal Garstang.

There is a post-script to draw my attention to the T in his signature. I gather that although he was called Tom as a child at home, he quickly changed it to Trevor when he adopted the *Maraschal* as an actor.

I was very interested to know that Trevor's Uncle Tom had traced his family's origin to an Anglo-Saxon who landed on the east coast of Northumbria at Jarrow, as that very morning I had received from Sara a copy of the story which follows. It is introduced by a statement that in 1737 the account of the birth, marriage and death of Betty, Countess of Iddon, had been lost from the register kept at Longton Hall. Betty Iddon married Thomas Garstang who lived 1803-83, and some of this branch of Garstangs were born at Longton Hall, but it is not clear if the title of Counts or Countesses of Iddon was ever that of the Thorald Gar, as suggested. No such title is mentioned in the *Complete Peerage*.

When sending the story of Thorald Gar, Sara said that it had been found among the papers of her aunt Alice after her death. Sara continued:

> She had no children. I knew her very well—the only member of that generation except my father-in-law that I knew. She was a charming lady—very sweet and very good in every way.
>
> The children of Thomas, Betsy and James are all dead but there must be grandchildren somewhere. I hope you will get news from Olive, her mother and father (Albert) had many children.

One of the most striking features while I have been copying these letters from members of the Clan has been the intense interest in the name Garstang shewn, not only by the writers, but also by strangers whom they have happened to meet. The name, and the story of Vikings landing from Scandinavia, leads to the writing of romances like *The Garstangs of Garstang Grange* published in 1869 as mentioned above in Chapter I, p.18.

This story might well have been called: "The Iddon romance of Longton Hall". It begins: "In the year A.D. 803 Oswald Thorald Gar landed near the present Newcastle as stated in the ancient *Records of Jarrow on Tyne*."

This no doubt refers to the *Anglo-Saxon Chronicle* begun by Bede after he went to reside in the Abbey at Jarrow founded by the Abbot Ceolfrid in the fifteenth year of King Egfrid's reign. The dominions of King Egfrid extended from the Humber to the 'Frith' of Forth, and he had given to the abbot Benedict all the land drained by the river Wear; so he built two monasteries one at Wearmouth and the more famous one at Jarrow. Bede places an event of the struggle with Anglo-Saxon invaders against each year, and in A.D. 449 Hengist and Horsa, the descendants of Woden, fought against the British. In 642 Oswald, king of Northumbrians, was slain by Penda, and in A.D. 657 Penda himself died.

In the *Romance of Longton Hall* Oswald Thorald soon after his landing in 803 is killed in battle by Penda, but his son gains a victory and reigns as King Edwin, followed by his son Egfrid who lost the throne in 827 when Egbert became king of England.

The *Anglo-Saxon Chronicle* states: "Oswald's brother Oswy was 7th Bretwalda, the 8th was Egbert K. of the W. Saxons. Egbert led an army against the North-humbrians, and they there offered him obedience and allegiance, and with that separated."

The Longton story states that the Thorald Gars later reigned as governors until they joined William the Conqueror on a Crusade to the Holy Land. They then lived partly in France having adventures with the kings of England up to the time of Henry VI, after which they give away all their possessions, except the castle of Hexham, to the Percy's, and moved westwards to Oswaldeston, Stang, and Longton about 1440. "They then adopted the name 'Gar-of-Stang', and became staunch supporters of Lancashire and the Red Rose." The early part is said to be in Saxon times.

By 'Stang' is meant no doubt Garstang, as it was already mentioned in legal records, and Oswaldeston was spelt *Osbaldeston* when I was a child; it was one of our favourite picnic haunts and an old house with a moat had been made to serve as a farm. To us it added to the charm and was known by us as 'The moated Grange.' The Ribble flowing below the wood was another attraction.

This makes a wonderful story, and I should like to know if Betty Iddon of Tarleton invented it to amuse her son Henry Garstang when a little boy in the eighteen thirties, or if it was Thomas, the eldest brother of James Iddon, who by it awoke the histrionic talent of his sons Albert and Norman, or their cousin Trevor.

Of Albert and Norman's families I have heard nothing, but perhaps I may do so before the book is quite finished. I had often wondered what had happened to policeman Ronald who saved the cat in my brother's day. Then last week, in January, 1969, I received a letter via Alec from Ronald's widow, Jane Ellen (née Jones). She thanks Alec for his information about *From Generation to Generation*, and then continues:

> My late father-in-law, James I. Garstang, did indeed meet Professor Walter Garstang many years ago and was, I believe, able to supply him with some information; it is with his name that I head the enclosed genealogical table which I have completed as far as I am able down to my grandchildren; although as you can see the name Garstang no longer exists in this branch of the family. Ronald was born in 1903 and died in 1963, leaving one daughter Gwyneth born 1930.

Gwyneth married David Brown Williamson, and they have four children, Katherine born 1955, David Ronald born 1957, Judith born 1963 and indeed still carrying the name, John Garstang born 1965.

Mrs. Ronald Garstang now lives in Radcliff near Manchester.

I am grieved to add that I have just received an announcement of the death of Frank Garstang on January 28 1969 peacefully at Birkenhead General Hospital.

Albert and Olive of South Africa

On the 8th of February 1969 I received an answer from Olive Rhodes with a full description of her father's wonderful work in South Africa, as an enthusiastic organiser and teacher to take the aims of Methodist Missionaries to the Zulu and other African peoples where the early Missionaries had already penetrated.

Olive's father, Albert, was born in 1866, and when he was seventeen years old he began to work for Missions in Oldham and Rochdale. He volunteered for African Mission work, and was appointed to work in Buffalo Flats in 1889, and later moved to Ndwedwe, in 1893 he returned to Buffalo Flats and was appointed House Master under the Governor of the Edendale Training Institution; there he taught in the school and had charge of the students' industrial work.

After three years Albert's health broke down, and he settled in Newcastle for 22 years in a timber business, but serving also as Local preacher, Sunday School Superintendent and Circuit Steward. He then helped to found the church in Port Shepstone, but in 1934 the strain and advancing years enforced his retirement from full pastoral responsibility. He is described in the Methodist magazines from which I am taking these details as a 'man of frail frame and burning zeal'.

Olive adds that her father taught himself the Zulu language by translating from the Zulu Bible with the aid of a dictionary. In 1894 on April 23rd he married Henrietta Jemima Dicks, one of a family of 13 who had travelled out from England in a sailing boat. Albert and Hettie had seven children, Tom, Betsy, Harry, Richard, Olive, Georgina and Jessie.

Albert's health broke down again in 1901, and he decided to take his eldest son Tom to England for treatment and to see his relations, he arrived in June and returned to Africa in October, having gained in health through his faith and courage. He was a member of the Town Council in Newcastle for 20 years but never gave up his work for spreading Christianity.

Hetty died in 1946 and two years later Albert again visited his family in England, but he died soon after his return to South Africa. George Henderson wrote of him "as the most Christ-like man he had ever met."

Olive's full name is Olive Irene, her first husband died, and in 1953 she married Frank Cecil Rhodes, but he died in 1965, she says he is not related to the explorer. One daughter lives in Rhodesia and Olive says Rhodesia is a lovely country.

Olive concludes her letter: "A number of our family will be interested in the book when it is published, so I hope you will let me know, and we wish you every success."

Olive's eldest brother Tom has a son Anthony Garstang B.Sc. he is a Civil Engineer, and married Noel M. Coleman. They have two sons, Richard is a student at Natal University. The younger son Edward and the elder daughter Mary are also studying for degrees.

Tom's second son, Michael Garstang, B.Sc. Meteorology, is engaged in research in Florida State. He married Elsabe Mostert, and they have three children: Stephen, Raymond, and Elizabeth Michele.

Olive's first husband was T. van Rooyen, they had three children: Graham who married 1st Lenore Eady, 2nd Sylvia Greggor; Una Natalie who married

1st Lionel Sandy, 2nd L. Bailey, B.Sc. (they have one son Stephen); and a daughter Ruth who died in 1951.

Olive's brother Harry was killed in the war 1917, and Albert Richard died last year in 1968.

Olive's sister Betsy May married Ernest James Mann, and their daughter Valerie B.Sc. married Ernest Prout a doctor of Cape Town University. The younger daughter Sybil Mann gained her B.A. degree and married Professor A. Noble of Grahamstown University.

Pedigree III.14.
John Garstang of Liverpool and Preston.

On January 7th 1930 a John Garstang then in Liverpool wrote to Walter about his ancestry. He had been born in Preston and had lived there until 1920; his father still lived there and would like to know more about the Clan if possible. His great-grandfather's name had been Hugh, born in or near Longton, a Chapelry in the parish of Penwortham. This was confirmed on January 22nd by the father of John, and the father's name was also John; as the son was a police-constable we can distinguish him by calling him P.C. John to save confusion.

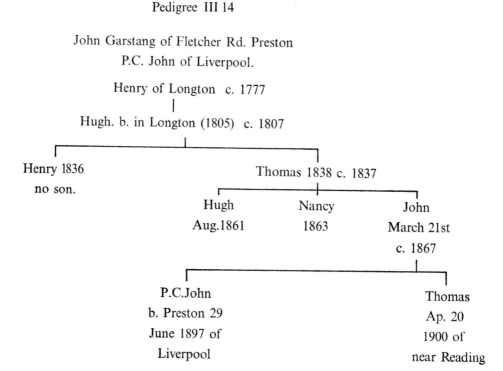

Pedigree III 14

John Garstang of Fletcher Rd. Preston
P.C. John of Liverpool.

Henry of Longton c. 1777

Hugh. b. in Longton (1805) c. 1807

Henry 1836   Thomas 1838 c. 1837
no son.
            Hugh   Nancy   John
            Aug.1861   1863   March 21st
                                         c. 1867

       P.C.John   Thomas
       b. Preston 29   Ap. 20
       June 1897 of   1900 of
       Liverpool   near Reading

It is the custom to allow 30 years for one generation therefore as P.C. John was born in June 1897, we can assume that his father John was born in 1867, *his* grandfather in 1837, his great-grandfather in 1807 and *his* father in 1777, all approximately. A relative, Henry, was manager at Horrocks, Crewsden and Co. and died 1928.

In the Pedigree table III.12 there is a Henry Garstang, farmer and weaver, born in 1777 whose father lived at Longton and his son was Hugh, a dredger engineer on the river Ribble probably born about 1807 as his elder brother was born in 1803. We can therefore assume that P.C. John was descended from this Hugh Garstang and belonged to the same family group in all probability as Frank the ex-mayor, and James Iddon the printer.

Pedigree III.15.

James Holmes Garstang
88 *Mount Rd. Higher Tranmore, Birkenhead,*
Cheshire.

On December 5th 1930 James Holmes Garstang wrote to Walter:

> In reply to yours of the 3rd instant I am afraid I will not be able to help you much. Personally I was born in Liverpool in August 1868. I had two brothers, William Frederick and Henry, but both are dead. My father, Henry Garstang, lived at Moody's Farm, Heapey, near Blackburn in Lancashire, I think. I cannot say whether he was born there or not. He had three brothers, William, Robert, and John; I think there was a sister too, but I never heard much about the family. William came to Liverpool, but he died about 40 years ago (1890?). Robert went to America and I believe he was frozen to death! His Grandson is in Indianapolis, U.S.A.
>
> John went to Canada and I have not heard from him for years. My father born in 1833 died 1897, he was a Coal-merchant in Liverpool.

During the next month Walter received a letter from the "cousin" of James Holmes Garstang, *William Frederick,* who lived in Edge Hill, Liverpool:

> My Great Grandfather was Roger Garstang of Preston or Chorley. His sons were: William, John William, and Henry.
>
> My Grandfather was William, a coal-merchant in Solway St., Liverpool, he married three times.
>
> My father, William Fred, died in March 1927 aged 61. His brother, James, was the Manager of Masbu and Gladstone, wine-merchants in Birkenhead, Cheshire.
>
> His sister Anne, a spinster in Wodsworth Lodge Lane in Liverpool would be able to give you more information of her father's relations than I can, as I am writing only from the memory of what I have been told.
>
> My father married Mary Wenrow of Liverpool.
>
> My brother Henry is 35 years old and I am aged 31, he is a motor driver and I am a Railway Checker at L.M.S.R. Park Lane Station, Liverpool.
>
> There are some of our relations in U.S. America and Canada, and the following information is copied from a Newspaper from America, dated June 7th 1895:
>
> 'Mr. William Garstang, the present incumbent of the Presidential

Chair of the Master Car Builders Association, is Superintendent of motor power of the Cleveland, Cincinnati, Chicago and St. Louis Railway. He was born in Wigan, Lancashire, on Feb. 28th 1851, his father occupied a position on an English Railway of Road Masters. *The elder Garstang* came to America in 1857, followed by his family in 1859. He located at Toronto and laid the track on the *Grand Trunk Railway* to the East of that city.

William Garstang obtained his education in the Public Schools of Cleveland, Ohio; he began Railway service as a water-carrier to his father, and in 1863 entered the Cleveland shops for six years. Afterwards he was a machinist and Gang-foreman in the Shops of the Atlantic and Great Western Railway for 11 years at *Gallion and Kent, Ohio*. He was the general foreman in the Locomotive and Car Department of the *Cleveland and Pittsburg Railway* for 3 years at Cleveland and Wellsville; then Division Master Mechanic of the old *Bee Line* between Cleveland and Cincinnati for one and a half years and between Gallion and St. Louis for three years.

When Mr. Ingalls assumed the Presidency of the Chesapeake and Ohio Railway about the first appointment he made was that of *William Garstang* to the position of *Superintendent of Motive Power* with headquarters at *Richmond*, Virginia.

William was there from 1888 to April 1893, and on April 1st of the latter year he was promoted to the position of Superintendent of Motive Power of the Cleveland-Cincinnati-Chicago-St. Louis Railway, and has his *Headquarters at Indianapolis* where he is one of the most popular and useful members of the Master Mechanics Association.'

This William Garstang was an uncle of mine, I think there is one son and two daughters still in the United States, and another uncle still in Toronto.

When James Holmes sent his pedigree he wrote: "My father looked a proper Lancashire man, he was very tall being 6ft. 1½ inches, and I weighed him once at Preston station, he weighed 19 stone!"

He also explained that his cousin William, son of John in Canada, went to the Boer War and came to England when the war ended. James Holmes then went to the Preston Guild with his cousin William, and his own brother William, after which his cousin returned to Canada.

The Guild Festival is celebrated every twenty years; the first recorded meeting, dated back to August 29th 1328, was held in memory of John the Baptist to whom their Church was dedicated at that time. The custom developed from the Councils or Moots established in each important settlement by the Angles for the dispensation of justice, and from which representatives would be sent to the chief town of the district to hold a Wapentake or Hundred moot as a Court of Appeal. Preston was given the right because of its position at the mouth of the River Ribble where it served as a port for coastal traffic.

The name 'Preston' developed from 'Preostatun', due to the fact that a Priest proclaimed silence before an 'ealderman' introduced the business of the day. The 'freemen' who had the right to attend settled matters at the end of discussion by loud cries of 'Nay' or in Scandinavian fashion by a shaking of spears and clash of shields with a cry of 'Aye'.

Note. In Pedigree III.13 the names Holmes and Holden occur as wives. The father of both James Holmes and William Frederick married three times. There is uncertainty about the name of the ancestor who married Margaret of Heapey. William Frederick gave 'Roger' as his great grandfather from Preston or Chorley, so perhaps there is a generation missing after Margaret of Heapey.

PEDIGREE III.15

Heapey and Liverpool.
James Holmes and nephew William Frederick.

William and Margaret Garstang of Heapey

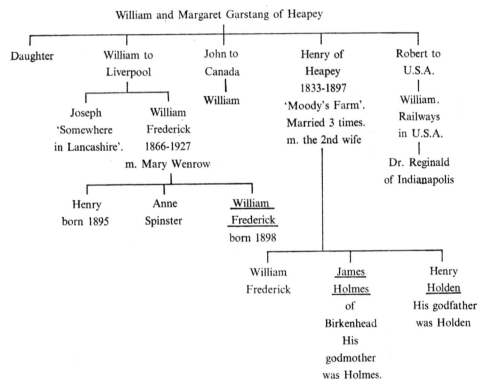

J. V. Garstang, son of
William Frederick in Liverpool.
Ronald, son of Henry.

One of the letters written to Alec at the end of 1968 came from the son of William Frederick Garstang of Liverpool.

He gives his grandfather's name as William Frederick and his father was also William Frederick living in Liverpool, born January 17th 1901, married Christina Deboo and died last year, 1968.

The writer gives his name as J. V. Garstang, he has a son James born July

16 1952, and a daughter Joyce born February 5 1958. He was married in St. Catherine's church June 5th 1948 to Kathleen Chambers.

In December 1930 James Holmes Garstang said he was born in Liverpool in 1868 and had two brothers William Frederick and Henry. His father was Henry of Moody's Farm, Heapey and his brother William went to live in Liverpool and died about 1890.

In January 1931 Walter had a letter from William Frederick also from Liverpool. He said that his father was also called William Frederick, born c.1866, and his grandfather was William, a coal merchant in Liverpool.

These two accounts are difficult to understand and do not agree in some generations, but it seems that the J. V. Garstang who wrote on December 17th 1968 is the son of William Frederick, born January 1901 according to his son, and in 1898 according to Pedigree III.15, given by James Holmes to Walter.

Early in January 1969 I had another letter from this Liverpool family: Ronald, son of Henry Holden, who is said to be 35 years old in 1930 when his brother James Holmes wrote to my brother Walter. This date tallies with Ronald's date of Henry's birth 27-9-1894 and his death in September 1954; he married Clare Eva Cortina. Ronald continues:

> My father had two brothers, William and James, also a sister Elsie, the youngest of the family.
>
> I have two brothers living in Winsford, Cheshire where my home is now: Stanley James born 26-3-1930, married Cathleen Clark in June 1955, they have five sons, James 18-6-56, Michael 25-10-57, David Stanley 2-10-60, Andrew 12-8-65, Mark 2-8-68.
>
> The other brother in Winsford is William John born 16-11-33, he married Valerie Kenneth in 1957 and they have two sons William Kenneth 26-6-58, Barry John 25-10-60 and two daughters Gillian Valerie 29-5-62, and Susan Coral 1-2-65.
>
> Ronald married Annie Welsh 24-3-56 (he was born 16-3-35), and they have one son Ronald John 17-7-65 and three daughters Karen Ann 11-7-57, Susan 17-10-59, Ann 15-62.
>
> My other brother Harold and my sister Beryl are still living in Liverpool. Harold George was born 5-4-42 and married Isobel McCarthey in 1967, they have one daughter Julie Ann born 20-11-67. Beryl Elizabeth was born 16-7-37, and married John Ashton in September 1956.
>
> My sister Dorothy May born 16-5-31 married John Murray in 1954, and they live in Belfast.
>
> This is about all the information I have been able to gather at the moment, should any more become available in the near future I will be only too pleased to forward it.

In January 1930 in a letter written to Walter, William Frederick of Edge Hill, Liverpool said that his grandfather William was a coal-merchant in Solway St. Liverpool and he married three times.

Today January 17th 1969 I had a second letter from James Victor G. And he explains that his "grandfather ran the coal merchant business under the family name 'Garstang'. The other William Frederick, my father, had to close down the business on the death of my grandfather. He then became a checker at the L.M.S. Park Lane Goods Station." He continues: "I was christened James Victor in St. Catherine's church in Tunnel Road, and my son James was born in July 1952, he is now studying for A. Levels at Liverpool Collegiate Shaw Street school. My daughter, Joyce Marion, born February 1958 is also still at school. My occupation is Tanker Driver with Esso at Dingle."

History as well as names repeats itself in this family, as the William Frederick who wrote in 1930 and was the father of James Victor, said that his brother Henry was a motor driver, while the William who emigrated to U.S.A. became among other important posts, the Superintendent of motor power in the Chicago etc. Railway according to the writer of 1930 already quoted.

Pedigree III.16.
James Gordon Nicholson Garstang
of Geneva.
The Garstangs of Heapey, Liverpool, Preston, Teignmouth, Geneva.

In June 1963 I wrote to Jack Garstang at the London Polytechnic after my niece Pauline had seen his name as the author of a book on Athletics. My letter was passed on by him to his parents who happened to be staying with him in Geneva; he is now working at the International School in Geneva where my letter had been forwarded. His parents sent me a wonderful picture postcard of the 'Palais des Nations Unies' and said they would be home on June 14th and would then write to me from South Devon.

Jack's mother, Edyth Garstang, afterwards wrote to say that her husband, James, prior to his retirement had been H.M. Inspector of Taxes under the Board of Inland Revenue and was living in Blackburn in 1905, and had also lived in Preston, Longton, and many other towns in Lancashire. His father's name was Joseph.

She continued in her letter:

Sixteen months ago I met an American lady who ran me home in her car. We chatted a while and then exchanged names. Most people have difficulty in spelling my name, but she wrote it down without any hesitation. When I commented on the fact she told me that her daughter was married to a Professor at Oxford, and she had heard her speak of Eustace, the son of John.

Unfortunately she lost the paper upon which she had written the name and address of her new friend.

Edyth continued:

Joseph, my husband's father, came from a branch of the Garstang family of West Derby, a suburb of Liverpool, but went to live in Blackburn in 1905 and finally settled in Brinscall.

Our son to whom you wrote is Head of the International School of Sport in Geneva. He is the author of a number of books, of which the publishing rights of one have been purchased by an American firm in New York.

After I had answered this letter, Edyth Garstang wrote on June 26th. She explained that she had been to Dawlish where the American lady had been living when she mentioned Eustace and my brother John, and though the lady had returned to America, Edyth G. found that our friends in Oxford were Sir Humphrey and Lady Waldock who had been Eustace's friends ever since his undergraduate days!

Edyth wrote as so many other Garstangs have remarked:

We have never in all our lives during all our travel met another Garstang. We have always been the only Garstangs in the Telephone Directory.

My husband was born in Wheelton between Blackburn and Chorley in 1898, went to Preston in 1920, Longton in 1926. Our son was born in a Nursing Home on the *Garstang* road in Preston in 1927. He was named 'James Gordon Nicholson', but is known as 'Jack' from College days and appears to like it. He has a daughter 'Jacqueline'. We also have a daughter, Jean Doreen Evans, who has two children, David and Celia.

Thank you for the Chapter headings. It does sound exciting.

This information gave me a clue and I remembered having seen that a Garstang had gone to live in Liverpool and that some one in his family was 'living somewhere in Lancashire', so I hunted through the pedigrees which I had typed for this Preston section, and found that a Joseph of Lancashire belonged to the whole group of Longton Garstangs that we have been considering. We may conclude that all these families had their origin in Heapey where a Henry Garstang lived in 1475, another Henry of direct descent died in Heapey in 1754, and he might well have been the grandfather of William in the table sent by James Holmes; or Margaret's husband's name may have been Thomas as suggested by James Iddon. A little more new research is needed!

In any case Margaret of 1738 from Heapey seems to be an ancestor of James Gordon Nicholson Garstang of Geneva.

In July Edyth Garstang wrote again to say that she had heard from Mrs. Robina Waldock who was staying with her daughter in Montreal. She continued:

Two sisters married two brothers, so Lady Waldock in Oxford is her sister, and they are from New Zealand. They met Mrs. John Garstang and her two children, Eustace and Meroë, on board ship in 1926 going to Marseilles to meet your brother.

Talking with my daughter about never meeting other Garstangs, she said she had often read about Professor John's excavations in the papers, and one day in London when she gave her name in a jeweller's shop, an Air Force officer asked her if she was any relation to the Professor. She is very interested in your forthcoming story of the family, and she has seen the tomb of Henry Garstang in Cirencester Church.

James Gordon Garstang's grandfather was Joseph Garstang of the West Derby suburb of Liverpool, he went to Blackburn in 1905, finally to Brinscall

Pedigree III 16 Longton and Heapey

Ancestors: (Thomas of Longton 1738) One of these
(William of Longton) married
Margaret Heapey
Henry of Heapey 1777-1843 m. Jane Atherton.
He is given as ancestor of James Iddon

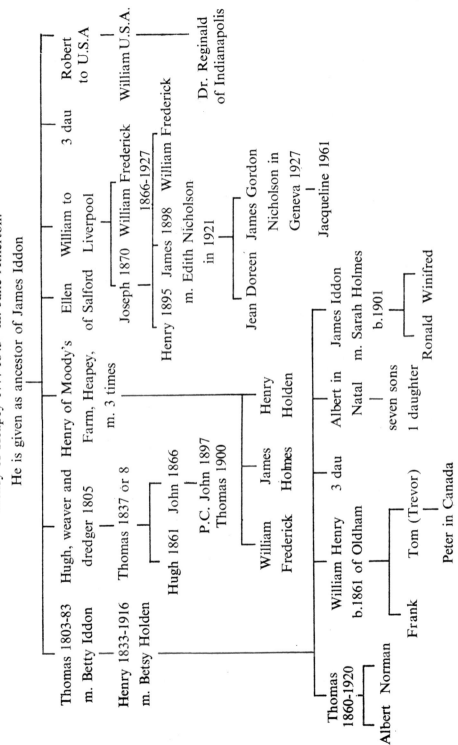

in Leyland parish. He would be the 'Joseph' in James Holmes Garstang's pedigree shewn as 'living somewhere in Lancashire'. Joseph's Grandfather and Grandmother were William and Margaret of Heapey, and so the husband of Margaret of Heapey could be written in as William the son of Thomas living at Longton.

The family names supplied by Mrs. Edyth Nicholson Garstang have been added to construct her Pedigree III.16.

Ancestors from Penwortham.

In Pedigree II.3 it was seen that Garstangs had migrated from Penwortham to Tockholes, but some stayed near Preston.

In 1377 John, the son of William Garstang of Penwortham, and Joan his wife, remitted certain rights to Thomas le Molyneux of Cuerdale for 100 marks; and sixteen years later for 20 marks down and a pair of gloves annually for 14 years, they agreed to hand over two messuages with 66 acres of land and meadow in Levesey (Livesey) to Louis Garstan and his heirs; or, in default, to Louis's brothers and sisters in succession: William, Nicholas, Alice, and Margery. In 1401 John of Garstang was pledged in a suit for dower when his son Louis brought a suit against Roger of the Rhydding for a dower consisting of certain lands. In the same year Thomas of Gayrstang of Faryngton, senior, and many others, were to have answered an indictment at Lancaster Assizes, but the sheriff failed to find them.

By the above references the Garstangs now seem to have moved from their original settlement to places beyond Preston, and for the first time Blackburn appears in the story. Joan was probably the second wife of John, whose children by his first marriage for 20 marks and a pair of gloves annually, were to receive two dwelling houses, the out-houses, and attached land as well as 66 acres of land and meadow in Livesey. It seems as though Roger of the Rhydding may have been a son of the second marriage and had cleared trees from some of the woodlands (which the father had pledged to Louis and his heirs) and had taken possession of the Rhydding or Clearing for his own use.

A dower could be either a widow's share for life of her husband's estate, or property brought by a wife to her husband.

Penwortham was an attractive village on the south bank of the Ribble two miles south-west of Preston. Water and marsh here reach out to good pasture land where sheep farming would succeed.

The estuary of the Ribble was at one time protected here by an important castle under the authority of the Earls of Chester, but now only 'Castle Hill' remains in memory of its former greatness.

Of the priory founded by the Benedictines in 1087 can still be seen the ancient timber and plaster walls, timber ceilings, and large open fire-places.

In the church of St. Mary, built in the 'perpendicular' period, the armorial bearings and fragments of stained glass in the windows, have been transferred from an earlier church building; and on St. Thomas's day a dole amounting to about £70 is still distributed to the poor of the parish in accordance with an ancient 'Charity'.

Pedigree III.17.
Thomas and Colin Garstang of Preston and Penwortham.

There is a family of Garstangs descended from Thomas of Penwortham born in 1790, and in their pedigree, which has also wide connexions, the town of Leigh comes into the picture.

Leigh is a market town and parish in the Archdeaconry of Chester, about 12 miles west of Manchester and connected with West Leigh and Pennington. 'Leigh' was pronounced by the inhabitants with a peculiar gutteral sound, which according to *The New Gazetteer* by Stephen R. Clarke, 1830 "is quite unattainable by a stranger".

Failsworth is also mentioned in the pedigree and this town is 4 miles to the north-east of Manchester.

Walter received the pedigree from Thomas Garstang in a round-about way: he knew T. F. Wardle of Devonshire Hall in the University of Leeds who gave him the name of Thomas Garstang, Head of the Gray Department of Thomas Wardle Ltd., New Silk Works, Leek, Brook, Staffordshire; on January 13th 1930 Thomas G. wrote as follows:

> I am in receipt of the interesting documents re the History of the Garstangs, and I would be glad if you would inform me if you have got into touch with any of the family who are in Preston, Burnley, or Blackpool, Freckleton, and Leigh?
>
> Perhaps you will be interested to know that my father is still living and is about 90 years of age.
>
> I have also four brothers and about ten cousins married and named Garstang.
>
> Yours truly,
Thos. Garstang.

63 Northfield Rd. New Moston,
Manchester via Failsworth.

Walter hoped to be able to go and see the old father, but in the meantime he received another letter from James Iddon G. saying that he had met a Mrs. J. Halstead living in Burnley whose maiden name had been 'Florence Garstang'. He had been told that "Mr. Halstead is a loom overlooker at Simpson and Baldwins, but I could not find him there. Then he had heard that I was looking for him and he called to see me. Incidentally he entertained us with some of his war-time experiences. He is a 'taper' at the factory, that is a man who applies sizing to yarn preparatory to weaving."

James Iddon had not explained how Florence Halstead had been a Garstang before her marriage, so Walter mentioned her in his next letter to Thomas of Failsworth who had a good deal to do with Burnley, and Thomas replied:

H

The James Iddon Garstang of Burnley I do not know, but the Florence Garstang, Mrs. Halstead, is the eldest daughter of Elijah of Boston, U.S.A. Her mother's maiden name was Macintosh of Burnley when she married my brother Elijah, and I think she died before he went to Montreal where he married his second wife.

As you are no doubt aware this family tracing is a very tall order . . . at the same time I will give you any information I can. I am glad Mr. Wardle gave you my reply to your previous letter, I met him quite by chance as he was returning to the University after the Christmas vacation.

That would be the University of Leeds where Walter was then Professor of Zoology.

The name *Elijah Garstang* was so unusual that Walter remembered at once a visit he paid to Colin Garstang in New Hall Lane, Preston, in September 1927. Colin had told him of five relations, one of whom was Elijah, and another Thomas; so this looked like a link and Walter got out the notes he had made while Colin, at first a little tardy and then gradually thawing as he saw Walter's eager interest, poured out the story of his family, but without dates. He had only in recent years found out to his surprise that there were any Garstangs other than his Preston-Penwortham-Leigh group. "Yes," he agreed,

Uncle Elijah lived in Burnley and married a Burnley girl, he was attached to Thomas Wardle's firm then, where Uncle Tom works, he went to Canada when his wife died and then to U.S.A. and took a second wife to Boston where he worked as a Loom fixer, his old trade.

It was when Colin heard that his Uncle Tom had written to Walter that he became more eager to give his family's history; it began with Thomas of Penwortham who was buried in the churchyard there. "His eldest son John". said Colin,

married a Roman Catholic and his first child, Tom, emigrated to America, was burnt out of his home in 1166 Missouri Street, San Francisco during a bad earthquake, then he removed to Alameda, but his children were born in Otago, New Zealand.

After a little conversation on Walter's part, Colin continued:

The second son John still lives in Surrey St. Preston, and his son Aloysius is a Language Professor in Xavieran College, Victoria Park, Manchester. Uncle Colin came next, and I'm called after him, it was just a fancy of his father's to call him 'Colin' after Colin Campbell. Uncle Colin was at first in the cotton business like most people, but he helped to invent the way to make 'flannelette', and he's now an Insurance Agent here in New Hall Lane, Preston. He got on well enough to 'set up' my Father's family in Leigh where most of us work in the Co-op Mill.

After a pause Colin went on:

Now besides Uncle Colin's father, John, and my Grandfather, Richard or Dick as they called him, the old Thomas of Penwortham had a third son 'Tom'; he left Preston to work in Burnley, and now he resides in

Freckleton. He was the father of Elijah and had five daughters and four other sons: John or Jack used to work at Wardle's firm, then went to America, Richard is an Engineer in Freckleton, and Tom, who wrote to you, lives near Failsworth, but he's mostly at the Silk Works in Leek, Staffordshire.[1] His youngest brother, Harry, helps his sister Elizabeth Ellen, now Mrs. Armstrong, with a Boarding House in Blackpool. So now I think I've told you all I can."

Walter was more than pleased with all this information and found some of the dates concerning different members of this family, then Thomas wrote again from his new home at New Moston, near Failsworth, and gave him a few more details: his Uncle John in addition to his three sons had a daughter, Mary Ann, who was in the Roman Catholic Convent at Ribbleton, Preston. He continued:

I have not seen Tom for many years, he was always a roamer all over the world, but John and Colin I saw last year.

I have also not seen any of the family of Richard and Lizzie, ('Old' Thomas of Penwortham's youngest son) for about 35 years. Richard was a Power-loom Overlooker as also were his four or five sons, but the whole family left Burnley for Leigh about 35 years ago.

My own Father, Thomas, second son of Thomas of Penwortham, is still alive about 90 years old. He lives at Freckleton opposite the 'Coach and Horses', and he is the one left who could give you the information you still require re the Garstangs of Penwortham, Longton, Farington, Leyland, Croston, etc. I have not been to see him myself for about two years, but I have no doubt that he would be pleased to help you in this matter.

Thos. Garstang.

Jan. 30th, 1930.

In Tom's letter he had said that his father was about 90 years old, and as Walter was not able to go over to Freckleton at once, he wrote in his notes that when he did manage to motor there he was sad and disappointed to find that the old Thomas had died.

About June 29th 1963 I received another letter from James Rowland Garstang in Southampton; he had written to Mrs. Richard in Freckleton, and on July 9th she answered bringing the family of her husband Richard of Freckleton up to date; it will be seen later that Constance was Richard's 2nd wife:

We were indeed surprised to receive a letter from you last week. We have been making enquiries about the Garstang family and if we hear of anything of interest we will certainly let you know. My husband, Dick, really Richard, does not remember his Grandfather or even hearing his name mentioned. Of the present generation of a family of ten, (the children of Tom and Betsy of Freckleton) only the youngest are still living, the youngest Harry is in Blackpool, then my husband, and Jane at Broughton.

[1] Richard, the engineer in Freckleton, would be the Garstang mentioned by James Rowland on p.128.

We are of course interested to know more of the History being written about this family.

Yours sincerely,
Constance M. Garstang.

James Rowland sent her the chapter headings of this book when he replied to thank her for writing. James Rowland had received Constance Garstang's address from the Manager of Messrs. Bibby's Mill at Freckleton on June 4th 1963:

In reply to your letter I feel sure that Mr. Dick Garstang of 'Balderstone', Lytham Rd., Freckleton, is the person you seek. The house in which he lives is adjacent to the mill which is known as 'Balderstone Mill', and belongs to J. Bibby and Sons. I often speak to 'Dick Garstang', he is hale and hearty and cheerful as ever. Hoping this information is of value to you.

Yours truly,
J. Bateson,
Mill Manager.

Lancashire people are therefore just as helpful as they used to be. They really are eager to help and interested in others, not just in their own pursuits. (For James Rowland's own Pedigrees see III. 19 and 20).

This family beginning as it did with so many brothers and sisters of such varied interests had spread far and wide, and I have been for years trying to find the family to which a Lieut. Frank Garstang belonged. He was not the Birkenhead Frank, nor the Frank connected with the Bleach works in Leyland, but Walter had heard of him in the following way.

Lieutenant Frank Garstang of Burnley and Preston.

On October 17th 1944, Walter received a letter from R. J. Garstang of 26 Cotterills Lane, Birmingham:

I hope you will not think me impertinent, but it gives me a great thrill to be writing to you, especially as I bear the same surname as yourself, but I am afraid not quite so famous.

On the 6th of October I went to a lecture at the Chamber of Commerce in New Street, Birmingham, the speaker being Lieutenant F. Garstang, talking about his experiences from Normandy to Belgium which proved very interesting.

After the lecture he was answering any questions the audience put to him appertaining to his experiences of course. When the meeting was over and the audience had dispersed, I went to Lieutenant Garstang and asked him if he would answer me a personal question. He said certainly, so I asked him if he could tell me how many people in England would have the same name as himself, it being such an uncommon name. He said he could not tell exactly, but he thought there might be a dozen or so.

Then he said that if I were to write to you I could get an answer to all I wanted to know about the Garstang Family. He gave me your address, Sir, and he advised me to write.

I know there is a small town near Preston named Garstang but I have never had the pleasure of coming in contact with any relation of my father as he died when I was too young to remember him, but his Christian names were the same as my own—Richard John—but my mother never told me much about him.

So if you would enlighten me in any way I should be very grateful and hoping you will be so kind, and oblige.

Yours truly,

R. J. Garstang.

As I have not found any further correspondence with Richard John I tried writing to his address in Cotterills Lane, Alum Rock, but the lapse of time may have prevented my letter reaching him.

Walter read notices in different newspapers about Lieutenant Frank and learned that he was a reporter of the *News Chronicle*. He saw articles by him about his discoveries concerning the chief operators of the black market, who, he said, "began their illicit trading only 18 weeks after the war had broken out."

Frank had been invited to the wardroom of naval headquarters and met the men who "fought in the bravest naval engagement of the war, fighting the *Scharnhorst,* the *Gneisenau,* and the *Prinz Eugen."*

About the same time Walter had received a notice from a friend about a similar lecture to be given by Lieut. Frank in Droitwich, Worcestershire, and his friend had written above the title: 'Worth hearing'. The lecture was under the organisation of the Ministry of Information:

An eye-witness account by Lieut. F. Garstang from the Normandy beaches to Belgium.

Before the war Lieut. F. Garstang, R.A.O.C. was a journalist in Fleet St. He went to the war early in 1944 to Normandy. The audience will hear of his experiences with the British and Canadian armies in the fighting for Caen, Thiery Harcourt, and Falaise. He will describe the spectacular bombing of Caen by the R.A.F., and he will also give his impressions of the liberation of Paris, the race into Belgium, and the liberation of Brussels. He will sum up the position of the armies of liberation that are now poised for the liberation of Germany. He describes the Beach landing of tanks and other vital equipment.

That is a brief summary of the advertisement on the back of the announcement about the Lieutenant's lecture.

At last I wrote to the R.A.O.C. depot and they sent on my request to the Army Record centre, but they refused to send any address, so I wrote to Frank and asked the Record centre to forward it. I received this reply on January 20th 1969 some days later:

Lieut. Frank Garstang, R.A.O.C.

Thank you for your letter dated January 16th 1969.

The letter you enclosed has now been forwarded to the above-named.

Now at last I have received an answer from his son, John A. Garstang of Preston:

In answer to your letter of January 16 I can tell you that my father is ex-Lieut. Frank Garstang and is the same person who delivered the lectures in Birmingham etc.

He was born in Burnley in 1905, but his father Elijah Brown Garstang was brought up at Salmesbury Farm near Preston. There were ten children in the family, and he belongs to the Preston branch of Garstangs.

John adds that he is writing for him as his father is not well but John will willingly answer any further questions. So at last by reference to Walter's first letters from Thomas above, we see that Frank must be a brother of Florence Halstead in Burnley.

To make sure that Frank was the brother of Florence Halstead (née Garstang) of Burnley, I wrote to John again and received this answer written February 4th 1969:

My mother and father live with us as neither of them enjoys the best of health, and my father is unable to work.

I have only one sister, she is ten years older than I am and has four sons ranging from 10 to 17 years of age.

My mother's maiden name was Nellie Haworth from Burnley, and Mother and Father lived there until just before the war, then they moved to Chorley and finally to Preston itself.

I was born in Reedley near Burnley in 1938, but I have lived nearly all my life in Chorley or Preston, and my wife and I have two small children, a boy of eighteen months and a girl of six months.

I have been a schoolmaster for $8\frac{1}{2}$ years, and at present I am teaching handicapped children in a special school near Preston.

My mother tells me that Elijah did have a daughter called Florence who married a Mr. Halstead. Elijah's first wife died and he married a second wife in Canada. I believe that my father's sister, Florence Halstead, died only recently in Burnley.

We do not know, however, whether Elijah's second name 'Brown' was a family name or not, but we will try to find out.

Now I am looking forward to reading all about the Garstang Clan when your book is published. If I can help you with any other details you have only to ask.

My father was born in 1905 so he will be 64 this year. I hope you will find the few details I have included of some interest.

Best wishes,

John A. Garstang.

I shall be able to write to John to tell him that by a very lucky chance his distant cousin Derek Garstang in his letter written on January 28th 1969 happens to mention that his Great-grandfather Thomas born in 1840 married 'Betsy Brown', and as the same Thomas was Elijah's father, the name Brown was passed to the eldest son. Before I had received Derek's letter I had only the information that Thomas married 'Betsy', so I had asked John if he knew anything about the name 'Brown' which he had given as Elijah's second name.

I have been able to add Frank's name and that of Derek of Lytham to the old pedigree I had made from the information sent by Colin to my brother Walter, Pedigree III. 17.

Thomas of Penwortham 1790-1869 died in
June, bur. Penwortham.

mar. to Ann -who died Ap. 17th 1868 aged 66 years.

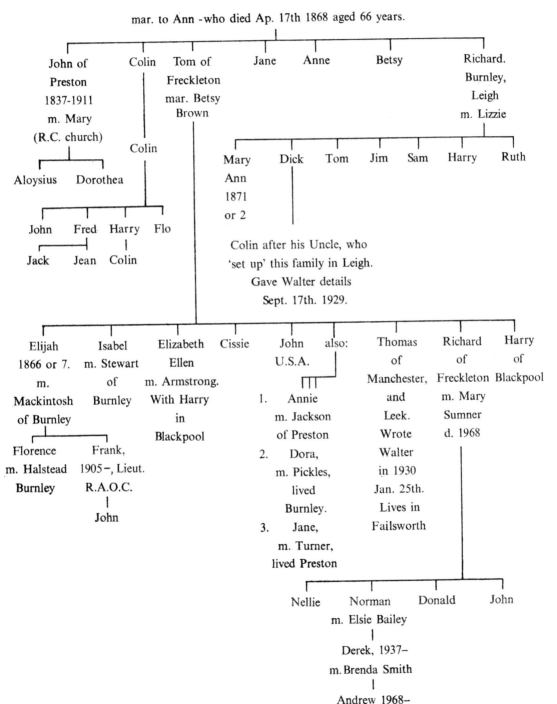

John of
Preston
1837-1911
m. Mary
(R.C. church)

Colin

Tom of
Freckleton
mar. Betsy
Brown

Jane   Anne   Betsy

Richard.
Burnley,
Leigh
m. Lizzie

Colin

Aloysius   Dorothea

Mary
Ann
1871
or 2

Dick   Tom   Jim   Sam   Harry   Ruth

John   Fred   Harry   Flo

Jack   Jean   Colin

Colin after his Uncle, who
'set up' this family in Leigh.
Gave Walter details
Sept. 17th. 1929.

Elijah
1866 or 7.
m.
Mackintosh
of Burnley

Isabel
m. Stewart
of
Burnley

Elizabeth
Ellen
m. Armstrong.
With Harry
in
Blackpool

Cissie

John   also:
U.S.A.

1.   Annie
m. Jackson
of Preston

2.   Dora,
m. Pickles,
lived
Burnley.

3.   Jane,
m. Turner,
lived Preston

Thomas
of
Manchester,
and
Leek.
Wrote
Walter
in 1930
Jan. 25th.
Lives in
Failsworth

Richard
of
Freckleton
m. Mary
Sumner
d. 1968

Harry
of
Blackpool

Florence
m. Halstead
Burnley

Frank,
1905−, Lieut.
R.A.O.C.

John

Nellie   Norman   Donald   John

m. Elsie Bailey

Derek, 1937−

m. Brenda Smith

Andrew 1968−

Derek Garstang of Lytham St. Annes

January 29th 1969. Derek Garstang has just telephoned to say he has posted the particulars of his family to me. He said that Harry Garstang of Blackpool was his Great Uncle, so he too belongs to this group of Garstangs from Penwortham.

He wrote on January 28th 1969, from Lytham Hall Park, Lytham, as follows:

Thank you for your letter of the 22nd January, 1969; I am sorry I have not been able to reply earlier due to pressure of work.

My Great-Grandfather was Thomas Garstang who married Betsy Brown. They had ten children, five girls and five boys. My Grandfather, one of the five boys, was Richard Garstang who was born at Habergam Eaves, Nr. Burnley, in June, 1881. He married Mary Henrietta Sumner.

They had four children, (Nellie) Ellen?, Norman, Donald and John. My father is the eldest son, Norman, who married Elsie Bailey, and I am the only son of this marriage.

In December, 1962, at 25 years of age, I married Brenda Mary Smith, and in July last year we had our first child, a boy, Andrew Richard Garstang.

For four months last year we had four generations of Garstangs since Andrew was the first Great-Grandchild of my Grandfather to carry the family name. Unfortunately my Grandfather died in November aged 87 years. He is survived by his second wife Mrs. Constance Garstang (née Ollier).

I hope the above-information is of some interest to you, and don't hesitate to write again if you require further detail.

Meanwhile, I have lived in Lytham all my life, and the Windmill, the Green, and the 'Old World Charm' remain. The donkeys still emerge in the summer months, and the town is very popular with visitors.

Lytham Hall Park is mostly agricultural land and is not available to the public. In recent years a small area of the Park has been developed with a good class of property, and this is where I reside.

I work in the County Education Offices in Preston as an Administrative Officer.

I look forward to reading your completed work when it becomes available.

Yours sincerely,
Derek A. Garstang, A.C.C.S.

Pedigree III. 18.
The Lancastrian Society.

In May 1963 James Rowland Garstang wrote to me again to say that when he had been staying to work in Newhaven lately he had heard of some more Garstangs:

The landlady of the digs where I was staying shewed me a Programme of an entertainment given by the Lancastrian Society of Sussex for the benefit of Old Age Pensioners at Brighton. The leading lights were H.

Garstang, A. and A. H. Garstang—probably a family unit—I have now written to Brighton to find out the origins of the Garstangs concerned, and I will let you know the result if any.

On June 29th James Rowland was arranging to call and see me on his way to Preston. His letter continued:

> I hope by then that I shall have heard from A. H. Garstang in Brighton. I telephoned to him and he has promised to let me have a letter this week. His name is Alfred Harold. He said that his father's name was Thomas, one of a family of five or six brothers, four of whom were Colin, Samuel, James, and Richard. His Grandfather was born in Preston, his father moved to Burnley then to Leigh.

I remembered this family quite well as 'Colin' was a key-word, so when James R. G. brought me the pedigree from Alfred Harold, all I had to do was to add the new names to Pedigree III. 17.

Alfred Harold places the name 'John' as the first ancestor buried in Penwortham, and James (in addition to Albert) has a son whose name is not given. He does not mention 'Colin' as the son of Richard and Martha, but I have added his name as it was he who gave the information to Walter.

In September 1963 I heard from James Rowland that the Brighton Garstangs were in charge of the entertainment section of the Lancastrian Society of Sussex in Brighton. About the same time I had a letter from Doris to say that a friend of hers had said in one of her recent letters that 'Peter Garstang goes round helping with *Lancaster* Marionettes'. As the only Peter Garstang of whom I know is in Canada, I asked James Rowland to see if he was one of the Brighton Garstangs. He replied:

> I telephoned the Garstangs at Brighton to-night regarding Peter but they don't have any information on him. Alfred Garstang has been in the Lancastrian Society there for the last fourteen years. He was President four years ago and had possession of all the Society's archives, but there was no mention of any other Garstang. However apparently the Society is holding a Social evening next Thursday and Alfred is going to enquire if anything is known of Peter. I am interested in the whole Clan, not just in the Preston Section.

There is a Peter Garstang Totty mentioned in Pedigree II.8. of the Darwen Branch, and as a small boy he liked the name 'Garstang', could it be he? More investigation wanted again!

In answer to Alec's appeal the writer of the Brighton note gave some more information about the family. He thinks that most of his predecessors lived and died in Leigh or the neighbourhood, except Richard who married Martha Hulme, the sister of Elizabeth's husband Charles, and they lived in New Zealand where they were later joined by Ruth. These are all the sisters and brothers of Mary Ann in Pedigree III. 18 and she was born c.1841.

Alfred Harold (the writer in December 1968) is the son of Thomas and Mary Sargent (the Tom of the previous group). He is the youngest of nine children of whom five died in infancy and the eldest, James Edward, was

Pedigree III.18.

A continuation of Pedigree 17 by Alfred Harold

of Sussex.

Letter headed by the <u>Red Rose.</u>

(Lancastrian Society).

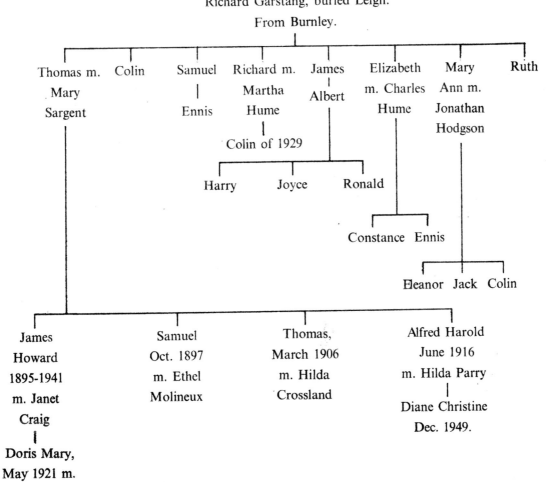

Thomas (John) Garstang buried in Penwortham

1790-1869

Richard Garstang, buried Leigh.

From Burnley.

Thomas m. Mary Sargent   Colin   Samuel   Richard m. Martha Hume   James Albert   Elizabeth m. Charles Hume   Mary Ann m. Jonathan Hodgson   Ruth

Ennis

Colin of 1929

Harry   Joyce   Ronald

Constance Ennis

Eleanor Jack Colin

James Howard 1895-1941 m. Janet Craig

Doris Mary, May 1921 m. William Williams.

Samuel Oct. 1897 m. Ethel Molineux

Thomas, March 1906 m. Hilda Crossland

Alfred Harold June 1916 m. Hilda Parry

Diane Christine Dec. 1949.

husband George had a father George and a grandfather George, but still I cannot trace them nearer than to their cousins in Leigh.

The letter continued:

My husband's father went to Madras where he died of fever when 42 years old, leaving his widow with her two sons, one being my husband George, and the other, Harry; she also had a daughter Alice who married Edward Sullivan of Cheetham Hill, and she has a son Anthony.

My brother-in-law Harry lives in Bradbury, Cheshire, and has a son Geoffrey.

My mother-in-law's name was Elizabeth (Mills), my father-in-law, George, had two brothers, Harry and John, both born and reared in Radcliffe near Manchester, all worked in the Pioneer Cotton Mills. They lived at one time in Black Lane, where Arnold Garstang is still living.

My maiden name was Malgrave, and my son Edward married Elsie Farnworth, their son Michael is sixteen years old. Elsie came from Bolton. That is all I can tell you.

Yours sincerely,
W. M. Garstang.

Two more of the letter-writers belong to this large group and between them give some very important details. The first is from the widow of Fred Garstang, living in Pinner, Middlesex:

In reply to your letter of the 13th instant (referring to Alec's appeal), I regret to say that my husband, the late Fred Garstang, died on October 11th 1964.

I am afraid I know little of his antecedents, but he had a son and daughter by his first marriage (there are no children of the second marriage) who might be able to help you. The son, Jack Garstang, lives at Hillingdon, Uxbridge, and he has two sons, one born November 22nd 1965 and the other on April 12th 1968. The daughter, Jean, is Mrs. Alan Batchelor of Eastcote, Ruislip, and they have an adopted family.

There is also a brother of my late husband, Mr. Harry Garstang of Preston, who has one son, and a sister, Mrs. Arthur Parsons.

This is the only information I can give you, and I regret I cannot be more helpful.

As I have no address of a Garstang in Uxbridge sent by Alec I wrote to Jack after receiving his step-mother's letter and received a very full and interesting reply written on January 9th 1969. When I had been typing the pedigree table from Walter's notes made when he interviewed Colin in 1927, I was always puzzled because he called his cousin *Colin* his *uncle*. Somewhere I was short of a Colin! Now at last I was about to find him, as in his letter from Uxbridge Jack said:

My great grandfather Colin was a Works manager of Horocks of Preston and had several children; my grandfather, another Colin, I think was the eldest, he also worked for Horocks as a travelling salesman manager and he died between 1935 and 1945 followed by his wife Naomi who had lived in New Hall Lane after his death.

Great grandfather Colin invented something important to do with the stripe-printing of cottons. He had several brothers and sisters with children one of whom became a monk and another a nun known as Sister Dorothea of Rochdale I think.

Looking back to find the name of this son—Aloysius—I see why I missed out 'Great-grandfather' Colin from the pedigree, for Colin had said to Walter 'Uncle Colin came next' meaning after John, but I thought he meant after Aloysius. He also said that his 'Uncle Colin' helped to invent the way to make flannelette, so with stripe-printing to his credit, he must have been something of a genius.

Now we must go back to Jack's letter:

The eldest son, John, of grandfather Colin was killed in the first world war, unmarried. Fred, my father came next, he married Nancy Eugene of Tottenham, London, in 1928 when he was thirty; I was born in 1932 and Jean two years later.

My mother Nancy died in 1952 and after five years Father married Cecily Curl, a widow in Norwich. He died in 1964.

The youngest son of grandfather Colin is Henry of Preston, his wife's name is Amy, and they have one son, Colin, who was born in 1931. Grandfather's daughter, Flo, married Arthur Parsons of Bury and now lives in Preston without any family.

Now for myself. I am Fred's son Jack, and in 1964 I married Anne Florence Cold of Chelmsford in Essex, and we have two sons, Brian, 1965, and Tony, 1966.

My sister Jean in 1958 married Alan Batchelor of Ruislip, and they have adopted two children.

There is a Professor W. Garstang I think of Manchester University tied in somewhere. He wrote a book on Bird Song published about 1910 or 1920. Some time ago some one in great-grandfather's family did a comprehensive family tree of the Garstangs and gave my Aunt Flo a copy.

My father, Fred, worked in a mill in Preston for a time, did not like it, and went to evening classes in Manchester, joined the Marconi Company, and served as radio officer on passenger ships. He went all over the Atlantic and Mediterranean until he gave up the job in 1929 having met my mother on S.S. Avoceta. He then worked for several firms including Hoovers and Colombia Radio Co. having been made Sergeant-major (WO I). He joined up in July 1939, but stayed in Britain during the war.

He was invalided out in 1946 due to injuries received during the first world war in the trenches in France and was on sick pay for several years. From about 1948 he worked at the Army Ordnance Depot in charge of a repair shop at Greenford, and when that closed down about 1960, for the Home Office, Stanmore.

Father's brother Harry started work in car repairs, and later for Siemens Lamp Works and English Electric Aircraft in Preston, where his son Colin also works.

On leaving school I worked in the Post Office Research department on electrical engineering, where I have remained except for two years National Service in the Royal Signals.

My sister Jean trained as an Infant Teacher and practised until she adopted the first child in 1964. Please let me know when the book is published as my sister and I are both very interested.

Yours sincerely,

J. Garstang.

I have been able to alter the pedigree which I had made from Colin's conversation with Walter, and have included Jack's great-grandfather Colin, also the nun Dorothea. I had written to Jack to ask a few more questions about his father, and in replying he wrote:

My father in 1945 obtained Associate membership of the British Institute of Radio Engineers, and in 1928 he had been admitted as an associate of the Institute of Wireless Technology while he was working on the ships for the Marconi Wireless Telegraph Company Ltd., who in those days supplied all the Radio Officers for reputable Lines. They were not under the command of the Captain only under Marconi, but that company was taken over first by Cable and Wireless Ltd. and in 1948 by the G.P.O. My father-in-law is a Director in Marconi Co. Ltd. at the moment.

I think I was told that grandfather Colin was one of several brothers and sisters. He was a non-practising Roman Catholic and when he was dying he would allow only his cousin Dorothea to see him, saying that she was the only person who treated him in the right way.

This story of Jack's about his grandfather Colin being a Roman Catholic is a good introduction to another family of Garstangs moving from the Preston area to the coast of North Lancashire, as they now seem to be connected with Jack's family.

Garstangs of Ulverston and Barrow-in-Furness.

Two letters from John Faint Garstang of Ulverston and his distant cousin, Mabel Garstang Round, of Barrow-in-Furness, are better dealt with together as they give details of the same relatives. Mabel says that the family originally came from Preston, and that her grandfather's father was connected with a Roman Catholic family of Garstangs. John Faint G. also begins his story with this great grandfather whose name was *Henry*. The only Garstangs obviously belonging to the Roman Catholic Church as far as I know were Aloysius and Dorothea with their mother who had married John of Preston, the brother of Colin (Pedigree III.17), and I therefore place them in that group.

Great grandfather Henry left Preston for Ulverston and chose a sea-faring career, probably in the eighteen thirties. He became a master mariner and was shipwrecked finally and lost at sea while serving as second mate.

Henry's son *John* 1855-1929 left school at 12 in Barrow-in-Furness to become a sailor. He rose to the position of first mate of a sailing vessel, and then became a Pilot with the Harbour Board. He married Elizabeth Quine who was of genuine Manx stock and came to the mainland of North Lancashire to work in a vicar's household as nurse to the children. There she first made friends with 'grandfather' John's sister, and then of course with John whom she married, at first much to the disappointment of her Manx relations.

They settled down in Barrow where at that time there was much activity in the docks, and in addition to his work as pilot John became a member of the Barrow life-boat crew for many years. During that time they had eight children and 'grandmother' Elizabeth died in 1932 at the age of 76. Of the daughters only two, Mabel and Lily, are still alive; the eldest son, *Harry,* has a son and two grandsons, the second son, *John* (1890-1967), married Hetty Faint (1889-1962); he gave up the seafaring life and became a skilled trades-man.

The family of John and Hetty Faint consisted of six daughters: Dorothy, Muriel, Lilian, Mildred, Olga, and Elfrida; the elder son, Walter J. Garstang, died suddenly last summer (1968) and his widow, Elsie, passed on Alec's appeal for news to her niece Mabel Garstang Round, so as she is not yet married I suppose she is the daughter of one of John and Hetty's daughters.

The younger son of John and Hetty Faint is *John Faint,* the writer of the first letter I received from Alec about this group.

John Faint was born in 1928, and has three daughters, Fiona, Alexandra, and Charlotte; so as his brother Walter J. and Elsie had two daughters, Alison and Anne Marie, John Faint ends his very interesting letter on a sad note as too many other Garstangs have also done:

> On our side of the family it would appear that the Garstangs are dying out, both my brother and I having only female children; but my father's brother Harry has a son and two grandsons.

Pedigree III.19.
James Rowland Garstang.
Ancestors from New Longton.

In May 1963 I had written for the first time to a Mr. Garstang because the Passport Official in Southampton had remarked that the name on my niece's passport was the same as that of his 'boss'! I could not have chosen a better moment, as I had reached a stage in these Preston relationships when I needed a living Garstang to help me out of the bogs. He answered in a very few days:

> I actually work in the Immigration Dept. of the Home Office and your letter was sent to me by my friends in the Customs.
>
> In answer to your enquiry all my relatives come from Preston, Lancs., and its environs. I was born in *Freckleton* near Preston, and my father was born in *Preston,* his name is *Richard.*
>
> His father, my Grandfather, *Joseph Rowland,* was born in *Preston,* also his uncles, *Thomas and Elisha,* were born in Preston.
>
> I am writing to my father to see if he remembers anything more regard-ing his forebears.
>
> I expect you are a relation of Professor John Garstang the Archaeologist? I once had occasion to go to the Royal Free Hospital, London, with one of

my sons and the specialist remarked on our name and mentioned that the Prof. was one of his patients.

This would be during the time when my brother John was living in Hampstead Way with his daughter Meroë (Fleming) as her husband is a pathologist at that Hospital. In his letter James R. Garstang then describes his interest in the tomb and buildings of the wool merchant Henry Garstang in the church at Cirencester, laying stress on the stained glass window where an angel is portrayed holding the Garstang Coat of Arms (a blue shield with three lozenges), and he adds that he often passes through Cirencester en route to Freckleton; it was very curious that by the same post I received from George Squibb the copy of the Garstang arms which his wife Bessie had painted years ago in Cirencester Church. There is also in Bessie's notebook a sketch of one of the corbels in which an angel holds up a shield bearing Henry's initials 'H.G.' and his Merchants Mark.

In concluding James Rowland gave me more details:

My wife, Aileen Nancy Charters, was born in Preston, married 25th March 1940, a school teacher.

I have two sons, James Howard and Richard Graham. James is reading Chemical Technology at Edinburgh University, and Richard is trying to get into Medical School.

Although I was born in Freckleton, all other members of the family came from Preston. I recall now that there was a separate family of Garstangs in Freckleton who were no relation to us, the father was the engineer at the village cotton mill.

His name was Richard too.

I had never heard of the Garstang Hall at Tockholes until you mentioned it in your letter.

The Freckleton you knew is vastly altered now although the village Green still remains. Now the land is pretty well all built up on the way to Lytham. At the Warton end is the big English Electric Aerodrome where aircraft are built. A great deal of the river bank and foot-path have been closed in order to make room for the run-ways, and the old road across the marsh no longer exists, but for many years has been replaced by a wide motor road from Preston.

The boat-builders, Allonson, still have their yard by the river though, and they still build yachts and small boats; also the Marsh itself is very much as it was and is given over still to cattle grazing.

I shall be making a trip to Preston at the beginning of July, or sometime during that month I expect when my elder boy, James, is on vacation from Edinburgh, and we could pass through Oxford en route. He is very keen on tracing the Garstangs history, so as you suggest we could perhaps meet you then. My father has not yet replied to my letter, but I hope to hear from him shortly.

This was a great help as I knew no living Garstangs in that area, but in Colin's letter to Walter he had said that a Tom Garstang had left Preston to work in Burnley and had then retired to Freckleton and his son Richard was an engineer there, so he might well be the engineer at the mill in Freckleton mentioned in this letter from James R. G. as not belonging to his family.

The father was 90 years old in 1930 according to Tom of Leek's letter. We kept hearing of this Richard in Freckleton! James said he would write to Freckleton. So the problem of these two families was solved after James

Pedigree III.19.

James Rowland of Longton, Freckleton,

and Richard of Preston.

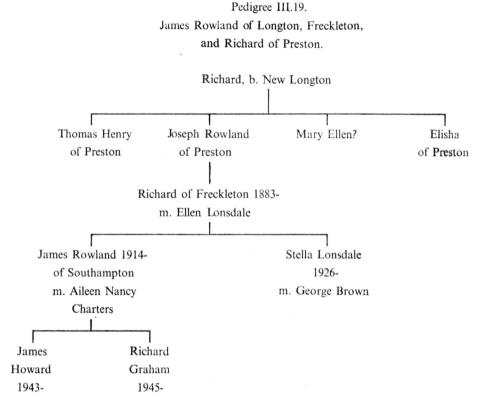

Richard, b. New Longton

| Thomas Henry of Preston | Joseph Rowland of Preston | Mary Ellen? | Elisha of Preston |

Richard of Freckleton 1883-

m. Ellen Lonsdale

James Rowland 1914-
of Southampton
m. Aileen Nancy
Charters

Stella Lonsdale
1926-
m. George Brown

James
Howard
1943-

Richard
Graham
1945-

wrote to them and received the answer from Mrs. Constance G. as given already above on p.115. James enclosed this amusing poem about farmers of Garstang in his letter to me.

Veni Garstang, ubi nata
   Sunt armenta fronte lata,
Veni Garstang ubi male
   Intrans forum bestiale,
Forte vacilando vico
   Huc et illuc cum amico,
In juvencae dorsum rui
   Cujus cornu laesus fui.

From *Lancashire Plain and Seaboard*, Herbert C. Collins. p.95.
Published by J. M. Dent and Sons Ltd.

A rough translation brings out the rural atmosphere in the following jingle: (with my apologies!)

I

I came to Garstang where the broad-browed cattle breed.
I came to Garstang where alleys to the market lead.
Thither with my good friend I came,
Staggering along, and he the same,
Both swaying thus from side to side
I with a heifer's back collide.
No more of Garstang could I see,
That heifer's horn had punctured me!

Pedigree III.20.
The Garstangs of Preston and Longton.
Richard, son of Thomas Henry.

On January 7th 1930, R. Garstang of New Hall Lane, Preston had written to my brother Walter to explain his Family Pedigree; he was living with his father:

The householder at this address is *Thomas* Henry Garstang who is my father. His father was Richard G. who was born at New Longton in 1825, and married Mary Morland at Preston on April 12th, 1856.

He had three sons all born in Preston; Joseph Rowland born July 29th 1857, Thomas Henry, May 20th 1861, and Elisha, May 21st 1863.

Joseph Rowland died in the first few years of the present century (between 1901 and 1905 I think) leaving the following children: Richard, living at Moss Avenue, Lea, Nr. Preston, Minnie since dead, Elizabeth Ann now Mrs. Whiteside residing at Freckleton, Rose now Mrs. Nichols at Church Avenue, Preston, and Elisha serving in the Royal Navy.

Thomas Henry has one other son besides myself viz. Thomas Stopford of Avenham Lane, Preston.

Elisha has two surviving sons and one daughter: David living at Ship Lane, Hutton, Nr. Preston and James who is living I think in Porter St., Preston. The daughter is Mrs. Owen.

I have found records of Margaret Garstang born at Bamber Bridge on Sept. 10th 1843 and while nobody seems to know definitely she appears to be the daughter of the Richard Garstang born at New Longton in 1825! She died in Burnley a few years ago.

There is an Elizabeth Garstang born at Accrington in Feb. 1864 of whom I can get to know nothing, and two other children, I think of Richard's family, Richard born 1871 and Elizabeth born 1869, both died young.

This is all I am able to unearth at the moment.
Yours faithfully,
R. Garstang.

This letter was written in 1930 and now in 1968 on December 23rd Richard writes again, this time in answer to Alec's appeal for the latest news:

I thank you for your letter of the 13th December and I well remember the letter sent by Prof. Walter Garstang. I am afraid I have little new in family history to offer, beginning with Grandfather Richard of New Longton near Preston, born c.1823.

Of the next generation Joseph Rowland, Thomas Henry (my father), and Elisha you have the names already, there were two daughters who died young, the name of one was Mary Ellen.

I have records of several people of my father's generation who through early deaths or removals I never knew. I expect they were the children of my grandfather's brother in New Longton.

(Among these he gives the Elizabeth born 1864 in Accrington and she is in our earlier pedigree as a sister of Elisha; he is probably right as he gives Margaret born 1843 in Bamber Bridge, while all Richard's sons were born in Preston where the next two on his list were also born: Elizabeth Ann 1869 and Richard, 1871.)

Richard continues:

Joseph Rowland had a family of two sons and two daughters, all of whom I know to be dead except Elisha. My father had one other son beside myself, Thomas Stopford, he died in April ten years ago. Incidentally his widow is the M. Garstang to whom you wrote at 522 New Hall Lane in Preston.

(This is the address given by Richard when he wrote to Walter.)

My uncle Elisha had three sons: David, Joseph, and James, all of whom are dead and one daughter Mary (Polly) aged now 84 and residing with her daughter.

I have two children: a son John Rowland who is a scientific official in the Ministry of Agriculture, and one daughter who is now a student at Leicester University reading French.

Her name is Judith Mary, and the son John Rowland is at the Experimental Husbandry Farm at Gledthorpe on the edge of Sherwood Forest.

This letter introduces both Joseph Rowland, who must be the grandfather, and Richard the father, of James Rowland who had done much to help the Quest but whose family I had not been able to connect with any of the other pedigrees. I wrote at once to tell him of this discovery among Walter's archives.

On June 29th 1963 James Rowland answered my letter, he had been to call on these newly found relations and was disappointed that they knew no more of the family:

Many thanks for the pedigree, that is certainly our family. . . . I have also heard from my Father in Preston, but he does not remember any ancestor before Richard of 1825 whose photograph I happen to possess! . . .

I suppose the great difficulty is to find the right Parish Records before 1825? I wonder if New Longton Church Register would help?

We are looking forward to seeing you next week when I shall be more free. I've been too busy these last few weeks.

James Rowland is now H M. Inspector of Immigration for Scotland and N. Ireland in Glasgow and has bought a cottage in Lytham for his holidays and retirement when it comes, so I hope he will then be able to carry on with the Quest. His two sons are still at Edinburgh University: James

Pedigree III.20 with 19 added.

The Garstangs of Preston, Longton, Freckleton.

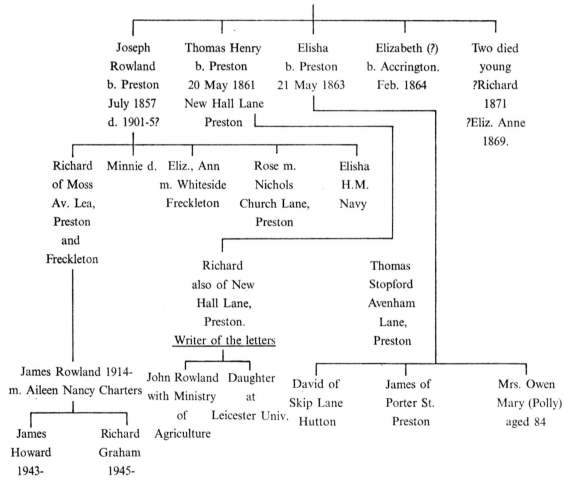

Richard, b. New Longton 1825
m. Mary Morland, Preston, 12th April, 1856.

Joseph Rowland b. Preston July 1857 d. 1901-5?

Thomas Henry b. Preston 20 May 1861 New Hall Lane Preston

Elisha b. Preston 21 May 1863

Elizabeth (?) b. Accrington. Feb. 1864

Two died young ?Richard 1871 ?Eliz. Anne 1869.

Richard of Moss Av. Lea, Preston and Freckleton

Minnie d.

Eliz., Ann m. Whiteside Freckleton

Rose m. Nichols Church Lane, Preston

Elisha H.M. Navy

Richard also of New Hall Lane, Preston. Writer of the letters

Thomas Stopford Avenham Lane, Preston

James Rowland 1914- m. Aileen Nancy Charters

James Howard 1943-

Richard Graham 1945-

John Rowland with Ministry of Agriculture

Daughter at Leicester Univ.

David of Skip Lane Hutton

James of Porter St. Preston

Mrs. Owen Mary (Polly) aged 84

Howard has taken his degree and is engaged on Chemical engineering on the scientific and industrial side.

Richard Graham is in his third year on a dentistry course at present, and may stay there to qualify as a doctor as that was his main hope since boyhood. In 1969 he married Elizabeth Anne Hardie, a graduate of Edinburgh University.

On November 19th 1968, I received a picture post card from James Rowland; a fortnight before he and his wife had visited our favourite village of Ribchester where John began the excavation of the Roman camp while still at the Grammar School as a scholar. James thought we would like to see the picture of the Museum which was built to house at first the finds from the camp. I well remember helping John to drag a huge measuring chain there when I was about 14 years old. We dragged it from Blackburn where we lived, several miles away.

Early in February I had another letter from James of Glasgow in answer to my enquiries if he knew Richard and his children, he writes:

I have not been in touch with Richard Garstang since before the war— we met our wives at the same Psychology class in Preston.

So indeed they were not like so many cousins who have been surprised to hear of the relationship from me.

Pedigree III.21.
Richard Garstang of Southport.

On September 16th 1928 Walter met Richard Garstang of Bolton Road, Southport who remarked several times that, although he could not remember the name of his great grandfather, he was sure that he was in some way connected with a farming family in Longton—the Parkers. This was luck for Walter, as the Garstangs of Longton were as much of a puzzle to him as those of Preston and Freckleton, so he asked as many questions as possible, among them the name of the inn keeper at the Virgin's Inn in Preston. Richard of Southport said the inn had been pulled down and the site used for the Preston Free Library, the host, Thomas Garstang, having afterwards moved to the 'Golden Lion'. He was the grandfather of Richard and had died at the age of 75 years, probably buried in Longton but possibly in Preston Cemetery. Richard himself had formerly worked as a 'traveller' and had resided in Avenham Rd. Preston, but had retired to live in Southport. He had no son.

From all the information given to him by Richard of Southport, Walter made Pedigree III.21.

Note to Pedigrees 17-21.

Pedigree III 17 of Thomas of Penwortham 1790-1869 deals with so many families, and with so many children in each family, that it fails to answer to the facts as given in each letter received. My brother met Tom, son of Richard of Burnley and Leigh, he also talked to Tom's nephew Colin, but

PEDIGREE III.21.

The Garstangs of Longton and Preston, with Southport.

From Richard of Preston and Southport.

Thomas (?) , Richard's Great-grandfather a farmer in Longton

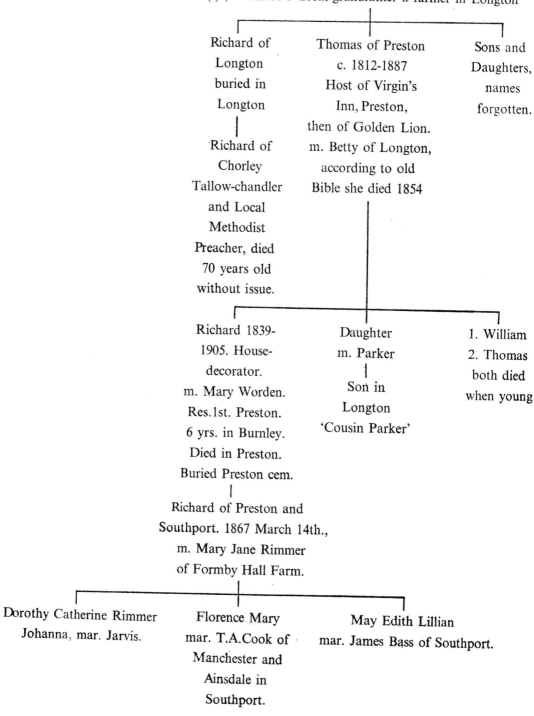

Richard of Longton buried in Longton

Richard of Chorley Tallow-chandler and Local Methodist Preacher, died 70 years old without issue.

Thomas of Preston c. 1812-1887 Host of Virgin's Inn, Preston, then of Golden Lion. m. Betty of Longton, according to old Bible she died 1854

Sons and Daughters, names forgotten.

Richard 1839-1905. House-decorator. m. Mary Worden. Res.1st. Preston. 6 yrs. in Burnley. Died in Preston. Buried Preston cem.

Daughter m. Parker

Son in Longton 'Cousin Parker'

1. William
2. Thomas both died when young

Richard of Preston and Southport. 1867 March 14th., m. Mary Jane Rimmer of Formby Hall Farm.

Dorothy Catherine Rimmer Johanna, mar. Jarvis.

Florence Mary mar. T.A.Cook of Manchester and Ainsdale in Southport.

May Edith Lillian mar. James Bass of Southport.

I have dealt only with letters. The chief difficulty lies with the descendants of John of Preston 1837-1911; he married Mary, a member of the Roman Catholic Church, and unfortunately in those days there was no ecumenical movement so, as one letter explained, the younger half of the descendants remained Protestants and did not know much about the Roman Catholic half. Now, in June 1969, I think the Colin put in the Pedigree as brother of John of Preston did not exist, and his son Colin, together with *his* four children in the pedigree, were all the children of John of Preston and therefore the brothers and sisters of the priest Aloysius and the nun Dorothea.

(Compare the letters quoted on pp.124 and 136.)

Curiously, the explanation of the mystery is due to the Joseph William of U.S.A. (see p.139) giving me the addresses and names of Wilfred Garstang of Garstang, Bernard of Freckleton, and Mrs. Bell Ingham of Preston, and I give extracts from her letters, for, as she said in her first letter: "My mother used to love to talk about the Garstangs, and that you see has come down the female line, and I still have the old family Bible." The letter continues: "Thomas Garstang was her grandfather, and she used to take me to the grave in Penwortham churchyard. I don't know if it is still there as a lot of graves have had the headstones removed and a garden made for burial of the ashes. This Thomas and Ann had at least two daughters, Ellen, my grandmother, was the youngest, and Ann, who married Mr. Hodge, went to live near Bolton. I do not remember the names of all the sons, but there was a Richard which is a family name, a Thomas, and I think a Joseph but I am not sure where he came. My grandparents Thomas and Anne, were hand-loom weavers. They had then very big rooms built at the back of their kitchens, the hand-looms were in there, and they were built for the Flemish weavers 200 years ago. Well, most of these have been knocked down now to make way for shops, and the others are to come down shortly, but before that happens I will get a photo taken and send you one. I enclose now a copy of the mourning cards of my great grandparents."

Mourning cards of Ann and Thomas Garstang of Penwortham, Preston.

In Memory of
Ann Garstang,

who died 17 April 1868 aged 66 years, and was interred at Penwortham Church April 21st.

'Farewell dear friends and relatives all
I'm going to obey the Saviour's call.
I always strove to do my best,
And now I've gone to take my rest.'

In memory of
Thomas Garstang,

who died 13 June 1869 aged 79 years, and was interred at Penwortham Church on June 15th.

'Go home, dear friends ,and shed no tears,
I must lie here till Christ appears,
And when he comes, I hope to have
A joyful rising from the grave.'

Mrs. Ingham's letters then explained the next generation:

"My grandmother Ellen Garstang married a man called Smalley, and my mother when she married changed her surname from Smalley to Barnes, so that was my name until I married my husband who died over twenty years ago.

"My mother had a great friend called Mary Ellen Garstang, my grandmother and her father were cousins; she married Tom Downing and moved to Freckleton from Preston in 1912. She had a brother Thomas and another called Elisha who both had sons, Mary Ellen had no family of her own but she was my godmother. There was a Joseph who might have been their father, but he had been an invalid for a long time before he died. When I was young I used to cycle to Freckleton with my dad to see them. It is about 8 miles from where I was brought up. Mary Ellen and her husband used to come and stay with us, she used to live in Porter Street, Preston, before they went to Freckleton."

(Compare Pedigrees III.19 and 20 with 19.)

Mrs. Ingham continued in another letter: "I am 68 now, I had a lovely home and I never thought that I would have to leave it. I have one daughter, Jean, who was married 6 weeks before her dad died, she and her husband, Thompson, and their two girls lived with me until they went to Canada, Calgary in Alberta, 12 months ago last March. I do miss them so much. I came to live in this bungalow the week after they went. We have a warden whom we can call if we are ill. It is really nice, quite in the country with nothing but fields at the back, and my brother lives quite nearby with his daughter and two boys of 7 and 10 years. She comes nearly every day to see if I want any help or errands doing.

"I had a Bernard of Freckleton to see me on Saturday and we had a good chat about our Garstang relations. He is descended from the John Garstang who married a Roman Catholic, he was the son of Thomas and Ann of Penwortham, and was my mother's uncle, brother to my grandmother Ellen. He died 22 July 1911 aged 74 years and was interred in Preston Cemetery. He had a son John who lived in Fishwick View, and *he* had a lot of sons and one daughter, Agnes; Bernard Garstang of Freckleton is a descendant of these Garstangs and quite a different branch from those we knew. Then there was Richard whose first wife was Rose and his second wife I never knew. (See p.115 where the second wife, Constance, writes to James Rowland G.) We called his sister Cissy, and you mentioned Elizabeth Ellen in your last letter."

About the same time (June 1969) I had a letter from the Bernard Garstang of Freckleton mentioned by Mrs. Ingham:

"I must say with each letter I receive come more surprises, and with them so does the Garstang family grow. To add to the Joseph William and Ray in America, a John Garstang, son of Richard of Freckleton, stated how he met some of the Garstangs who came from overseas during the war, and strangely enough I was in barracks outside Plymouth where I met my name-sake with the New Zealand Navy." (See Alfred Harold's letter p.121 in which he states that Richard and later Ruth, the children of Richard of Burnley and Freckleton, went to live in New Zealand.)

In Mrs. Ingham's letter quoted above she states that John of Preston had a son John who lived in Fishwick (Preston), and it is this John with whom Bernard begins his pedigree when writing to me. He knows of Richard, who died 1968 in Freckleton, had married 1. Mary (Rose), 2. Constance, and whose son and grandson are living in Warton, also he had heard of Harry of Black-pool, whose widow in her letter to me assured me that Harry's brothers Elijah and John went to America and died there.

Bernard traces his pedigree from John of Fishwick who had one daughter Agnes and six sons: Frank (2 sons, 1 daughter), Edward, Leonard (1 daughter), Wilfred (1 son, 4 daughters), Joseph (4 sons), and Alphonse who is a head teacher at a priests' college in the Midlands. Bernard is one of the four sons of Joseph, his brothers being another Joseph (2 daughters), Robert (2 sons), and Edward who was the youngest and is deceased. Bernard himself has 2 sons and 2 daughters; he has consulted his uncle Wilfred in Garstang about the family relationships, and will try to get more information from his uncle Alphonse.

Wilfred told him that four of the family worked in the Horocks Company's cotton mills: the ancestor John, son of Ann and Thomas of Penwortham, became manager of the Preston mill, and three of his sons were salesmen; Mrs. Ingham mentioned that one of her great-uncles working there invented flannelette weaving; and another (pp.124-5) invented printing in colour for woven cotton. Also Henry Garstang, a relative of John living in Fletcher Road, Preston (Pedigree III. 14.) also became manager of Horocks Crewson and Co., he died in 1928. So the hand-loom weaving in the home of their ancestor, described by Mrs. Ingham, must have developed enthusiasm for the new steam-looms. (Invention of steam looms, see pp.140-1.)

Bernard ends his letter by saying that he is painting a picture in oils of old Preston to send to Joseph William in Salem, and he adds: "When I see my surviving son at this moment I don't wonder our ancestors came over in the Viking boats—tall, blonde, blue eyes, he has all the characteristic markings."

Like so many of us, Bernard was born in Blackburn.

Mrs. Bell Ingham of Preston, after she had described how her mother's great friend in Freckleton was her second cousin, Mary Ellen Garstang, explains that her grandmother Ellen was the cousin of Mary Ellen's father, (pp.129, 136). She continues: "Mary Ellen had several brothers, but no sisters when I knew her; there were other children who died young. I have heard the name Roland mentioned but I never knew him. It was Elisha and Thomas whom I knew. First, let me tell you about Elisha: he had a daughter and three sons, I think the daughter is still living, she will be about 80 or more now; she married George Owen and had one daughter; George's sister, Eliza Owen, married the brother David and they had one son who married

Jean Cragg and they have a son and a daughter; David died about fifteen years ago, but his widow is still living.

"Their brother Elisha was quite a character: he was a vegetarian, and would only eat brown flour in bread, cakes, and pies. His wife used to long for a bit of white bread, so Mother would smuggle her in a small white loaf which he would have said was only fit for the hens. They came to live at Ashton then went to Belmont where his wife died; he came to live in Penwortham and lived till he was 85 years old.

"Thomas was quite a different person. He married Sarah Stopford, she was awfully nice; they had two sons, Thomas and Richard. Thomas was weaving-manager at Horrocks's mill, he married Emily Jones and had one daughter, they are both now dead. Richard got married and I have lost touch with him as I am not able to get about as much as I used to do." (See p.136.)

On 1 August 1969 James and Aileen called to see me on the way from Glasgow to Poole, having called to meet Alec in Sheffield in the afternoon. We had a good laugh about the sayings of Elisha as they agreed with Mrs. Ingham that he had been an exceptional man in every way; they saw him frequently when they lived in Preston soon after their marriage.

Amongst other Garstang recollections James told me that David Threlfall, who won the £10,000 bet on the U.S.A. astronauts reaching the moon, was the grandson of Rose Garstang. She was the sister of James Rowland's father, Richard.

James also left with me a typed description of St. Helen's church in Garstang, given to him by the Vicar, the Rev. E. S. Pickup and drawn up by him for the use of the many visitors who frequent the famous old church. It is known, he writes, as 'The Cathedral of the Fylde', mother of eight neighbouring parishes and with architecture of almost every age since the Norman Conquest. The piers in the nave on the North are late twelfth century, they have circular capitals and are nine inches taller than those on the South, these have octagonal capitals and were added about a century later. The vicars are traceable to 1190, and from 1241 to 1539 Cockersand Abbey served the Church.

While James and Aileen were in the Garstang church-yard Aileen copied an inscription written in Latin on a gravestone. It was in memory of Nicolai Brodley de Garstang who died when she was 84 years old, also of William who died 14 May 1825 also aged 84 years, and of his wife Margaret who died 9 June 1830 aged 72 years. (William born c.1741, Margaret c.1758).

Pedigree III.22.
Some Garstangs of U.S.A.
Margery, Joseph William, Ray and James.

On March 4th 1913 my brother John received a letter from Los Angeles in California, U.S.A. from a Margery Garstang:

In looking over books in our Public Library we found a book entitled

'The Land of the Hittites' written by you, Prof. John Garstang, Liverpool, England, and the name being the same as that of my Father, who came from England when a boy of seven years, I thought perhaps that you might be able to give me some information regarding our ancestry in that country.

My Father, John Garstang, is now 77 years of age and is the eldest son of a family of six living children. He was born in Preston, England, but his Father, Richard Garstang, was born in Blackburn and became a foreman of some weaving establishment there. Then he came to St. Louis, U.S.A., (the year I do not know) and ran the first steam loom in that city. He had a brother, Colin, who was also a weaver, but my Father's brother, Richard, became a very successful business man in St. Louis as a boiler-maker, and is now retired and still living there. My Father is more of a learned man than a successful business man and has lived here for 60 years as a highly respected citizen.

My brother Richard, who was given the family name after three former Richards of earlier generations, is a Lawyer, having first served as Prosecuting Attorney in Missouri, and other members of our family are doctors or lawyers. I taught in a Missouri school for three years, and then retired on account of ill health and resided in California with my Uncle Richard.

My Father's Grandfather was Warwick Garstang who married Betty Jackson, but that is all I know, so that any information you can give us about our English ancestors will be very highly appreciated.

Notes.

Margery's father was born about 1836 and by calculating 30 years for one generation we arrive at approximate dates for the rest. The father John went to U.S.A. when seven years old about 1843.

There seems to be some connexion here with Pedigree III.21 as there are sons whose names were forgotten and four Richards do occur in succeeding generations.

On the other hand the name 'Colin' was popular in the Penwortham families of II.17 etc., a very large family group.

Pedigree III.22 continued in U.S.A.
Joseph William of Missouri.

In Margery's letter of 1913 the earliest ancestor was given as Warwick Garstang who married Betty Jackson, and their two sons, Richard and Colin were both weavers.

Richard was born in Blackburn c. 1806, he married and took his son John born in Preston, and Richard probably born in Preston, to St. Louis, Missouri, U.S.A., in 1843.

John, born in 1836, left a Journal about his travels where he gives the date 1842 for their first arrival in St. Louis with his step-mother Sarah and sisters Elizabeth, Sarah, and Margery, also two step-sisters, Rosanna and Catherine. Later a half-brother Joseph and his sister Sarah Jane were born.

In 1875 the father, Richard, who had become a famous boiler-maker, founded 'The Garstang Company' for making steam engines to be used for

Pedigree III.22.

Pedigree given by Margery Garstang of Los Angeles, California, U.S.A.

in 1913, her father was then 77 years old.

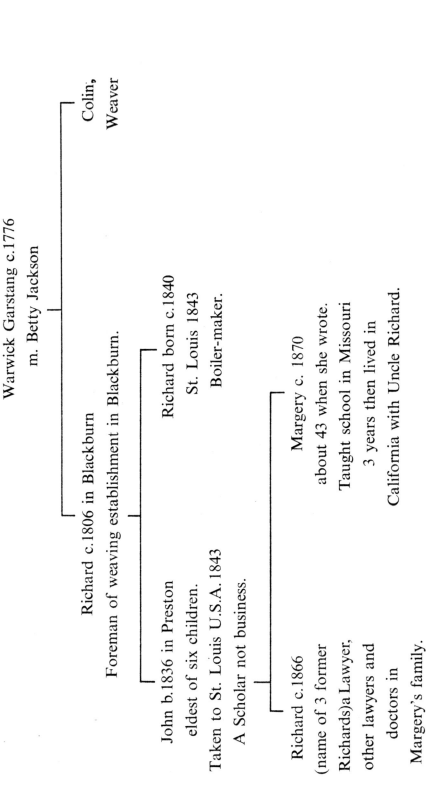

Warwick Garstang c.1776
m. Betty Jackson

Colin,
Weaver

Richard c.1806 in Blackburn
Foreman of weaving establishment in Blackburn.

Richard born c.1840
St. Louis 1843
Boiler-maker.

John b.1836 in Preston
eldest of six children.
Taken to St. Louis U.S.A. 1843
A Scholar not business.

Margery c. 1870
about 43 when she wrote.
Taught school in Missouri
3 years then lived in
California with Uncle Richard.

Richard c.1866
(name of 3 former
Richards)a Lawyer,
other lawyers and
doctors in
Margery's family.

the first time in steam-boats, and mills for weaving-looms. The company lasted until 1910 when Richard (John's brother) retired to Los Angeles.

Information has been added in 1969 by letters to me from two more of Richard's descendants still in U.S.A.

On April 16th, 1969, Joseph William Garstang of Salem, Missouri, U.S.A., had a notice printed in the Lancashire Evening Post to say that he hoped to visit Preston soon to see the places in England that his Garstang ancestors had known. This was forwarded to me by James Garstang of Glasgow and John of Chorley. So I wrote to Joseph William to see if he knew about the Margery who had written in 1913, and I have received letters in reply.

Joseph William retired at 65, after working for 41 years with the 'Multiplex Display Fixture Co.' of St. Louis, beginning as shipping clerk and ending as factory manager. He married Agnes Tieman, and has no family. He was born in St. Louis 17th April, 1901, his grandfather being Joseph, the half-brother of John who wrote the Journal.

"I have been told," Joseph William said in his letter, "that my grandfather Joseph built the first water tube boiler for the Heine Co. of St. Louis, working with a brother named Richard who owned the Garstang iron works or Boiler Co. My grandmother, Joseph's wife, was Maggie Conners, they had three boys and four daughters. My father was born May 15th 1876, married Tille Kaufholz who was my mother, his name was Herbert P. Garstang, and like his father, Joseph, he was a boiler-maker in St. Louis. They had a large boiler placed in front of their 'Plant' with a sign saying: *This first water-tube boiler was built by Joseph Garstang.*'

Herbert P. had two brothers: Richard who worked in a St. Louis printing works, and Ben, who died young. His four sisters were Barbara who died in her teens, Madge who married L. Zimmermann, Rose married Jack Keely, and the youngest, Katherine, also married. He himself had two sons younger than Joseph William; the second, another Herbert, worked in the McDonnel Aircraft corp. in St. Louis where 38,000 people were employed. He married as did the youngest son, Edward, and each has two children. The three daughters of Herbert P's family were Emma, who married J. Patterson and lives in St. Louis; the second, Eleanor, of whom Joseph William writes: "After Eleanor's marriage had broken down she retained her maiden name, Garstang, and about 30 years ago she wanted to find work when she had been left alone. I thought a temporary job in the company where I was employed would suit her, and she was put in charge of the mailing department. She was still there when I retired in 1966. Soon afterwards she retired when she reached the age of 62 and said she would like to live in the country near me. I begged her to come and live with us, as my wife is a semi-invalid and needs company, but she insisted on having her own home not far away from us."

"The third daughter, Ruth, married Charles Marchand, who owns a Tavern. Ruth is a school teacher, and her son, Timmie, is in a college in Missouri. The daughter, Tina, and the son are both married.

"Ruth said she would write to you and send any further information she knows about the family. Our youngest brother, Edward, is still employed by the *Curtis Air Compressor Company* as a foreman. The lawyer, Richard, mentioned by Margery in 1913, could have been my grandfather's nephew whose son I knew, and he was also a lawyer, his name was James.

"There is also a Dr. Garstang, but I am not sure of his name."

So far Joseph William's family history agrees with that of Margery's letter, except that while she gives *Warwick* as the father of Richard and Colin, and *John* as the elder of the two boys taken by Richard to U.S.A. in 1842 or 3; the family there call the boy *John Robert* and his grandfather *Richard*. However, whether John's grandfather was Richard or Warwick, his grandmother was *Betty Jackson;* and if, as Margery says, her brother Richard was so-called after three former Richards, perhaps the ancestor's name was *Richard Warwick*.

We have not yet succeeded in finding a Richard Warwick who married a Betty Jackson, but in his Journal John gives one generation further back than Margery, and the archivist in Preston kindly looked up the reference:

"Thomas Garstang of Longton, weaver, m. Jenet Sumner on 8 May 1759 in Croston, near Preston.

"The following baptisms of their children given:

8 Oct. 1759 Thomas.
3 June 1764 Thomas.
17 April 1774 Thomas.
3 Nov. 1776 Richard.
28 Feb. 1779 Henry.
24 Aug. 1783 Margaret."

The genealogy of his family is placed by John (Robert) at the end of his Journal of which we give extracts. It has been in the keeping of his grandson, Ray Garstang, whose letter follows the extracts.

Genealogy of J. R. Garstang of Missouri

Great Grandfather	Great Grandmother
Thomas Garstang	Jenny Sumner
Grandfather	Grandmother
Richard Garstang	Betty Jackson
Father	Mother
Richard Garstang	Sarah Blackist
born 1802	Step-mother
	Sarah Parker

John Robert Garstang, born February 21st, 1836. Married to Miss Mary Elizabeth Mahon of Osage County, Missouri, May 7th, A. D. 1865.

JOHN ROBERT GARSTANG'S JOURNAL

"I was born in Preston, a town in Lancashire, England. On the 21st day of February A.D. 1836. My mother, Sarah Garstang, died in England, when I was about four or five years old. My father, Richard Garstang, married again, and emigrated to America, with the intention of going to Nauvuo in 1842 with his family, consisting of his second wife Sarah, myself, and younger brother

Richard, my eldest sister Elizabeth, Sarah, and Margery the youngest, and two step-sisters, Rosanna and Catherine. We arrived at St. Louis Mo. in the fall of 1842; and in the spring of 1843 started up the Mississippi river, on the steamer "Maid of Iowa". Arrived at Nauvuo, where we remained until the latter end of June 1844, when we returned to St. Louis, where my father and his family still resides, up to the present time April 1856.

There was an addition of five by birth to our family: James was born in Nauvuo, Benjamin Collin, Joseph, Emily, and Sarah June in St. Louis; but we lost three by the death of James, Benjamin Collin, and Emily. Then Elizabeth married John F. Carol, and Sarah married William Weeks. Also Rosanna my step-sister, married John Ellis Gracy of St. Louis.

On July the 7th 1855 I left St. Louis again and arrived at Great Salt Lake City on the 2nd of November."

While there John Robert joined the 'Church of Jesus Christ of Latter Day Saints' and returned to St. Louis 1856.

In 1857 his step-sister Catherine married N. R. Vandyke, and in 1860 his sister Margery married Alexander Boote.

GARSTANG'S APPLIANCE CO.
Ray Garstang

Belle, Mo. 65013,
Missouri.
May 17, 1969.

To Mrs. S. G. Gurney.

I got a letter from Joseph William Garstang, Salem, Mo., with a copy of your letter to him about the Margery Garstang letter written about 1913; she was my aunt.

My grandfather, John Robert Garstang, born at Preston, England, Feb. 21, 1836—died Nov. 6, 1927, married Mary Elizabeth Mahon, born May 7, 1865, died March 15, 1928. 6 Children:

1. Guy T. Garstang, born July 11, 1866, died May 22, 1933 with leukaemia. (Was my father.) Married Lena Crutsinger, Linn, Mo., Nov. 16, 1886. Died Oct. 29, 1948, cancer. 4 children, all living:

Ray Garstang, born May 19, 1908

Robert T. Garstang, born Oct. 13, 1910

Thomas Garstang, born May 27, 1915

Dr. Wm. E. Garstang, born Nov. 17, 1923.

2. Gertrude Garstang (never married) born Oct. 27, 1868, died Nov. 2, 1927.

3. John Richard, born April 11, 1874, died Feb. 23, 1962, was a lawyer at Chamois, Mo., was Prosecuting Attorney of Osage County about 20 years. Married Leona Ernstmeyer, born Feb. 16, 1881, died Mar. 8, 1962. 6 children:

Marion Richard Garstang (living) a lawyer in Washington D.C.

Alma Garstang (dead) don't have dates of birth (about 1912) and death (about 1965) married Game

Janet Garstang (dead) born Nov. 19, 1910, died April 19, 1963 married Ross W. S. Garstang, living at Chamois, Mo.

Loraine Garstang Ernst, nurse in Jefferson City, Mo.

Carmine Garstang, born April 24, 1913, died Feb. 3, 1928 (died with 'flu and pneumonia).

4. Mildred E. Garstang, born 1870, died 1954. Was a school teacher and Baptist Missionary. Never married.

5. Margery Ann Garstang, born 1872, died 1947. She was a school teacher at Chamois, Mo., St. Louis and Los Angeles, California, she is the one who wrote the letter you mention in your letter about 1913. Never married.

I have a daughter named Margery Ann after her; she is married and has two children now.

6. Roscoe Richard Garstang, born 1876, died about 1951. (Don't have at this time exact dates). 2 children:

John Richard, living in Rialto, Calif., U.S.A. Real Estate Business.

Mary Ellen, married and living in Calif.

I visited Wilfred Garstang at Garstang, England, in the fall of 1966 and went to the Library there and read some of the History of Garstang but did not have time to do very much research on the history of the family.

I hear you are writing a book about the Garstang family and am sure all the Garstangs in U.S.A. will want one.

There are a lot of Garstangs in Davenport, Iowa, U.S.A. I have their history and will send you a copy as soon as I can get it made. They came from Lancashire, England, in 1836 approx. Will send you our family tree history as soon as I can get it together.

Yours truly,
Ray Garstang.

The following was taken from *History of Davenport and Scott County, Iowa,* Volume 13. Published in 1910.

James Garstang

In the years of an active business life James Garstang was connected with carpentering in Davenport and helped to erect many substantial structures here. Now in his seventy-fifth year he is living retired, the fruits of his former toil supplying him with the necessities and comforts of life. He was born in Lancashire, England, February 29, 1836, a son of Collin and Anne Garstang. The father was a loom-maker in England and came to the United States in 1849 with his wife, his son James coming in 1853. After travelling to a considerable extent in this country he ultimately settled in Davenport, where he remained until his death, which occurred in 1867.

James Garstang came to the United States four years after his parents had taken up their abode on this side of the Atlantic, although they returned to England and brought him to the new world. They landed at New York and all came to Davenport, James Garstang arriving here on the day that he was seventeen years of age. He attended school to a limited extent here and afterwards drove a team and was employed in other ways until about twenty years of age, when he began learning the carpenter's trade, which he found a congenial occupation, following it continuously until his retirement. As he prospered in his undertakings he made judicious investments in realty and now derives a substantial income from his property interests.

On the 30th of March 1865 Mr. Garstang was married to Miss Mary Baker, a daughter of William Baker and a native of England. She was born October 19, 1839, and came to the United States at the age of sixteen years. Her mother had died in England and her father died at sea while they were crossing the Atlantic. Mrs. Garstang lived to the age of sixty-nine years, passing away November 12, 1908. There were two children of that marriage, Colin and William Edward, but the latter died at the age of two years. The former was born December 7, 1867. There are now two grandsons, Clifford S. and W. Lloyd.

Mr. Garstang continued actively in business in Davenport for years and was always found reliable, painstaking and faithful in the execution of his work. His industry and careful management at length brought him a gratifying measure of success and with the retired men of affluence he is now numbered.

(Dec. 1969.) Alec has just sent me the names of five more Garstangs in St. Louis: Edward W., Guy, Herbert R., James E., and G. Heating Co.

Pedigree III.23.

Some Garstangs of Australia.
Mrs. Alice Cowan of Ayrshire,
Frederick Wright and Percival Herbert of Sydney.

In 1928 my brother Walter received the following letter from Mrs. Cowan of Ayrshire:

> You will no doubt think it strange that I should write to you; I came across a small paragraph lately mentioning 'Dr. Walter Garstang, Professor of Zoology in Leeds University', and it is a strange coincidence that the same day I had a letter written to my brother Walter Garstang returned through the post from Sydney, New South Wales, Australia. It is ten or eleven years since I heard from my brothers on the death of my father, Frederick Wright Garstang, and as it is such an uncommon name, I felt I must write to you to see if you were any of our kin. I do not know why my brother was called Walter except that it was my father who wanted him to be called by that name.

After Walter had answered that letter, Mrs. Cowan wrote again:

> I think my father went to Australia about 1875, and I have never heard of the name Garstang until I saw yours. I heard my father mention the town Garstang, and have always had a longing to see it. I shall certainly try to do so. Thank you for the picture post-card. I bring up my brood of four well-Garstanged, Ian Garstang, William Robertson Garstang, Frederick Garstang, and Annie. Ian is now a keen Rover-scout.

The writer then explained that her grandfather's name was James Garstang and her grandmother's maiden name, Eliza Wright. After their marriage

Pedigree III.23.

James Garstang m. Eliza Wright of Angel Place, Stratford, Essex.

Frederick Wright Garstang

born at above residence 26. Dec. 1847 emigrated to Australia between 1875-9.
married May 20th. 1880 Mary Jane Deas, born 1850, died 1914.
an Accountant at Ashfield, later Stipendiary Magistrate.
Resided in 1885 at Fairfield Terrace, Summer Hill,
Ashfield and after retirement at Auburn, Sidney.

| Fredk. Deas b.Feb. 1881 Bank Manager | Ethel 1883- | Alice Mary Isabel b.31 March 1885 at Windsor, Ashfield, N.S.W. Left Australia 1907 m. 1. McColl. 2. Cowan | Percival Herbert 1887- | Walter Treloar 1889- | Harry Ernest 1891- |

Ian Garstang — Annie Wm. Robertson Garstang Cowan

Fredk. Garstang Cowan

they lived in Angel Place, Stratford, Essex, where their first child, Frederick Wright, was born on December 26th 1847. When he was about 28 years old he emigrated to Australia, and he married Mary Jane Deas on May 20th 1880. After a few more details Mrs. Cowan gave the names of their sons: Frederick Deas, Percival Herbert, Walter Treloar, and Harry Ernest, their two daughters being Ethel and herself, Alice Mary Isabel, and she had left Australia in 1907. She had been married twice, her first husband being Frederick George McColl, and their children were Ian Garstang McColl and Annie.

The two youngest sons were William Robertson Garstang Cowan and Frederick Garstang Cowan.

On March 5th, 1969, Cecil Garstang of London sent me five names of Garstangs from the telephone directory of Sydney, Australia, where he had an office for Cook's Travel Agency; among these were P. H. Garstang and three having the initial 'W' in their names.

Alice Cowan had said that she had a brother called 'Walter' like my brother to whom she was writing, and also one with the names 'Percival Herbert.' As P. H. fitted Percival Herbert exactly and as he was not nearly as old as myself, the chances were that he was Alice's brother. So I wrote to him and received the following letter:

25 March 69.

Burwood, New South Wales.

"I was very pleasantly surprised and greatly interested to receive your Air letter dated 12 inst. and the subject matter set out therein. Your assumption that the initials 'P.H.' could possibly apply to myself is correct, as my Christian name is 'Percival Herbert' (Garstang). For your information I append details of our family:
Father Frederick Wright Garstang
Mother Mary Jane."

Here he gives the names of the four boys beginning with Frederick 'Deas', the mother's name according to Alice's letter; also the names of the two daughters, Ethel May, and Alice. Then he continues:

"From the facts set out in your letter it seems to me that the Frederick Wright Garstang you are enquiring about is my Father who was a Stipendiary magistrate in the state of N.S.W. He died during the First World War 1914-18 at the age of approx. 69 years.

"My brother Fred died three years ago at the age of 84. He had one son Robert who survives.

"Sister Ethel married about 1903, but as she left Sydney shortly after marriage, I am not clear as to the issue of her marriage.

"To the best of my belief Sister Alice left Sydney early in 1900 to go to Scotland to marry a sailing-vessel Captain named G. McColl. But unfortunately I have no further recollection of her life. Your reference to Mrs. Cowan intrigues me as she says she is the daughter of Frederick Wright Garstang who emigrated to Sydney in 1875, and that she had two brothers named Percival Herbert and Walter respectively.

"I have no record of Father's arrival in Sydney, but the various ages of our family seem to tie up. Could Mrs. Cowan have re-married to take the name of Cowan? If so, she could well have been my sister Alice.—I would be grateful if you would go into the matter further and advise me of the outcome.

"I myself married Grace Furcher Sneddon in 1910, and celebrated the Eighth Anniversary of our Golden Wedding last December, my wife Grace and I are each 81 years old. We have two children, both living, the eldest Ellen Grace, 57 years old and married to George Smith, O.B.E., barrister of Sydney (no family) and Phyllis Joyce, 53, who married Allister Turner just retired as Chief Engineer of Tin Mining Production by the Anglo-Oriental Co. of Malaysia; they have one daughter, Susan Elizabeth, 19 years old.

"The 5th born son of our family 'Walter Treloar' is now 79 years old, married, and had two daughters named 'Boralie' and 'Elvy' and one son named 'Walter'.

"My brother Walter lost his wife recently, and the remainder of his family still survive.

"The last of the Garstang family, Harry Ernest, left Sydney during the Second World War, we have not heard of him since he left. He would have been 76 years of age if he is still alive.

"I have heard of a few other people of the name of Garstang in past years, but none of them have been relatives of ours.

"Should I learn of any further details of Garstangs in Australia I shall keep you posted.

"Once again many thanks for writing to me in the above connection and with kind regards,

Yours sincerely,
Percy H. Garstang, J.P."

I answered this interesting letter to explain that his sister Alice had become Mrs. Cowan after a second marriage as he surmised, but so far I have heard no more from the family.

Some Garstangs of Nelson and Colne in Lancashire.
Ernest and Jeffrey, Richard and Harold.

In January 1960 I received a letter from Jeffrey Garstang of Harlow, Essex (the county from which Frederick Wright Garstang had emigrated to Australia):

In reply to your letter of December 13th, I was very pleased to hear about the book and hope that the information I can give you will be of use.

I know nothing of my grandparents or other relations on my father's side. He was born in Nelson, Lancashire in 1890. He worked as a cotton over-looker in the mills, and he married a Lancashire girl by whom he had three children: Doll, Dennis, and Jim. After his wife died he moved to Southall, Middlesex, where he met my mother. They married about 1939 and four years later I was born on September 24th 1943. I lost contact with Jim. Doll married and has four children; Dennis is still single and lives with my mother, he was born on May 5th 1930.

My father, Ernest Garstang died on November 6th 1964. I then got married to Maria Kearns on December 19th 1964. We now have three boys, Clive born September 30th 1965, Leigh born September 12th 1966, and Ian born July 25th 1968.

Would you be kind enough to let me know when 'From Generation to Generation' will be published and where I can get a copy. Thanking you very much.

Yours faithfully,
J. Garstang.

I suggested that there might be some connexion with the Frederick Wright Garstangs, but I have had another letter from Mrs. J. Garstang of Harlow, and her husband Jeffrey does not know of any relations in Australia. His family in Nelson owned some shops at the time his father left there for Southall, and Jeffrey himself has worked in a metal factory ever since he left school. In any case Jeffrey's father, Ernest, could not have been Percival Herbert's brother Ernest (who returned to England in the second world war), as Jeffrey's father's first marriage took place before 1930.

In December 1968 the mother-in-law of N. H. Garstang, to whom Alec had written, replied that he and her daughter were now living in Canada, and she had sent Alec's letter to his father in Colne.

Mrs. White continues:

I was just going away from home, Sabden Bridge near Whalley, as I am now on my own, and I go a lot to stay with my brothers in Lancaster.

Before you get to Lancaster there is a small country town called Garstang; it is very old, and I wondered if it was the town you mentioned in your letter. It is a lovely little place, very narrow. I could not stay long with my brother because Sabden where I live is in a hollow and we get a lot of snow, so I have just come back, but no snow has fallen yet.

So now I will close and I hope you will hear from my daughter's father-in-law in Colne.

On January 1st 1969 Harold Mayor Garstang wrote in answer to Alec's letter, and I think he must be the father of N. H. Garstang of Sabden, as his mother-in-law had said she was sending his appeal for news to his father in Colne. Unfortunately Harold M. G. does not mention the name of his son who emigrated to Canada, but he wrote from Colne.

I am sorry that I have no knowledge of my grandparents, he writes, My father, Richard Garstang, was born in the Leyland district, and came to Nelson about 1880. He was by that time married, and his brother Jack followed him soon afterwards.

My father had a family of eleven children, four sons and seven daughters. One of the sons emigrated to America, and two of the daughters to New Zealand.

I was born in 1896.

I have two sons, one born in 1922, and the other in 1929.
I am sorry I cannot be of more assistance.

Sabden is slightly north of the eastward line between Blackburn, Nelson, and Colne in Lancashire, Leyland is a few miles to the west of Blackburn.

As Harold's father went to live in Nelson in 1880 and had four sons born there, I should think that Jeffrey's father, Ernest, was one of them. More investigation wanted.

Garstangs of Stalybridge (Cheshire)

On December 24th 1968 Mrs. Joyce Pyrah, the daughter of Thomas Raymond Garstang and Clarissa (née Riley) wrote to explain their family connexions. She wrote from Norwood Green, near Halifax.

The following week January 1st 1969 Mrs. Charles Anthony wrote from Stalybridge in Cheshire, and luckily both mentioned a Frank Bromley Garstang as one of the sons of Charles Richard who was born between 1865 and 1875, and married Anne Tipping who died in 1939 two years after her husband.

Charles Richard had three sons. Charles Ernest b.1896 married Jane (Walsh), their three daughters Ella, Irene, and Brenda, had one brother, Brian.

The middle son of Charles Richard's family was Thomas Raymond whose daughter Joyce Pyrah wrote the letter, and she has two children: Carol Margaret b.1950 and Colin William b.1952. The second child of Thomas is Charles Raymond b.1928 and married Patricia Kenny who also has two children, Christina Ann b.1951 and Vivienne Lesley b.1953. He is now a Captain in the 2nd Canadian guards.

Now the third son of Charles Richard and Annie is Frank Bromley, and the only news that Joyce gives about him is that he was born in 1906, but Hilary, (the writer of the second letter) says:

The youngest son was Frank Bromley Garstang who married Anne (Cawley), they have two daughters and one son, Vivienne born 1936, Pamela born 1938, and Charles Anthony 1942. I married Anthony in 1966 and we now have one son, Adam born 1968.
Yours sincerely,
Hilary Garstang, N.D.D., D.A. (née Gummerson)

On January 28th 1968 Hilary wrote again after obtaining more details from her father-in-law:

My husband's great-great-grandfather was born and lived in Cadley near Preston, the great-grandfather was born in Bromley Cross and died in Blackburn where Frank Bromley, my husband's father, was born, but he lived in Ashton-under-Lyne and in Stalybridge; he now lives in Arnside in Westmorland.

As Garstang names tend to run in families, the name Ernest here suggests a possible connexion with the family of Ernest the father of Jeffrey and with the Ernest who left Australia for England. I have not found this name in any other pedigrees.

CHAPTER IV

THE GARSTANGS OF WHITTLE

It is a very curious fact that as far as Walter could discover the many branches of this Whittle group had known the story of their origin, and the history of their own families at least to the time of Charles I. We have therefore a wealth of information about their activities during different generations. That is a kind of illustration of the real friendship which seems to have been the rule between brothers, sisters and cousins of the group. There is difficulty then in choosing a short description of the characteristics most evident, but throughout their careers they show the same keen interest in the Christian Church and in their own local church as the other groups of Garstangs already mentioned. The bulk of the details must remain in the Clan archives, but a few individual services and achievements may reflect the stamp of their usual way of life.

At the time of the Tudors Leyland was the most important town in the neighbourhood, the Hundred of Leyland being bounded on the north by the river Ribble, and on the east by the hundred of Blackburn. To the north-west was a wide morass known as Leyland Moss, now in the parish of Penwortham, and the rest of the hundred consisted of flat grassland sometimes inundated by the sea. In *Domesday Book* the name is spelt 'Lailand' from Old English 'Laege' fallow, as in the modern local 'lay' for lying uncultivated.

The earliest church was built with Norman architecture and dedicated to St. Andrew. Later most of it was replaced by one of Early English design during the thirteenth century. In 1552 Thurstan Garstang, yeoman of Leyland, was one of the churchwardens, and with two companions he guaranteed to the king's commissioners in the sixth year of Edward VI's reign 'the safe custody of the bells and other property of the church'.

At the east end of the south aisle was built the Farington Chapel, and this contained brasses of the Farington family which had settled in the district by the river Lostock at the time of the Norman conquest. In the churchyard there remained several sepulchral slabs marked with crosses, and coffin lids also so carved, all dating from the 13th and 14th centuries.

1552 COMMISSIONERS OF EDWARD VI

By that time most churches were replacing some parts of their old windows and arches with the Early Decorated style of English architecture, but in such an out-of-the-way place as Leyland there was probably a time-lag. In any case the visitation of Edward VI's commissioners in 1552 was

151

nation-wide and after they had set aside a bare minimum of plate, such as the Chalice, and vestments for use in the services, the church wardens undertook to keep the rest safely for the use of the Crown.

A second reason for the postponement of alterations to the church may have been that until Henry VIII dissolved the monasteries in 1539 the Abbots, as in the case of Cirencester, had appropriated most of the tithes and other church income, leaving only a small stipend for the clergy. In Cirencester the wool merchants had been in a position to restore the church, but in Leyland in 1552 the money probably came through the king's commissioners. At the same time Thurstan Garstang in his office as churchwarden would be responsible for superintending many changes in the church services; for at the time when the Second Act of Uniformity was passed a second Prayer Book was issued in which the words "Take eat this etc." were added to the sentence spoken by the priest when administering the Bread during the Holy Eucharist. After 1553 he would have new difficulties to face while Queen Mary's ministers were seeking out prominent heretics to be burned for their Protestant faith.

At the time of this survey of Lancashire by Edward VI's commissioners in 1552 there were other Garstangs living in Leyland and district, some of them probably descended from the Thomas of Gairstang of Farington who failed to attend the Lancaster Assizes in 1401, Farington being only three miles to the north of Leyland and three miles south of Preston.

Among these Garstangs was William who was certified by royal commissioners for legal matters, as holding one acre of pasture and one of arable land in 'Whittell in the woods' belonging to the Leyland chantry and rated at 3 shillings yearly.[1]

They all seem to have had about the same amount of land, but in 1558 another Thomas Garstang got into some trouble in Leyland itself, being involved in a law-suit as occupant of a certain messuage and garden with 'common of pasture and turbary'. The right of cutting turf or peat on the Moss often seems to have led to a dispute. In 1558 Queen Mary died and Elizabeth I came to the throne determined to restore law and order in both Church and State, thus presumably Thomas could rely on a fair trial.

THURSTAN GARSTANG'S FAMILY

Although we cannot trace the relationship of these four Garstangs to each other, George Squibb discovered the name of Thurstan's father and of their Manor House. Eleven years before Thurstan undertook the responsibility of guaranteeing the safety of the church bells of Leyland, that is in 1541, 'Nicholas Williamson and his wife Mary (Crook) together with George Smalley and his wife Katherine (Crook) demised the Manor of Crook for 21 years to William Garstang in Whittle-le-Woods at £6 16s. rent.[2]

[1] In the case of Rex v. Langley in 1552. The information about these three Garstangs, William, John and Thomas comes from Lancashire and Cheshire Record Society, XL p.133 and LX, p.57.
[2] From *Victoria County History*, Lancs. VI, p.34, n.4

Both William and Thurstan Garstang must have died before 1564 as in that year Crook Manor was leased to Cecily and her son William. Cecily is then described as 'the widow of Thurstan Garstang' and the lease was granted by Henry Richardson and his wife Katherine with John Ward of Denford Northamptonshire and his wife Mary.' Katherine and Mary were the Crook heiresses of the previous transaction who had evidently been widowed and re-married. In any case as the Manor House had been granted to the elder William for 21 years and after 23 years it was legally in the hands of Thurstan's family. we may fairly assume that William was Thurstan's father.

William and Margaret Garstang kept Crook Manor House under the lease until 1569-70 in which year the owners of the estate, the two daughters of Anthony Crook, sold the property to the Claytons. The two daughters were Katherine Richardson and Mary Ward as in the previous transaction; they had inherited the property but their homes were elsewhere and Cecily Garstang had continued to live in the Manor House after she had married Oliver Breres.[2]

Probably Thurstan and Cecily had other sons after the birth of William, as there are two Garstangs in Leyland Hundred described as Yeoman in the same way as Thurstan. In 1554-5 "Oliver Garstang of Whittill in the Woods, husbandman, declared that James Gerstane, gent. was seised of one messuage or tenement and 12 acres of land, meadow, wood and pasture in Whittill, and two years before, i.e. 1552/3, he had demised and leased it to Thos. Pingcoke and Anne his wife, for their lifetime at a yearly rent of 20s. and 3d." Probably James was a brother of Oliver's, and after his death the property would become Oliver's. In the parish register of Chorley, 5 miles south of Leyland, a Scandinavian name meaning a Churls' clearing in a wood, William Garstang, the son of Oliver is registered in 1559; and in 1574 Oliver's name appears again in the Records of the Chetham Society with that of Lawrence, "as yeomen of Leyland Hundred required by the General Levy of the sixteenth year of Queen Elizabeth's reign to provide each a long bow, a sheaf of arrows, a scull and a bill".

A 'bill' in the reign of Elizabeth I meant a halberd, a military weapon now obsolete which combined a battle-axe and spear. At that time the Queen's army was made ready to oppose the military preparations by the Roman Catholic Earls under the encouragement of the Pope, France and Spain, to place Mary Queen of Scots on the English throne.

In the meantime William, Oliver's son, continued to live in Whittle and, although there are many William Garstangs at this time who are difficult to distinguish, an entry in the Preston Guild Roll of 1602 of a William Garstang recorded as a 'Stallinger' probably refers to him. It implied that as he did not live in Preston borough, he could not claim full municipal

---

[1] From *Victoria County History*, VI, p.35. There are two hamlets 'Crook' in S. W. Lancs., one near Standish between Wigan and Chorley, and the other near Wardle North of Rochdale, from O. Norse 'krokr' bend.

[2] *Victoria County History*. Lancs. VI, p.35, n.1.

rights, but he was licensed to take part in the business of the Guild.

William Garstang of Whittle in 1590 made "a feoffment of 3 messuages in Whittle". His son Andrew died before him, leaving two daughters, Anne and Ellen who, when their grandfather William died in 1638, became the heiresses of his estate. At that time he held "2 messuages in Whittle of Thomas Standish of Duxbury", in Leyland Hundred two miles south of Chorley. This may have been Oliver's son, but all there is to connect the two Williams amounts to his registration in Chorley and his dealings with Thomas Standish near Chorley.[1]

WILLIAM, GUILD ALDERMAN'S SON, CHRISTENED AT STANDISH

One of the William Garstangs lived to the north of Preston at Bank Hall, Broughton, in the parish of Preston where he was registered as an 'In-Burgess' in the Preston Guild Roll of 1582, and in that of 1602 as a Guild Alderman. On October 6th of that year he served as a juror when he was described in the Quarter Sessions Roll as "William Garstang of Preston, Gentleman". His wife, Margaret, probably came from Standish, as their only son was christened 'William' there in 1602. Standish was a pleasant village in the Hundred of Leyland, $3\frac{1}{2}$ miles to the north-north-west of Wigan. Shortly before the christening of little William Garstang, the rector, Richard Moodie, was the chief benefactor in the building of a handsome church with a spire in the Late Perpendicular style and dedicated to St. Wilfred, an Anglo-Saxon thegn's son. This Rector conformed to the Protestant faith, but he is represented in his Franciscan habit lying on his altar-tomb in the chancel of his church.

The child, William, later married Agnes Bilsborow in 1624 in Preston, and it was he who with his wife and servants died in the Plague of 1631, as related at the beginning of Chapter 3 above by James Iddon Garstang (p.93).

In the list of Recusants accused under the Law of 1561 (when there was danger of a Roman Catholic plot against Queen Elizabeth I) we read that "William Garstang of Preston, Amounderness, is indebted to the Queen in the sum of £80, by reason of his recusancy".

In 1628 "The names and due additions of all such Popish Recusants convicted of the age of 17 years, or above, and all non-communicants of the age of 21 years, and above, as are chargeable by the Act of Parliament to pay 8d. a powle (i.e. a head) as they were presented at Chorley on the 4th day of August 1628. All the parishes of Leyland Hundred lack Garstang Recusants except Whittle-le-Woods: 'mort—Margaret uxor Lawrence Garstang 16 d.'"

On September 13th 1621, a certain Margaret Garstang of Whittle-le-Woods was given a conspicuously spectacular funeral at Ormskirk and was buried in the High Chancel.

If this Margaret can be identified as the recusant wife of Lawrence

Victoria County History. VI, p.35, n.14.

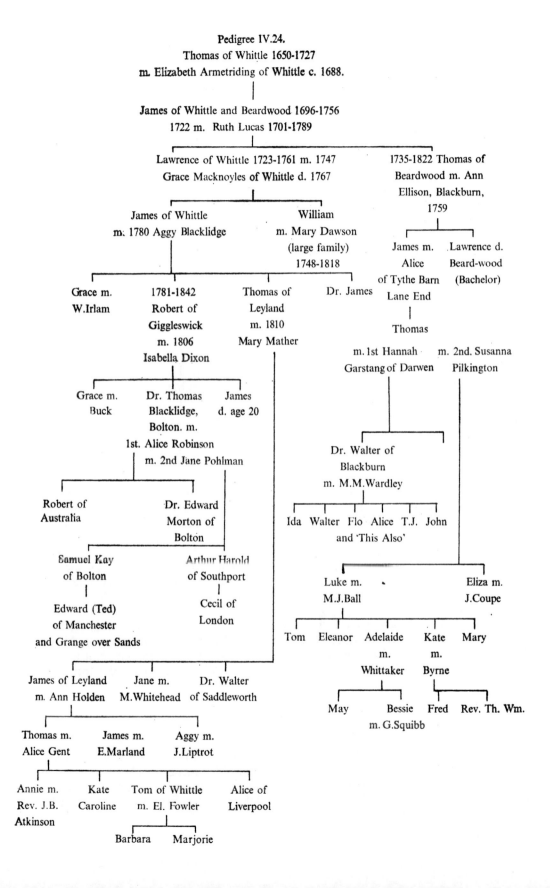

Pedigree IV.24.

Thomas of Whittle 1650-1727
m. Elizabeth Armetriding of Whittle c. 1688.

James of Whittle and Beardwood 1696-1756
1722 m. Ruth Lucas 1701-1789

Lawrence of Whittle 1723-1761 m. 1747
Grace Macknoyles of Whittle d. 1767

1735-1822 Thomas of
Beardwood m. Ann
Ellison, Blackburn,
1759

James of Whittle
m. 1780 Aggy Blacklidge

William
m. Mary Dawson
(large family)
1748-1818

James m.
Alice
of Tythe Barn
Lane End

Lawrence d.
Beard-wood
(Bachelor)

Thomas

Grace m.
W.Irlam

1781-1842
Robert of
Giggleswick
m. 1806
Isabella Dixon

Thomas of
Leyland
m. 1810
Mary Mather

Dr. James

m. 1st Hannah
Garstang of Darwen

m. 2nd. Susanna
Pilkington

Grace m.
Buck

Dr. Thomas
Blacklidge,
Bolton. m.
1st. Alice Robinson
m. 2nd Jane Pohlman

James
d. age 20

Dr. Walter of
Blackburn
m. M.M.Wardley

Robert of
Australia

Dr. Edward
Morton of
Bolton

Ida Walter Flo Alice T.J. John
and 'This Also'

Samuel Kay
of Bolton

Edward (Ted)
of Manchester
and Grange over Sands

Arthur Harold
of Southport

Cecil of
London

Luke m.
M.J.Ball

Eliza m.
J.Coupe

Tom Eleanor Adelaide
m.
Whittaker

Kate
m.
Byrne

Mary

James of Leyland
m. Ann Holden

Jane m.
M.Whitehead

Dr. Walter
of Saddleworth

May Bessie
m. G.Squibb

Fred Rev. Th. Wm.

Thomas m.
Alice Gent

James m.
E.Marland

Aggy m.
J.Liptrot

Annie m.
Rev. J.B.
Atkinson

Kate
Caroline

Tom of Whittle
m. El. Fowler

Alice of
Liverpool

Barbara Marjorie

Garstang, we may assume that the Priest in Ormskirk shewed sympathy with her, while in Leyland a more strict obedience to the Law might be observed.

In 1654 the estates of Thomas Garstang, a tanner of Brindle, were sequestered for recusancy, although as the records report "he had but little land and that in Herefordshire". (See p.19, Pedigree II. Thomas Garstang the Tanner 1604-1670).

For non-attendance at the church services the fine was £20 a month, and in cases where the fine was not paid the recusant's lands were seized and sold for the sums due to the Queen's Exchequer.

This brings us to the time when a James in Whittle who married a wife from Brindle and died c.1630 can be directly traced as the ancestor of the James Garstang who left his son Lawrence in Whittle as blacksmith and took Thomas to Blackburn as described in Chapter 1. (Pedigree IV. 24).

Pedigree IV. 25.
Thomas of Leyland m. 1810 *Mary Mather*

For Christmas 1929 Walter sent us all a typed copy of his researches into the Garstang Clan up to date, and in thanking him I said: "Now I will be able to put them into a story as I promised!" However, Daisy's last illness, followed by that of all the others, intervened, and only now is it possible to finish it.

Early in that year Daisy was staying in Liverpool with John and wrote to Walter:

A certain Alice Garstang wrote to John, not being sure from a letter she had received from her brother Tom, whether the Professor Garstang who called on him in Whittle was John or not. I suppose it was you who called and missed him?

However, John, thinking that if two 'Alice Garstangs' met together we might get some more history, invited her to come here today, as she lives in Liverpool. She has only just gone and has left some very interesting pedigrees, letters, notes and photographs of old Garstangs for you and John to see.

Alice G. gave us addresses of relations, she has five sisters and this brother Tom in Whittle. Dr. Thomas Walter Harrop Garstang of Altrincham is now in London, and his son Dr. Walter G. lives near Nottingham, his sister, a Mrs. Milne, with one son who, Alice says, looks like John, lives here in Liverpool.

In Pedigree 25 can be seen Alice's near relations.

Once when writing to John, Alice said:

We have lived in Whittle for thirty years, and it is a fact worth considering and I think of some significance, that old Whittle people—I mean really old inhabitants who speak the dialect—always and invariably pronounce Garstang as *Gairstin*, although the dialect pronunciation of *Gar* is not like that in any other instance.

This supports the views of James Iddon Garstang which I have already mentioned: "When I was a boy in Preston," he wrote, "few of the older people put any 'ah' sound into the name. It was more like *Gay-es-tin* or at best *Gairstun*".

Towards the end of Chapter I a visit is described which my mother enjoyed in Leyland when Thomas, the son of James Garstang and Ann (Holden) showed her a little book about two lambs, so that she could tell me the story. This Thomas and his wife (Alice Gent) were the parents of the Alice Garstang who lived in Liverpool, and after making friends with John and Daisy gave so much information to Walter about her immediate family; among the papers was the following programme of her father's investiture as a Freemason.

Carnarvon Lodge, Leyland, No. 2376

Festival of SAINT JOHN   DECEMBER 8th 1902

"To-night the Brethren hold High Feast
I'll warrant they're a merry company."

INSTALLATION
of

Bro. THOMAS GARSTANG,
W.M. Elect,

at

THE MASONIC ROOMS,
Public Hall, Leyland,

on

Monday, December 8th 1902

Installing Master:
W. Bro. J. Houseman, P.M.

Investing Officer:
W. Bro. J. Shutt, P.M.

"Be a pattern to others, and all will go well."

The uniform of a Freemason is illustrated by the photograph of Uncle Whewell shown on Plate IV.

Although Alice lived in Liverpool she put in writing most of her news about the Clan so that John could pass it on to Walter:

Perhaps it would be best to begin with my Father, Thomas, who married Alice Gent, and who was, I think, rather badly hit by the 'slings and arrows of outrageous fortune.'

He was very interested in Natural History. Our walks with him as children were a pure delight. I still remember, as a mere baby, being lifted up to see a chaffinch's nest, and Father's warning not to touch, as the mother bird would know, and resent any interference. I sometimes wonder if the quick flash of blue, which meant a Kingfisher, is ever seen now in what used to be a haunt of theirs in Whittle, and whether anyone still finds Reed Warblers' nests along the canal bank where he showed me one.

He was to have been a doctor, and was with that intention, apprenticed as was usual in those days, to a doctor, in this case to 'Uncle James' of Clitheroe, but Uncle James died, and as there was not enough money to continue Father's training, the whole scheme fell through. His next plan was to become a teacher, but the Head Master turned out to be a complete bully and a confirmed drunkard, then I think Father in vulgar language 'punched his head', and that was that! Now comes a little light on part of your letter, we had some relatives in Bradford named Morton (hence I suppose connected with Dr. Edward Morton Garstang whom you mention). They owned a cotton mill and were quite wealthy, so Father went to work for them. My Father did a good bit of Church work there for All Saint's Church, the Vicar being Dr. Kenyon who later became Bishop of Adelaide and Father went out there with him for a time. When he came back we moved to the old house at Whittle and bought it. He did some quite amazing work among men. He had a men's Bible Class and kept a big room in his office, which they could use exactly as they liked; they had debates, discussions, and chess tournaments etc. When Father died these men, over 200 of them, gathered on the Village Green and walked in procession to the Church where they sat all together as a mark of their great affection. So I wouldn't have had my Father any different although he tried various businesses, but seemed to do none of them very well, but under his guidance we all grew up with a strong love of animals and birds.

Later I tried to instil this into the school children I taught. One of them arrived at the old house one evening with a couple of young Blue Tits, completely featherless, which she had rescued from some boys because they had destroyed the nest. One of the Tits died, but I succeeded in rearing the other. We called him 'Oliver' because he 'asked for more' so persistently. We intended him to fly when he was grown, and so he did, but he would not leave us and always slept indoors, flying in and out as he liked, always with a swish of his wings as soon as the door was opened to the garden in the morning. Half a hard-boiled egg was kept on the kitchen dresser for his delectation and he kept the rose-trees completely free of green fly. He had no sense of fear, but sat on people's shoulders or heads, or upside down clinging to one's ear! Sometimes he sat on Father's pipe before it was alight, and once I had to apologise for my writing in a letter because he flew on to my pen. Eventually he got a little mate who couldn't understand him retiring every night into the house. She used to call him for an hour every evening

William Whewell

Thomas Blacklidge Garstang
M.R.C.S.Eng., L.S.A.

for a time, and then I think she persuaded him to elope, for both disappeared and we never saw them again.

Alice enclosed two old papers, one beautifully printed on rice paper with an elaborate border design of flowers and headed:

The

WEATHER PROGNOSTICATOR, through all the lunations of
each year for ever.

Then it gives the phases of the moon for winter and summer and according to the hour of each change is given the state of the weather and temperature, such as "The nearer the time of the moon's change, first quarter, full, and last quarter, is to midnight, the fairer will the weather be during the seven days following."

Although it had not been possible for Alice's father to be trained as a doctor, his younger brother had been provided with sufficient means to finish his education by his uncle, Dr. James Garstang, who had moved from Clitheroe to Lytham, and had taken the younger boy, Walter, as his apprentice. After qualifying, he (Walter) practised as a doctor in Saddleworth. He married Hannah Harrop, and their son, Dr. Thomas Walter Harrop Garstang, in his 81st year dined with Walter at the Savile Club in London in October 1929, having met him first at Knutsford in 1891. The old doctor much enjoyed telling Walter all about his family and said on retiring that it would be a red letter day for him to the end of his life! Like his uncle James, he left Knutsford to spend his last years in Lytham.

Alice was devoted to Dr. T. W. H. G. as she called him, and in another of her long letters to Walter wrote:

The research work you have undertaken seems to me rather a colossal business—I had no idea there were quite so many Garstangs in existence! I have been in fairly close touch with T. W. H. G. for about 20 years, corresponding with him and seeing him from time to time. He had quite an admiration for my mother (Alice Gent), who in addition to a beautiful character had a keen and clever sense of humour which always amused him. He used to come over to Whittle from Altrincham to see us—something, I don't know what, caused dissension in his marriage. Only once has he in any way unburdened himself to me, when he told me his life had been a disappointing one. We expect to be seeing his son, Dr. Walter Garstang of Hucknall, some time this month when he hopes to be spending a week or two with his cousin George Milne. George's mother was T.W.H.'s sister, we see him fairly often, and next time we go to Moosley Hall where he lives, I will take your letter with me. My brother Tom would not be likely, I think, to carry on any research on family lines, so it is much better that all records should remain in your hands. Tom has been Chief Engineer for Dunlop's in Manchester for years, but his home is still in Whittle, and he contemplates some fairly extensive improvements as soon as it is possible to carry them out.

I spent last Thursday (Sept. 1945) with my great friend and cousin, Winifred Liptrot, she is now living in Ormskirk, and I have some pictures of the Church there. Like me she was a Teacher, and like me again she is now retired. She had a bad accident about 10 years ago and injured her knee so that she is now rather lame. Her mother was Aggy (Liptrot) my Father's sister, who died when Winifred was a baby.

Another relation of Dr. Thomas Blacklidge G. wrote to Walter to explain his connexion with the Clan. This was Dr. Buck of Cravendale, Giggleswick, Settle. He was the son of Grace Garstang, the sister of Dr. Thomas, and she married Richard Buck of Settle. In the following letter to Walter he refers to Dr. Edward Morton Garstang:

My dear Sir,

As my mother was a Miss Garstang, I am taking the liberty of writing to you to see if we are related, and also to see if you can help me with the Family Tree. Over a hundred years ago my Grandfather came here from Leyland or Whittle-le-Springs (Robert Garstang) to manage the Clayton Cotton Mills. He married a Miss Dixon and they are both buried in the Parish Church Yard.

I have an intuition that you are a son or nephew of my old friend Dr. Walter Garstang who was in practice in Blackburn over 50 years ago, but we could not then make out our relationship.

My mother's brother, Thomas, practised first in Blackrod, and next in Bolton where he died, and his son Dr. Edward Morton Garstang took on his practice. I have retired from Medical work and live in the old family homestead here where I shall be delighted to see you, if you ever come this way.

This is a great country for the Botanist and Geologist, but I believe your speciality is Zoology, as I think I have read articles by you bearing on that subject. I must apologise for troubling you, but hope we may eventually meet and with kindest regards remain

Yours sincerely,
C. W. Buck.

All these doctors were so confusing when I was reading these letters in 1964 that I could not sort them out at all, then by chance Mrs. Magda Polanyi happened to call to see me in Oxford. She said that her daughter-in-law lived in Altrincham and could send me news of two of the doctors.
Before the end of January came her reply:

Thomas Walter Harrop Garstang
M.A. (Oxon 1875) M.R.C.S., D.P.H. (Vict. 1897)
M.O.H. Middlewick, Knutsford, Bucklow etc.
Lived in Altrincham, died c.1932

His son was another doctor:

Walter Garstang M.B., Ch.B. (Vict. 1901)
Hon. Surgeon Hulme Infirmary
Brampton House, Hucknall, Notts.

So the following pedigree will show their relationship to their distant cousin Alice, and the others can be traced in Pedigree IV. 24.

Pedigree IV.25:

The three doctors,

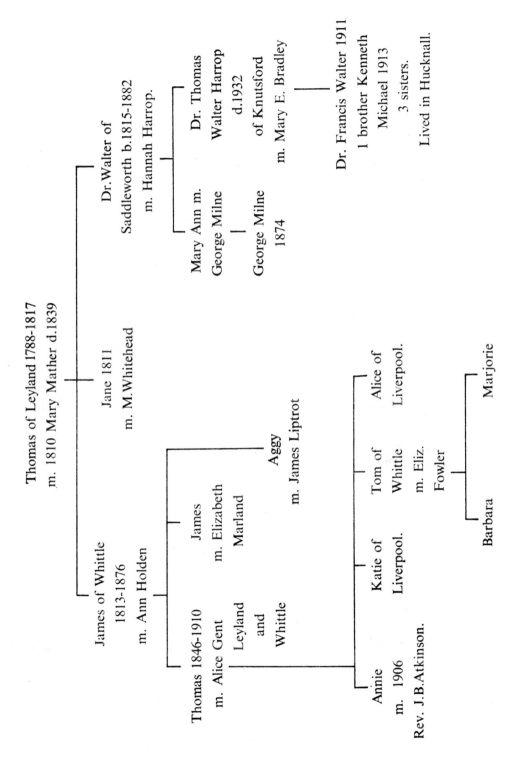

Thomas of Leyland 1788-1817
m. 1810 Mary Mather d.1839

Jane 1811
m. M.Whitehead

Dr.Walter of
Saddleworth b.1815-1882
m. Hannah Harrop.

James of Whittle
1813-1876
m. Ann Holden

Dr. Thomas
Walter Harrop
d.1932
of Knutsford
m. Mary E. Bradley

Mary Ann m.
George Milne

George Milne
1874

Dr. Francis Walter 1911
1 brother Kenneth
Michael 1913
3 sisters.
Lived in Hucknall.

James
m. Elizabeth
Marland

Aggy
m. James Liptrot

Thomas 1846-1910
m. Alice Gent
Leyland
and
Whittle

Annie
m. 1906
Rev. J.B.Atkinson.

Katie of
Liverpool.

Tom of
Whittle
m. Eliz.
Fowler

Alice of
Liverpool.

Barbara

Marjorie

From time to time Alice still wrote about little events in her family story: "My father bought Dolphin House from Mark Whitehead, his aunt Jane's husband, simply, I think, because it was built by 'Old' James, and 'Old Aggy', 1754-1838, and he thought it ought to be owned by a 'real' Garstang. One of the windows has scratched on it in old Aggy's writing:

> When I have no money and none can I borrow,
> Great is my grief and more is my sorrow.
>
> Aggy Garstang.

We have very quaint portraits of Aggy and James, and a letter from Thomas Garstang of Blackburn to Mr. James Garstang, Surgeon, of Clitheroe. For years I have been convinced that all the Garstangs are relatives.

There is a sampler I have, it was worked by Ann Holden and dated 1828, when she was 8, poor mite. It bears the legend

> Seek virtue, and of that possess
> Henceforth to God resign the rest.

I am afraid I know nothing of her family, but the sampler ought to go to you.

The old smithy was at the bottom of our garden when we lived at Dolphin House in Whittle, and during the whole of our life there for over thirty years there were Garstang blacksmiths at the smithy. We knew them well of course, but we never discovered if they were related to us in any way. One of our favourite occupations as children was watching the horses being shod there. The forge was worked by some brothers, the eldest was William, a fine character who owned the business.

In 1937 George and Bessie Squibb saw the smithy and in a note to Walter said "the farmer's wife at North Bank had known the last of the Garstang blacksmiths. Presumably they were descended from the William G,1748-1818, whom you note in your pedigree as having numerous progeny not traced. Your ancestor James who died in 1633 and his son William were both blacksmiths, and had two forges, but we could not find any one in Whittle who knew of a second forge". Here we must pause to investigate an unsolved problem.

Pedigrees IV.26-27 (Whittle) 28 (London).
Winifred and Ernest S. Garstang
of London.
Adam Garstang of Stepney.

In June 1963 I wrote to Miss Winifred E. Garstang in Upper Richmond Rd., Putney, whose name was among the Garstangs sent to me by Cecil Garstang from the *London Telephone Directory*. On June 18th she answered my letter as follows:

> Thank you so much for your letter of June 14th. Unfortunately I cannot give you much information about my ancestry.
>
> My father, Adam Garstang died in 1911 at the age of 45 years. He was

born in London, but his family came from the North of England. He had two brothers and three sisters.

I have always had a deep desire to find out about the family and I will not be satisfied until I have visited Garstang on the river Wyre. Hence your letter has given me a thrill and I would be most interested to know when your book is published.

I have only once met Cecil Garstang and then just for a few minutes at a luncheon at the Dorchester, but I too am connected with travel so I know of him quite well.

With my very best wishes, sincerely,
Winifred E. Garstang.

It was very interesting that Winifred Garstang remembered meeting Cecil at the luncheon because when he sent me the names he explained how once he had thought that his wife had inadvertently been listed as Miss W. E. Garstang and placed at a separate table, so he was astonished to find there was indeed a lady there with the same initials. He went to speak to her and found she worked in a Shipping Office in the city. Quite a coincidence!

Having answered her letter, Winifred Garstang wrote to me again on June 20th (1963):

I have paid several visits to Somerset House this week, but I have not yet discovered where my Grandfather James was born. It will be necessary to pay another visit.

My father was born in Stepney, London, in 1867, he died in 1911. He married Emily McDonald in Banfield in 1890, and at that time his father was already deceased. He would have been born about 1837.

His children now living are as follows:

Henry, Rose, Jack (baptised John),
Matilda, Lilian, Jessie
Ethel, Ernest, another son whose name I have forgotten,
Winifred and after me
Horace and Francis.

They are in chronological order, but I do not know the order of my Grandfather's family, the names are:

Adam, my father,
John emigrated to Australia, Henry
Albert, Frances, Rose
Eppie (probably Hephzibah from Isaiah LXII.4. meaning 'My delight in her', first used in connexion with the restored Jerusalem).

I will write to you again next week.

I wrote to suggest that perhaps Winifred's grandfather, James, was the James of the Whittle family of Garstangs who had married E. Marland and was the son of James of Leyland and Ann Holden. This James was mentioned once by Aggy Liptrot in 1877 in a letter to their brother Tom, but his niece Alice said in a letter to Walter that they had quite lost touch with that family.

We thought that he might have moved to London and neglected to send his address.

On July 24th Winifred wrote again to say that James of Leyland could not have been her grandfather as she had been searching in Somerset House again for a Garstang marriage about 1860 and found that a James had married Maria Hill, his father being William and his address Stepney Causeway, and she added: "as my father was born in Stepney this may be the answer, but I cannot be 100 per cent sure".

Meanwhile on July 10th 1963 I had received a letter from Winifred's brother, Ernest Sidney. He was living in Catford, London S.E.6, and has two sons, John and David; he married Doris Mabel Wilkes in Deptford in 1937.

On August 2nd while I was at Calthorpe in Norfolk with Eustace I received a letter from a nephew of Winifred's:

> I am Cyril William, the son of John William whose grandfather was a blacksmith. My son is Robert John, and I understand that a son is important for your work because of the name (Garstang). If I can be of any more assistance please write and let me know.

About the same time I had a letter from Robert's mother Lillian:

> My son Robert is 14 years old and 5 feet 10 inches tall and has blue eyes.
> He passed his eleven plus and attends a Grammar School where he will stay until he passes his exams. He is mad on football and all sports. He is studying History, Geography, English, and Maths. for G.C.E.
> I asked him to write to you but he seems to think that I am joking, especially when I told him that he was descended from the Vikings!
> Mrs. Green, who is my husband's sister, and Mr. Green, who is the son of a former Miss Garstang, have a daughter of 5½ years; they would both like to help you if you let them know.

Lillian added later:

> Robert was born on April 17th 1949 in the West Ham Maternity Home because the hospitals on the south side of the Thames were then full. I was born in Greenwich on January 8th 1925, and Robert's father, Cyril William, was born on November 17th 1922 and registered in Deptford.
> I would like to bring Robert to see you in Oxford some time. I enclose his photograph for you to see, it was taken last year, and I will enclose one of him as a baby. I will help all I can to find his ancestors if there is anything I can do.

When I had been staying in Norfolk with Eustace I had sent Robert a picture post card of the boats on the Broad at Stalham, and when we returned home I received a letter from him:

> I am very interested in our family background, and I should like to have the book when it is published.
> I attend the Eltham Grammar School; until you told me in your note I did not know that the Head Master at Roan School was in our family.

Football and stamp collecting are my favourite hobbies. I am looking forward to visiting you when I am on holiday.

Unfortunately after it was arranged that his mother would bring Robert to see me, she could not manage to come conveniently, and the expedition had to be abandoned. Winifred came and she met Ruth too and we had an enjoyable talk about the rest of the Clan none of whom of course she had ever met.

Winifred then sent me the certificates that she had found at Somerset House.

Birth certificate of Adam Garstang:
May 13th 1867, registered June 24th 1867.
Father: James Garstang, Hammersmith (blacksmith).
Mother: (Maria Hill) Maria Garstang, 42 Burgess St. Limehouse.
John Capes, Registrar, Stepney.

Adam's Marriage certificate:
June 21st, 1890. All Saints Church, parish of Newington, London county.
Aged 23, bachelor, Farrier, 34 Abinger St. Deptford.
Father: James Garstang, blacksmith, deceased.
Married: Emily McDonald Bandfield, aged 22 years, spinster, 131 Evelyn Street.
Her father: William McDonald Bandfield, clerk, deceased.
By Jas. J. Smyth, curate C. of E.
Copy in registration district St. Saviours, London, Somerset House.

Marriage certificate of James Garstang and Maria Hill.
Feb. 27th 1860 at St. Thomas's Church, Stepney parish.
Both of full age, bachelor and spinster.
James Garstang, blacksmith, 6 Stepney Causeway.
Father, William Garstang, blacksmith.
Maria's father, John Hill, Seaman, 6 Stepney Causeway.
James Roe, C. of E. officiating minister.

These three ancestors of Winifred were all blacksmiths. The address of James is 6 Stepney Causeway, the address of the bride's father is the same. Winifred had said that her father was born in Stepney.

The morning that I received the certificates from Winifred I also received by chance an advertisement of Dr. Barnardo's Home Headquarters. The address was 6 Stepney Causeway.

George Squibb also wrote after he knew about the certificates and advised Winifred to ask for the census returns in Stepney, and that I should apply to the Preston archivist for Garstang births.

Meanwhile I wrote to Dr. Barnardo's Home in Stepney Causeway and received this reply:

No. 6 Stepney Causeway.
With reference to your enquiry of the 9th instant, from a perusal of the Deeds in our possession, it would seem that in 1854 two properties passed from a Sir Tomas Edward Colebrook to a Mr. Robert Carter, but they were numbered then 19 and 20 Stepney Causeway.

In 1871 they were conveyed by Mr. Robert R. Carter to a Mr. John Solomon, and the conveyance here refers to them as numbers 6 and 8 Stepney Causeway.

They were then leased to this organisation in 1877 and the freehold was later acquired in 1908.

It would appear that between 1854 and 1871 the two houses were re-numbered from 19 and 20 to numbers 6 and 8 and, therefore, it is possible that the original number 6 which William Garstang gave as his home address in 1860 had no connexion with the house known from 1871 as number 6. I am sorry that this is all the information that I am able to pass on to you.

Yours sincerely,
R. Martin.

Then I wrote to the Worshipful Company of Blacksmiths in Old Bond Street, but the Clerk regretted to say that he could not "trace either the William Garstang referred to in my letter, or any other person by the name of Garstang".

After that disappointment I tried The Worshipful Company of Farriers, Martin Lane, Cannon Street, where there had been a change of Clerks in 1964. Mr. Scott replied:

I very much regret that I have no records which I think would help you with the particulars as to the Garstangs for which you ask in your letter.

The only suggestion I can make is that you insert an advertisement asking for this information in the "Farriers' Journal" which is published by the National Farriers', Blacksmiths' and Agricultural Engineers' Association, 48 Spencer Place, Leeds 7.

Many of the readers of this Journal are elderly farriers and it might be quite possible that they would open up a source of information for you. I am sorry I cannot be more helpful.

I wrote to the Association in Leeds and received the following reply from the General Secretary:

I was interested to receive your letter of the 5th instant (Oct. 1964) with reference to some Garstang Blacksmiths and Farriers but after consulting my records as far back as is possible I find that I am unable to help you in this matter. The Association was started in 1904 and most of the members who joined at that time have obviously now passed on. I will, however, try to make some enquiries in the areas which you specify, in the hope that something may turn up.

The Preston archivist had sent me not only the names of the children of William and Mary (Dawson), but also the fact that one son, Robert, was a blacksmith.

Robert's marriage certificate was not in Preston, but from the Bishop's Transcripts we learned that his wife's name was Margaret and their sons' names were given, but not their marriage certificates. That of the youngest son John was obtained from Somerset House; he was married in Manchester and had been a metal worker but not a blacksmith. So perhaps his brothers were married in London, in the parish of the bride.

Pedigrees IV.26 and 27

William of Whittle and Mary Dawson 1748-1818.

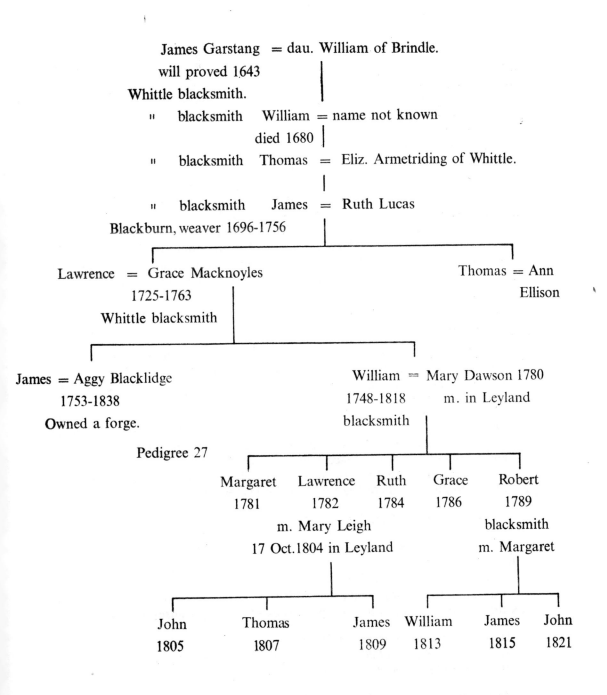

James Garstang = dau. William of Brindle.
will proved 1643
Whittle blacksmith.

  "   blacksmith   William = name not known
            died 1680

  "   blacksmith   Thomas   =   Eliz. Armetriding of Whittle.

  "   blacksmith   James   =   Ruth Lucas
Blackburn, weaver 1696-1756

Lawrence = Grace Macknoyles
1725-1763
Whittle blacksmith

Thomas = Ann
Ellison

James = Aggy Blacklidge
1753-1838
Owned a forge.

William = Mary Dawson 1780
1748-1818   m. in Leyland
blacksmith

Pedigree 27

Margaret   Lawrence   Ruth   Grace   Robert
1781   1782   1784   1786   1789
        m. Mary Leigh   blacksmith
    17 Oct.1804 in Leyland   m. Margaret

John   Thomas   James   William   James   John
1805   1807   1809   1813   1815   1821

It was impossible for Winifred to visit all the London church registers so we had to abandon that line of investigation.

As Winifred had reported that her father had been a blacksmith, and the certificates vouched for her grandfather and great grandfather being black-smiths, we felt that this William of Whittle, who had married a Mary Dawson, must have been an ancestor, because not only was his son a blacksmith but his ancestors, the Whittle Garstangs, had been blacksmiths for generations and generations. Walter had not investigated this family, but had written after his marriage to Mary Dawson, "large family of children not followed further".

In Pedigree 24 in this chapter above can be seen that this William was born in 1748, counting 30 years for a generation his son would be born about 1778, grandson 1808, great grandson 1838 and the next generation 1868 which approximates to Adam's birth in 1867.

We now turn again to Winifred's known ancestry, James and William who were connected with 6 Stepney Causeway, which we had also found to be the last address of Maria Hill's father, John Hill the seaman. Winifred then tried to find William's name in the 1861 census for Stepney of which we had been told the returns had recently been published and opened to the public. George Squibb said that he had understood 'Place of birth' would be one of the first questions answered. If not given there perhaps William might have moved from Stepney Causeway, and his name to be located in the Post Office Directory.

In her reply on September 21st Winifred disclosed how very frustrating these searches in the past can be:

I had a disappointing day on Thursday; I searched the Census Returns for 1861 and 1851 for the Stepney Mile End Old Town and New Town, but for some reason Stepney Causeway was not to be found. I phoned to Headquarters of the G.P.O. who turned to the 1860 postal addresses. These revealed numbers 2, 4, and 14, but *no* number 6! The Guildhall library searched the Poll records and the only Garstangs at that period were a Fred G. a potato merchant and coal merchant of Grafton St. Soho, and a James G. of Searle Place, a map mounter.

I have visited the Library today to search the Land-tax records. It was interesting to find there the name of the Dawson family at Stepney Causeway.

Where do we go from here?

What a surprising result after all the earlier disappointing researches in Stepney Causeway!

Winifred brought back these facts from the Land-tax Office:

The Land Tax Assessments for 1846, 1857, and 1858 give Samuel Dawson as the occupier of the following properties in Stepney Causeway:

House and garden assessed at £1-16-8.
Buildings, Richmond Garden, assessed at 12/10 and 7/6.
Rose ground and Paddock assessed at £2-15-0.

These pieces of ground were said to be on the west side of the footpath

Pedigree IV.28.

London. (By Winifred G.)

William Garstang, Blacksmith,

of 6 Stepney Causeway, for which in 1857-8

Land Tax paid by William Dawson.

James Garstang

Blacksmith, Feb. 1860 m. Maria Hill, father at 6 Stepney Causeway,

Marriage in Stepney

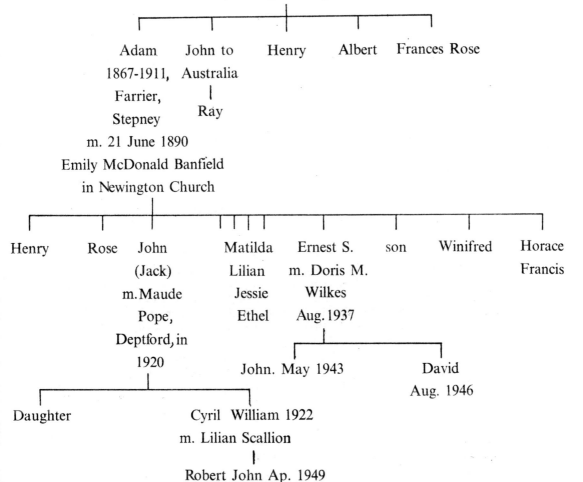

Adam
1867-1911,
Farrier,
Stepney
m. 21 June 1890
Emily McDonald Banfield
in Newington Church

John to
Australia

Ray

Henry   Albert   Frances Rose

Henry   Rose   John
(Jack)
m. Maude
Pope,
Deptford, in
1920

Matilda   Ernest S.   son   Winifred   Horace
Lilian   m. Doris M.   Francis
Jessie   Wilkes
Ethel   Aug. 1937

John. May 1943   David
Aug. 1946

Daughter   Cyril William 1922
m. Lilian Scallion

Robert John Ap. 1949

leading from Green Dragon to Heath Street, and the sums assessed were exonerated.

Now, although the Secretary of Dr. Barnardo's Home could not discover the name of the householder from whom they had bought the house 6 Stepney Causeway, we had the name of Samuel Dawson to show the connexion of William Garstang and his wife Mary, née Dawson, with Winifred's family in Stepney.

We would still like to see the will of William or Mary Dawson but the archivist requires a personal visit to study it. So probably a pedigree-minded Garstang will settle the question when next he goes to Preston. In the meantime Winifred is content with the progress she has made.

In December 1968 Winifred wrote in answer to Alec's enquiry:

> I still have not been able to go back with ancestor hunts before 1837 as you will appreciate how many records in various London churches were destroyed during the last war. Since then, however, two of the family have died:
> John William in 1967.
> Rose Ellis Emily in 1968.
> Should you wish for any further information I shall be staying for the next two or three weeks in Cheshire with my niece.

Pedigree IV. 29.
Arthur Garstang of Wilpshire, Blackburn, and Manchester,
and brothers.
Frank of Llandudno and Alan of Ferndown near Bournemouth.

In Walter's pedigree note-book dating back to 1928 the names of Arthur and Frank occur when they were both living in Wilpshire. In 1964 I received Arthur's address from Meroë and wrote to him; in answering he said:

> I have often wondered about my ancestry as *Garstang* is rather an uncommon name and does not appear to be of English derivation. The furthest back I can go, however, is that my father was born in 1861 and my Grandfather c.1828, he was the manager of *Bleach works* at Lower Healey near Chorley where he died in 1888. He had a number of sons besides my father, Robert, who died in 1910 when I was seven years old, so I was not in contact with any of the Garstang cousins.
> I suppose you know of the Garstang Chapel in Cirencester Church dating back to a Garstang in the wool trade, I believe, in the fourteenth or fifteenth century. I know of no Garstang in this area connected with woollen mills and I have been in or associated with textiles all my working life.
>
> I am most interested in your researches, and if I can be of any help I would be most willing to do anything I can.

In 1967 I received from Muriel a new business address of Arthur's and asked him for more details. He wrote:

> My new offices are in Preston New Road, Blackburn. My father was

Robert born in the Chorley area 1861 and died in 1910. His father was *James* 1827-1888, the manager of Bleach works in the Chorley area. I think my father was the youngest of several sons and one daughter, Florence, who married John Sharples, one time Mayor of Chorley.

As Winifred Garstang had become an expert during her own researches at Somerset House, I asked her to find if possible the marriage certificate of *James*. The result was correct in date and occupation: he married Mary Sumner on March 2nd 1851 in the Parish Church of Leyland and he was a *bleacher* by profession. The certificate was signed by his father *John*, also a *bleacher*, by William Sumner and a Margaret Garstang.

The next move was to ask the archivist in Preston to send me the names of any Garstangs who were married, born, or buried between 1825 and 1837 in Leyland and fortunately found the whole problem solved in the Bishops Transcripts:

Jan. 1 1825 John m. Ellen Jump, Leyland.
Dec. 24 1826 Margaret d. John and Ellen bap. Cuerden.
Dec. 11 1827 James s. of John and Ellen bap. Cuerden.
May 19 1829 Margaret aged 2½, buried.
Apr. 13 1830 Margaret d. of John and Ellen bap. Clayton.
Oct. 16 1832 Thomas s. of John and Ellen bap. Leyland.
Jan. 4 1833 Thomas aged 13 weeks, buried, Leyland.
Mar. 23 1834 Mary Anne d. of John and Ellen, bap. Bleacher Leyland.
Aug. 21 1836 Jane d. John and Ellen bap. Bleacher Leyland.

Cuerden is in the parish of Leyland, N.W. of Chorley.
Clayton-le-Woods is E. of Leyland, S.E. of Cuerden, both are villages on the R. Lostock.

As I remembered that a John and Ellen were also the ancestors of Henry Edward (Pedigree II.9.) I wrote to the Rev. Hugh Edwards at Holy Trinity Vicarage in Darwen where they had lived, and he replied: "Henry Edward Garstang's ancestors, John and Ellen, lived at 'Bowling Green' near Darwen, then moved to Manchester and were buried near there".

When writing to tell Arthur Garstang the result of the search of the archivist in Preston he said:

After receiving your letter I have been over to Chorley cemetery and there is no doubt that my grandfather James was the son of the John and Ellen who married in 1825.

James died in 1888 in his sixtieth year which tallies with the entry from Leyland transcripts of his baptism in December 1827. Also my grand-mother's name was Mary, like the wife of that James. I cannot see that they can be the same John and Ellen as those in Henry Edward's pedigree, although a 'bleacher' is the same as a 'finisher'. My ancestors would not be buried in Manchester.

Of course Arthur was proved right, but the archivist in Preston required a personal visit to examine wills, and I could not go to Preston. This John was probably the son of a Garstang already in one of our pedigrees.

Pedigree IV.29

Pedigree of Frank and Alan with Arthur Garstang of Wilpshire

John Garstang, Bleacher m. 1.1.1825 Ellen Jump, Leyland

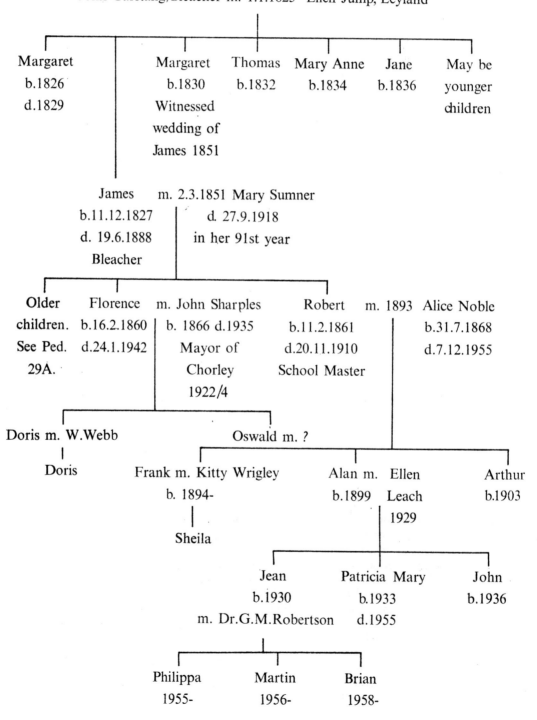

Margaret
b.1826
d.1829

Margaret
b.1830
Witnessed
wedding of
James 1851

Thomas
b.1832

Mary Anne
b.1834

Jane
b.1836

May be
younger
children

James   m. 2.3.1851 Mary Sumner
b.11.12.1827   d. 27.9.1918
d. 19.6.1888   in her 91st year
Bleacher

Older
children.
See Ped.
29A.

Florence
b.16.2.1860
d.24.1.1942

m. John Sharples
b. 1866 d.1935
Mayor of
Chorley
1922/4

Robert   m. 1893 Alice Noble
b.11.2.1861   b.31.7.1868
d.20.11.1910   d.7.12.1955
School Master

Doris m. W.Webb
|
Doris

Oswald m. ?

Frank m. Kitty Wrigley
b. 1894-
|
Sheila

Alan m. Ellen
b.1899 Leach
1929

Arthur
b.1903

Jean
b.1930

Patricia Mary
b.1933
d.1955

John
b.1936

m. Dr.G.M.Robertson

Philippa
1955-

Martin
1956-

Brian
1958-

As Arthur's ancestors had lived in and near Leyland I looked among the pedigrees for a John old enough to be married in 1825, but Arthur so far has not had time to discover more proof. William the blacksmith in Whittle who married Mary Dawson (see Pedigree IV. 26 and 27) had a son Lawrence as well as Robert, the suggested ancestor of Winifred. Lawrence was born in 1782 and married Mary Leigh in *Leyland,* they had a son John in 1805, and as he could have married Ellen Jump in 1825 we have placed Arthur's pedigree among the Whittle Garstangs until further investigations can be made.

It will be seen from Pedigree 27 above that the 'Margaret' who signed the marriage certificate of James could then have been Lawrence's sister or Robert's wife.

Recently I have received from Ruth the sad news in the *Daily Telegraph* of the death 'on July 19th, 1969, in hospital of Arthur Garstang, Somerset Avenue, Wilpshire, Blackburn, youngest son of the late Robert and Alice Garstang'.

On 4th August I received a letter from Arthur's brother, Alan, to say that the sadness was mingled with relief that Arthur had been spared a long and painful illness. His ashes were to be buried in Salesbury churchyard, near Blackburn and the house in Wilpshire where he had lived since 1911 when he was eight years old.

Pedigree 29 A.
John of Chorley and Joyce of Brampton, Cumberland.

On December 27th 1968 John Garstang of Chorley wrote to Alec G. about his ancestors and their position in the Clan. His pedigree is very interesting as it supplies the names missing from Arthur's of the brothers and families connected with Florence.

The writer's family begins with John, a formerly unplaced brother of Florence the Mayoress of Chorley, while Arthur's line descends from another brother, Robert. This is John's letter:

> I was most interested to receive your letter from "out of the blue" and regret the Christmas holiday prevented me from replying earlier. However I have been giving much thought to the matter. Strangely enough the letter arrived the day I was to go to our local cemetery with holly wreaths and I was able to take a quick opportunity to obtain dates, names etc., from family graves. I hope whatever information I am able to give will prove of use or interest. My mother who is now aged 86 was able to supply some information.
>
> I am able to go back as far as my great grandfather, James Garstang, who came from Leyland to Chorley to start a bleach works. His wife, a Mary Sumner, came from Eccleston, a village near Chorley. I have made out a 'family tree' which may be of help.
>
> James G's three sons, John, Thomas, and James all worked at the bleach works, as did most of their sons and also several of their daughters.
>
> Another son, Robert, was a schoolmaster at Barking, Essex, and he had, I understand, three sons named I think, Arthur, Alan, and Frank. Two of

these I believe were the founders of 'A. Garstang and Co. Ltd.', shirt makers from Blackburn.

James G's only daughter, Elizabeth Ellen Florence married John Sharples, Coal merchant. They later became Mayor and Mayoress of Chorley. They had a son Oswald and daughter Doris.

Regarding my own family, John who died before my birth, was my grandfather, his eldest son James died in 1918. The latter's wife was Olive Gertrude Haworth, sister to Sir Walter N. Haworth, a former Professor at Birmingham University, fellow of the Royal Society, and a Nobel prize winner, now deceased. They had three daughters, the eldest Eleanor is married to Professor Wesley Cocker of Dublin University, the second Joyce is a schoolmistress at Brampton near Carlisle, the third Ruth is married to the Rev. G. Batey vicar of Milnrow near Rochdale.

John's second son, Arthur, was my father. He was a Secretary at the Bleach Works until it closed down during the last war. The daughter Alice was unmarried.

I was an only son and married in 1948 Miss Betty Thompson whom I met whilst working for 8 years in the District Bank at GARSTANG! I enclose a cutting (about the name) taken strangely enough from the current issue of the Garstang Courier—no doubt you have already similar information.

I have two daughters only, so that the name 'Garstang' in my own family will not continue. The male Garstangs in Chorley of whom I am one now number three only I believe.

I should be interested to know when the book you mention can be bought, and where I could obtain a copy in due course. Incidentally, I suppose you would know that there used to be a Professor John Garstang in Archaeology at Liverpool University, now deceased.

It occurs to me that several years ago an American lady called to see me enquiring about an ancestor of her mother named Garstang. Unfortunately I no longer have her address, and somehow do not think that she was lucky enough to obtain much information to assist her in her enquiries.

With best wishes to 'one of the Clan'.

Yours sincerely,
John Garstang.

Written on the same day, December 27th 1968 came a letter to Alec from Miss Joyce Garstang of Brampton, Cumberland, the daughter of James who married Olive Haworth:

Thank you for your letter. My sister and I are very interested in the forthcoming publication about the history of the Lancashire Garstangs, and we should be glad if you would reserve three copies for us when it is published. By a strange coincidence my younger sister Ruth, wife of the vicar of Milnrow, nr. Rochdale, now lives at St. James' Vicarage, which was at one time the home of Pro. Walter Garstang's sister, I believe her married name was Elliot. My nephew (who lives there now) Peter Batey, is in his final year at Sheffield University, reading Honours Geography.

Our father James died in the 1918 flu epidemic and we left Chorley shortly afterwards, going first to White Coppice, and then to Cleveleys near Blackpool. I am at present staying with my sister, Mrs. Cocker, in Dublin

Pedigree IV 29A.

John of Chorley
Joyce of Brampton

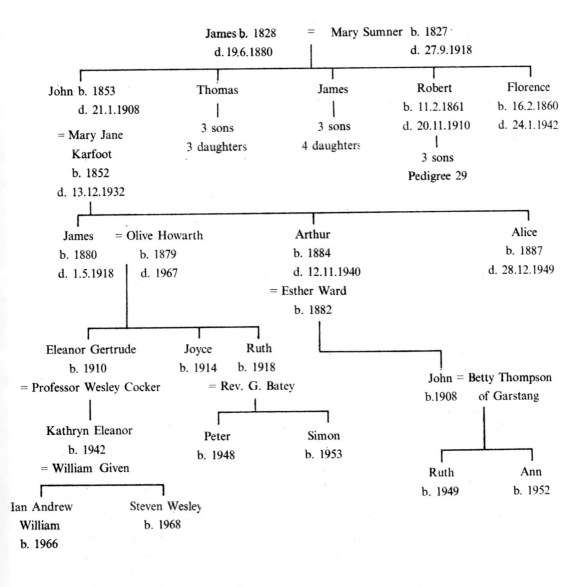

and would like to verify the names and dates of our grandparents when I return home to Brampton.

My cousin, John Garstang of Whittle-le-Woods near Chorley would be able to give you more detailed information of our branch of the family.

Whilst students at Birmingham University my sister and I were often asked about our relationship with Professor Walter Garstang, and we shall be very interested to find the connexion.

Yours sincerely,
(Miss) A. Joyce Garstang.

(There is a lovely little picture of Killarney lake at the bottom of each page of this letter. Yes, Joyce is quite right, my sister Florence married the Rev. E. Elliot and lived in the vicarage at Milnrow near Rochdale. S.G.G.)

John of Chorley enclosed another interesting paragraph cut from 'the current issue of the *Courier* published in Garstang, a newspaper he no doubt read when he was working in Garstang.

NAME OF THE PLACE

Strangers often ask how Garstang got its name, which is something the natives cannot answer entirely satisfactorily. The ancient spelling was Gayrstang and the explanation has been advanced that the name came from a Saxon baron Garri, and the stang part came from the Latin *stagnum* meaning a pool.

At the time of the Domesday survey, the name of the manor was rendered as Cherestanc. Soon after Garstang appeared as a fee of the Lancaster's, barons of Kendal and Wyresdale. William de Lancaster, steward to Henry II, appears to have given it to the Canons of Cockersand.

There is record of a Paulinus de Gairestang, a knight who "perambulated" the forests of Lancashire in the reign of Henry III.

The manor of Garstang subsequently passed to the Lindsays and an Earl of Bedford, and then to Margaret, Countess of Richmond and Derby, wife of Thomas, Earl of Derby.

Despite these sub-feudatory lords, the manor was part of the possessions of Cockersand Abbey until the Dissolution, and it passed eventually to John Rigmaden. It was leased to William, Lord Spencer, and went on to the Duke of Hamilton.

The lease expired, and the property was sold in 1752 to Sir Edward Walpole, and ownership came to the Kepples, continuing with them until the estate was broken up and sold.

All this shows how ancient a place is Garstang. The Roman road from Lancaster passed through the district, though they do not appear to have had a station here. So reasonably enough the name of the place could well have a Saxon origin, which has persisted right to the present time. As to the truth of this, we shall probably never know.

The first part is probably just an invention as they were not Saxons but Vikings from Scandinavia whose names have survived in those of towns and villages in north Lancashire. The Saxons arrived much earlier according to the *Anglo-Saxon Chronicle*. Also the wide estuary of the river Wyre could hardly be called a 'pool'.

The later history may well be correct as the various early 'men of Gairstang', like Paulinus of Henry III we have already mentioned, were generally working under officials of either the State or Church.

Albert Garstang
Whittle-le-Woods, Chorley.

On January 16, 1969 Albert Garstang wrote in answer to the appeal and he is connected with the Chorley Garstangs. He wrote:

> I did not know my grandfather's brothers, but Mr. John Garstang of Chorley may be able to help. My great grandfather, grandfather, and father were in turn Works Managers of the Local bleach-works which closed down during my father's time.
>
> My father was Chief Air-raid Warden and later Chief Fire Staff officer for Chorley during the 1939-45 war.
>
> I served in the Royal Air Force during that period, and I am now employed as Chief Audiology Technician at the Bolton Royal Infirmary.
>
> My son Hayden is an architectural assistant, he was married in August 1968.

Albert's grandfather's name was James and he gives the names of his seven children: Florence, Harold, Tom, Annie, Edith, Ellen, Albert.

Albert's father was Tom who, besides Albert the writer, had three daughters: Jessie, Phyllis, and Hilda.

Albert has two children: Stephanie who is married and lives in Sheffield, and the son Hayden the archiect.

John Garstang of Whittle-le-Woods, Chorley, has just written to explain that "the James G. who died in 1880 had amongst other children a son James who had four daughters and three sons, one of whom was Thomas, this Thomas is Albert's father. This Thomas and my father Arthur were cousins".

Pedigree IV. 30.
Arthur Harold Garstang, Southport and London.
Cecil and Edward Gerrard.

It will be seen from Pedigree IV. 24 that Dr. Thomas Blacklidge Garstang married twice. His first wife was Alice Robinson, the mother of Robert, who lived in Australia, and Dr. Edward Morton Garstang who carried on his father's practice in Bolton. A photograph of Dr. Thomas Blacklidge appears on Plate IV.

Dr. Thomas Blacklidge G. afterwards married Jane Pohlman of Halifax, and her children were Samuel Kay of Bolton, (the father of Edward Gerrard (Ted) and two daughters) also a daughter who lived in Dublin, and another son Arthur Harold who married Lilian E. Meacock. Their son is Cecil Garstang of London.

Just before the first World War my brother Walter was invited to a meeting in Southport by the President of the Southport Literary and Philosophical Society to hear a lecture by A. R. Forsyth, F.R.S. on "Universities: their Aims, Duties, and Ideals." He saw that A. H. Garstang was Hon. Sec. of the Society, and so at the very beginning of the Quest he met an unknown member of the Clan whose ancestors like ours were James of Whittle and Ruth Lucas, and before them were some of the earliest yeomen who had moved southward from Garstang.

In 1914 Arthur left Southport for Huddersfield, then Bradford, and in 1917 he was established in the London area. Two years later the names of Arthur and Walter appeared on the same list of "Lecturers who were willing to assist the Army Education Scheme" issued by the War Office in 1919. Arthur's lectures included "The Canyons of the Cevennes", "The Pageant and Palaces of Touraine", and "Heroic Belgium with its Cities and Scenery".

Walter lectured on the Songs of Birds of which he published a book translating their songs into music and syllables, and on various aspects of Life in the Sea.

Our first introduction to Arthur's son Cecil was when my nephew, 'Tim', the son of Walter, saw his name carved on the table with other distinguished pupils at Merchant Taylors School where Tim went as a Science Master. My correspondence with Cecil began in a still more curious way, as it was about thermometer scales when the B.B.C. began to announce temperatures in both Fahrenheit and Centigrade. Since then Cecil has helped me with ambiguous points in the Quest. He is the General Manager of Thomas Cook and Son, Ltd., the world-wide travel agents, and just as his father in the years following the first Great War encouraged travel in Britain as Secretary of the National Association of Railway Travellers, so Cecil has been associated with travel all his business life. In addition to his normal activities, which include dealing with incoming passenger traffic to Britain as well as outgoing movements, he was for three successive years, 1960, 1961 and 1962, elected Chairman of the Association of British Travel Agents. This entailed attending more than the usual number of official occasions and conferences. For example, in 1962 he represented the Association (A.B.T.A.) at a conference in support of the "Come to Britain" movement called by the British Travel and Holidays Association of which Lord Woolton was President, and Lord (then Sir William) Mabane was Chairman. The President of the Board of Trade, the Rt. Hon. Frederick Errol, M.P., attended the preliminary stages and these three gentlemen as well as Cecil made the opening speeches.

In one letter I asked Cecil if he had taken part in any specially interesting experiences, as travel must have come his way, and he replied:

> I suppose I have had a good many unusual journeys connected with my job and two such incidents occurred during the war. One so-called 'rough' night early in January 1941 when I arrived at Green Park Station from Piccadilly I found many other people sheltering there until the Luftwaffe departed. The Ministry in which I was working on a war job was only in Berkeley Square, so I decided to risk a dash to relative safety there. I had no sooner arrived at the Ministry than I heard a terrific crash and all the

lights went out. A bomb had fallen on Green Park Station, and all those whom I had left sheltering there were unfortunately killed.

The second memorable experience occurred some ten days after the hostilities ceased in May 1945. By then I was a Lt. Colonel attached to Shaef and my assignment led me to Berchtesgaden to the mountain villa known as the 'Eagles Nest' which was just as Hitler had left it fully furnished and equipped. I saw Goering's Art collection, which had been removed from his captured special train and placed in his Hunting Lodge. This was as large as a small Hotel; there covering the walls or just piled up against them we found masterpieces looted from half the picture galleries of Europe. Experts arrived from the liberated countries to sort and re-distribute the treasures to their rightful owners; among them we could identify some we had last seen in the Louvre, the Mauritshuis, and other famous Museums and Picture Galleries.

To turn to more peaceful scenes: in Australia I have visited the famous Club room on Sydney Cricket ground, but unfortunately not during a Test Match. Here I must explain that it is still the Lancashire cricket team which I most keenly follow with a strong sense of local patriotism, in fact I am known in the Office as a Lancastrian still.

Leaving the wonders of Australia I have visited the geysers in New Zealand at Wairaki, descended the Grand Canyon in Arizona, attempted quite unsuccessfully to shoot duck in British Columbia, entered the Temple of the Tooth in Kandy and of the Emerald Buddha in Bangkok, run the gauntlet between the Government forces and the Karen rebels on the way to Rangoon airport, both of whom sportingly held their fire to enable our coach to go through.

In East Africa I have had a close up view of all sorts of game. Once on my way back from India after a rather strenuous business trip to Singapore, Bangkok and Rangoon, I was asked to divert from Egypt to deal with certain matters in Nairobi, so I took the opportunity of visiting one of the big game reserves about 150 miles S.E. towards the Tanganyika border, an area of three or four thousand square miles. There are no settlements in it beyond a few hutments of Masai and no shooting is allowed, but unlike the Kruger National Park in South Africa where one must keep to the roads, one can go anywhere that a truck can take.

Since 1949 the number of visitors to Ambosali has increased, and though the game wardens do all they can to preserve the animals, the opening up of the country and pressure of civilisation in Kenya generally, has not I fear encouraged the growth of game. I set out with a young professional white hunter in a 15 cwt. truck and we reached the camp of three thatched huts (rondavels) by about 4 p.m. Actually just then the official camp it so happened was occupied by Sir Geoffrey de Havilland and a party of about six, so we set up our own tent a short distance away, although we all had dinner together. During the night a lion came round our tent, but as Kipling would say, 'That is another story'.

Next morning we set out just after dawn to see game, as that is the best time, in a landscape dominated by the snow-capped dome of Kilimanjaro. We saw many antelope, giraffe, monkeys, baboons, birds, and so on, but nothing more spectacular until we sighted a lone bull elephant having breakfast off a thorn tree just outside an area of bush of which the edge was well defined. Our truck was in the open as if it were in pasture land and the elephant in a copse. I had only a small camera with no telephoto lens, so we got out of the truck leaving the engine running. We quietly approached the edge of the copse, until we were within some twenty yards.

Now when I had tried to approach the animals we had seen on the way to camp in order to take a better photograph, they had all moved away, and so I suppose I had expected the elephant to do the same. But oh no! As soon as he heard the click of the shutter, his trunk went up and his long sensitive ears came forward. We knew that these were his signs of preparation for a charge. We just turned tail and ran, surely we accomplished a three minute mile! We piled into the truck, my companion pressed his foot hard down on the accelerator and fled. Looking back I saw the elephant watching us from the very edge of the copse and I felt a distinct impression that he was laughing at us!

About four years ago Cecil visited South Africa and Rhodesia and among other things went down a gold mine near Johannesburg. He sent me a description of the country which he had written for his Church Magazine, St. Peter's, Bushey Heath. Here are some extracts:

To the south of Bulawayo there rises from the bush a wild chaos of rugged hills in fantastic shapes and smooth domes, as if the molten granite had welled up in gigantic bubbles and been frozen as it seethed. This lunar landscape is alive with colour, browns, greens, and gold, which is wonderfully reflected in the iridescent skins of the lizards that bask in the sun or dart suddenly into the crevices. The horizon recedes as far as the eye can see, 50 or 60 miles, to distant kopjes, and still it is the same. Then near sunset there will emerge the graceful buck to water and the furtive leopard to prowl.

In the midst of this vast solitude sleeps the man who graved his name indelibly on a continent, Cecil John Rhodes, for these are the Matopo Hills, and here it was that he achieved one of his greatest triumphs. Here during the Matabele rebellion of 1890 Rhodes camped out alone in the midst of their stronghold, and because they respected his bravery he at length won their confidence.

Eight miles from the Matopo Hills lies the Anglican Mission of Cyrene where Africans are educated to secondary school standard, and for its school of African art. The interior walls of the Church are covered with African paintings, many of which recall Italian primitives.

280 miles north-west of Bulawayo lie the Victoria Falls whose majesty can scarcely be conceived. The stupendous volume of water, 4,000 tons a second, falls into a mighty cleft, and from this cauldron the river forces its way out through a zigzag gorge 400 feet deep. Trapped in the chasm, the spray surges hundreds of feet in the air forming rainbows vivid in the hot sunshine or visible under the brilliance of the tropic moon. The ground trembles, the senses are stunned, and the ear is deafened by the shouting of the waters.

On the southern edge of the abyss stands the man who first brought Christianity to this part of Africa when he discovered the Falls in 1855— David Livingstone. A plaque on the plinth announces that to celebrate the centenary of his discovery there was held near here in 1955 a gathering of people of different races, Africans and Europeans, who pledged themselves to pursue the ideals which Livingstone preached. His motto was 'Fear God and work hard'.

One year Cecil watched New York Yankees beat the Chicago White Six at Baseball, spent a week-end in the Yosemite Valley in California, wandered, quite unmolested as a solitary European, at night through the city of Marrakesh, and swam in the September amongst gaily coloured fish in the warm tropical waters of Barbados and Tobago.

Cecil ends his letter:

> I think that is a reasonable selection of some of the things that have befallen me, but lest you think I spend most of my time in travel, I should make it clear that I am an Office Worker who only gets away now and then!

On March 16th 1964 I received news that Cecil had just been invested by the Italian Government with the award of the Order of Merit of the Italian Republic.

In 1967 a Profile of Cecil was written by Simon Kavanaugh and published in continental papers as well as in England. Its title—"Nations listen as Mr. Travel talks." One paragraph explains the help that Cecil gives in bringing all the world within the reach of travellers: "Garstang's decisions and recommendations are of vital interest to the governments of countries all over the world, particularly to those of under-developed countries who see tourism as an essential source of foreign currency.

"He is frequently invited to suggest to Ministers of Tourism how African States, for instance, can profit from such dubious assets as swamps, jungles, elephant grass, and Amazon sized rivers."

Cecil's son John is in the motor car industry in London, Roger is an engineer also in London.

His cousin Elizabeth Pohlman Garstang was left a widow and married 2nd Charles Norman May who died in 1963. She lives in Knapton near North Walsham in Norfolk so I have been hoping to meet her when I am staying at Calthorpe Broad. On March 23rd 1964 she said in a letter to me that she had found the name of Robert Garstang in the Parish Register of North Walsham church:

> Robert Garstang, vicar, Sept. 30th, 1434, Reign Henry VI, Patron, the Abbot. By exchange with the last Vicar, Simon Dacke. Resigned 1447.

Elizabeth had received a copy of the Garstang of Whittle family tree from my brother Walter as far as he knew it when he was living in Leeds.

P. S. Hammond, husband of her daughter, Kathleen Elizabeth, was the Deputy Director of Agriculture in Ghana before he returned to farm in Norfolk.

In December 1968 Cecil wrote in answering Alec's note:

> Since writing to Mrs. Gurney the only development in my family has been that on September 5th 1968 my younger son, Roger, married Joy Patricia Davis of Bushy.
>
> I am not sure if you are interested in personal details, but you might like to know that I have been General Manager of Thos. Cook and Son Ltd.'s worldwide network for the past three years and also a director of the parent

company and subsidiaries. It has also just been announced that I am to be appointed Chairman of Sir Henry Lunn Ltd. (the Lunn/Poly travel agency).

In a recent letter to me he enclosed the following story:

One hundred years ago in the early summer of 1863 a group of twelve friends, calling themselves "The Junior Alpine Club", ventured forth on the very first tour of Switzerland to be organised by Thomas Cook and Son. One of the number, known as Miss Jemima—was deputed by her friends to write an account of the Trip in all its adventures.

In the spring of 1963, Thos. Cook's decided to celebrate the centenary of this expedition, and turning up the file of the event, Cecil and the rest of the group who were chosen for the celebration, were surprised to find that Miss Jemima was really Miss Jemima Morrell and that it was her father who had financed with others the setting up of Rowntree's famous chocolate and cocoa firm.

In May, the party, dressed in the dazzling costumes of 1863, set off on their fantastic tour, travelling round the original itinerary. They were met in every town and village by welcoming bands and choirs throughout Switzerland, all dressed in their age-old local costumes. They were officially welcomed everywhere and royally entertained. At the Riglu-Kulm Hotel they turned up the ancient register for July 8th 1863 and found the names of the original travellers, and who should have been there with W. W. Morrell and Miss Jemima but two Lancastrians from our dear old town of Garstang! So Cecil rejoiced that a Garstang had been one of the chosen few to repeat the journey, an appropriate chance indeed.

Edward Gerrard Garstang
of Fleetwood, Goole and Grange-over-Sands

When I was looking through Walter's papers I found that he used to stay with Edward G. Garstang and his wife Hilda at 'The Laurels', Hook Road, Goole, and for a long time I could not connect him with any relatives I knew and yet Walter seemed to be a friend of theirs. Then I read a letter from 'Hilda' written on October 21st 1929 in which she mentioned her husband as 'Ted'. At last the truth dawned on me that perhaps he was Cecil's cousin as Cecil always spoke of his cousin as 'Ted' whenever he referred to him. I feel as if I am in a Detective Story, so I asked Cecil and he replied:

Edward G. Garstang is indeed my cousin Ted, but he does not live in Southport or Goole any more, but in Grange-over-Sands.

So he gave me his address and though I had mentioned Cecil's cousin a good many times, this was the first time I had told him that I was trying to finish the story for which he had supplied Walter with material. So at last in the spring of 1963 he wrote again about the Quest, but to me this time:

I was delighted to hear from you this morning, and I shall be pleased to let you have any information I can. When I used to write to Walter I was Docks Superintendent at Fleetwood, then Steamship and Continental

Pedigree IV.30.

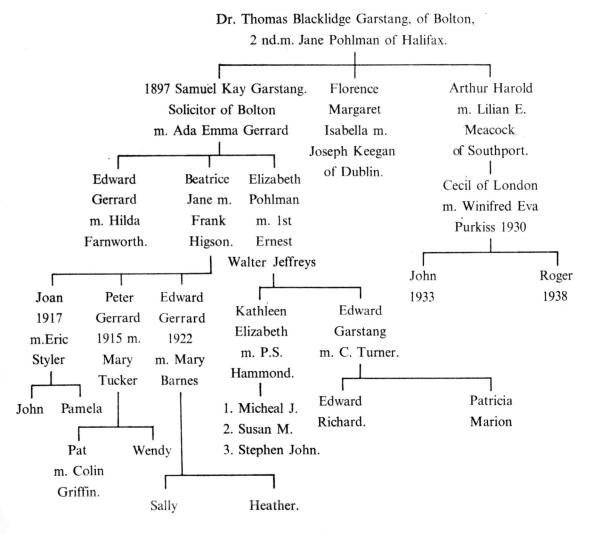

Dr. Thomas Blacklidge Garstang, of Bolton,
2 nd.m. Jane Pohlman of Halifax.

1897 Samuel Kay Garstang.
Solicitor of Bolton
m. Ada Emma Gerrard

Florence
Margaret
Isabella m.
Joseph Keegan
of Dublin.

Arthur Harold
m. Lilian E.
Meacock
of Southport.

Edward
Gerrard
m. Hilda
Farnworth.

Beatrice
Jane m.
Frank
Higson.

Elizabeth
Pohlman
m. 1st
Ernest
Walter Jeffreys

Cecil of London
m. Winifred Eva
Purkiss 1930

John
1933

Roger
1938

Joan
1917
m.Eric
Styler

Peter
Gerrard
1915 m.
Mary
Tucker

Edward
Gerrard
1922
m. Mary
Barnes

Kathleen
Elizabeth
m. P.S.
Hammond.

Edward
Garstang
m. C. Turner.

John   Pamela

1. Micheal J.
2. Susan M.
3. Stephen John.

Edward
Richard.

Patricia
Marion

Pat
m. Colin
Griffin.

Wendy

Sally   Heather.

Manager of the L.M.S. Railway, and later the District Goods Manager for the Railway Areas centred on Bolton—that was all North Lancashire up to the West Riding of Yorkshire, then District Goods Manager with head-quarters at Hunts Bank, Manchester, for an area stretching from Derbyshire to join up with the Bolton area. So I have had a reasonable Railway asso-ciation with many connections that in their day assisted our War effort. In 1927 I represented all British Railways at Stockholm in the International Convention.

Then he adds that his father was Samuel K. Garstang, Solicitor, son of Dr. T. Blacklidge Garstang (see Pedigree IV. 24) and that on February 4th 1963 he celebrated the 50th anniversary of his marriage.

In June 1969 Cecil's name appeared in the Queen's Birthday Honours List as having been awarded the C.B.E. It is a great pleasure to be able to record the honour as almost the last item in this Garstang book.

In August when I was staying at Calthorpe Broad House in Norfolk I was at last able to call upon Cecil's cousin, Elizabeth May, in Knapton. She still lives in the same village although her daughter and son-in-law occupy the farm, her former home. Elizabeth told me a charming story about her mother, Ada Gerrard, when as a girl of seventeen in Bolton (Lancashire) she was walking in the town with her sister; an old man stopped in front of her, smiling, and said: "Eh! Lass, thou art lovelier than th' angels in heaven!"

Just before I saw Elizabeth, Alec wrote to say that he had been to Grange-over-Sands, in North Lancashire, and called upon Elizabeth's brother, Edward Gerrard Garstang, and his wife, Hilda. It is no wonder that my brother Walter enjoyed going there so much, as Alec said: "Ted is a great chap indeed, and we all seemed to get along together like a house on fire!"

Pedigree of my father.
The family of Walter and Matilda Mary,
with that of his brother Luke and wife Mary Jane.

Enough has already been said about the first generation of my father's descendants to show that they bore the characteristics of Clan consciousness so evident in other families even if their connexion with each other had been forgotten. Only a brief summary of further events can be attempted and I will begin with the youngest in the hope that the last names will have the right significance.

My husband, Robert Gurney, was a keen Zoologist, and was awarded the Oxford D.Sc. Among his publications were *British Fresh-water Copepoda* in three volumes, *Larvae of Decapod Crustacea*, and *Trees of Britain*.

Our son, Oliver Robert, took his Oxford B.A. 1933 in *Litterae Humaniores*, D.Phil. 1939 in *Hittite*, appointed Reader in *Assyriology* in 1945 (with re-sponsibility for teaching Hittite), and Professor by Decree in 1966.

They were both fond of games, especially tennis and squash racquets, and in the holidays were never short of partners as Oliver was born with about 30 first cousins who stayed with us at different times while we lived in Norfolk. They all enjoyed Robert's sense of fun which can be illustrated by the quotations he placed after the title page of his three volumes on the identification of Copepods:

Vol. I:

One may not doubt that, somehow, Good
Shall come of water and of mud
And, sure the reverent eye must see
A purpose in liquidity.

Rupert Brooke.

Vol. II:

Wisdom will repudiate thee, if thou think to enquire
Why things are as they are or whence they come: thy task
is first to learn what is, and in pursuant knowledge
pure intellect will find pure pleasure and the only ground
for a philosophy conformable to truth.

Bridges, 'Testament of Beauty.'

Vol. III:

Little Girl: "What's that, Daddy?"
Father: "A cow."
Little Girl: "Why?"

—Punch.

In the second world war Oliver, trained in the artillery, was placed in the Sudan Defence Force, and took part in the campaign which drove the Italians out of Eritrea. In one of his letters he wrote:

Our Headquarters were at a small town called Shendi, 100 miles north of Khartum. Here for about a month we lived the life of a peace-time Bimbashi, learning to talk to the troops in their own dialect and to give orders to the gun crews in the special Arabic terms which had been invented for the purpose.
"When I travelled up into Eritrea I joined the Troop ensconced on a hillside where the Italian road suddenly came to an end although clearly marked upon the map. The Italians had been equally taken by surprise, and had left all their guns and lorries behind as they escaped on foot to the hills beyond. We then received orders to withdraw to the main road 100 miles back and proceed through Keren (which had fallen in the meantime) into the capital, Asmara. From there the next day we were sent down to the coast to take part in the attack on the great port of Massawa. We went straight into action and for half a day were bombarded by heavy shells from coast defence guns and mortars; but fortunately for us most of these missiles flew over our heads and burst behind us. Some days later, at a point where vehicles could not pass owing to the road being under repair, I encountered a genial person who looked vaguely familiar and on getting down to speak to him, I discovered that he was Richard Dimbleby, the expert B.B.C. television and radio broadcaster.

After this Oliver's unit followed the Italians up into Abyssinia remaining for three months at the foot of the escarpment leading up to Gondar. Eventually the unit was withdrawn and sent to attack the Italian positions from the other side, and after the enemy's final surrender Oliver's troop moved to take over the Italian post of Chelga.

A few more adventures followed, and then Oliver returned home in March 1945, first to help with German prisoner of war camps, and then to settle down to his University work in Oxford. On July 23rd 1957 he married Diane Hope, the daughter of René Hugh Essencourt. His choice of a profession was in part due to my brother John's thrilling stories of discovering inscriptions during his excavations in Egypt, Meroë, and elsewhere.

Among John's publications are the following: *Burial Customs of Ancient Egypt, The Land of the Hittites, The Hittite Empire, Joshua: Judges, The story of Jericho, The Heritage of Solomon, Meroë* (excavations and translations with Professor Sayce), *Prehistoric Mersin,* and finished after his death *The Geography of the Hittite Empire.* Characteristically John died at sea on our way back from his last visit to Mersin when, though very unwell, he insisted on explaining his excavations to the members of our cruise.

My brother John's children, John Eustace and Meroë, were born in the home of Marie's French parents in the Pyrenees, Eustace in September 1908 and Meroë seven years later while John was excavating in Ethiopean Meroë.

Eustace took his Oxford B.A. in Litterae Humaniores, became Classics Master in his old school, Rugby, and (after the war) in St. Andrew's College, Ontario, then finally Professor of Classics in McGill University of Montreal. He came from Canada on frequent visits to England, and in 1965 a long-standing heart trouble, contracted during an attack of diphtheria when three years old, had reduced his vitality, and he died here in the August of that year. Eustace was rather given to summing up the characteristics of his Garstang relations, and about Robert he once wrote to me:

> As for you, my dearest aunt, your life with Uncle Robert was always of incalculable benefit to the family. Where else could they breathe and relax and get the perspective of things, or get to know each other, but for the wonderful hospitality of your home at Ingham Old Hall? Much has been due to this alone.

His wife, Margaret Madeline Christian (Garrick) known as Peggy, returned in 1965 to Canada with the younger daughter, Patricia, born October 1944. Patricia had left school with seven First Class Honours out of eight papers set in the graduating class for Toronto University where after one year's attendance she had been granted a scholarship for a visit to England. Patricia has now taken her degree in Anthropology, has enjoyed a post-graduate course in McGill University with practical experience in Trinidad, and has an interesting job as Research Assistant in the Ontario Institute for Studies and Education. She has been sent on a year's project to an Indian Reserve on Manitoulin Island which is off the northern shore of Lake Huron. She is living with an Indian family and enjoys the work, having just attended a conference on Indian affairs in London (Ontario).

Eustace's elder daughter, Philippa Margaret Garrick (Garstang) born 1937 in Rugby, married Alex Sandor Hajdu, an engineer who escaped from Hungary after the rising. Their elder son, John Sandor Garstang (Hajdu) was born in 1961, and their second son, Michael Eric on October 28th 1964. They live in a ground floor flat in Peggy's house in Toronto, and in her letter about a month ago Peg says she loves having them there.

John and Marie's daughter, Meroë, after spending most of her childhood in Palestine, where John was then excavating, was educated at Cheltenham Ladies' College, took a massage diploma course at St. Thomas's Hospital in London and was awarded the C.S.M.M.G. There she met W. J. D. Fleming, for some reason unknown called 'Peter'. He was studying for doctor's degrees and was awarded first his M.B. and B.Chir. and later M.R.C.S., and L.R.C.P. They were married in July, 1938. After living in Reading and Oxford, his specialised interest in pathology took him to the Royal Free Hospital in London, and they then lived in Hampstead until 1963 when they bought an estate near Guildford, built a house with a space where Meroë's genius for garden design could succeed. Now with the son of an old friend of Peter's as partner, Meroë devotes her time to house building and gardening. Meroë thinks that soon she may retire from the Firm and let Hugh take her place.

Simon, the elder son, has always been interested in engines. He is working his way through the different stages of British Rail management in the Southern Region. He is now qualified to be an Assistant Station Master, but still pursues his studies at the southern depôt.

Hugh, the younger son, took his Oxford degree B.A. in French and Spanish, staying often with his French relations in the Pyrenees and travelling in Spain during vacations. He is now in charge of 'Reservations' in a Travel Agency in London. This work takes him to many districts abroad to investigate the accommodation offered to travellers, and he enjoys the journeys by air as much as his brother does by rail.

His love of travel is perhaps inherited from their grandfather, although his influence seemed to have passed by his own son Eustace. In 1963 I had sent Eustace the typescript I had written about the story of our childhood, and he replied:

Having read your typescript I feel closer to you all, even in Toronto. It filled in for me the missing years and explains my father, poetic almost, at first the quiet one of the family, establishing his personality by the originality of his pursuits. I'd no idea that his Ribchester 'dig' began during his school days. I can see now how he got started in his career.

You ask me about Uncle Walter: when I stayed there about the age of 12 he often took me for walks and told me about the birds, the butterflies and moths, and in the house played records of good music on a gramophone, teaching me to appreciate it. His whole attitude of distinction and culture had a profound influence on me during my early school days. Afterwards I saw him only occasionally at Oxford, but after the war he had the same stimulating effect on Philippa (aged 10) who was fortunate in being able to see and know him.

People talking to me about him, always with the greatest admiration, have also spoken of his influence, they have been either his pupils or Leeds colleagues who have travelled to Canada.

James, my next brother, experienced many tragedies. Eustace, with his usual insight into character and his apt way of expressing it, once said to me when talking about the sadness of his life: "Uncle James had such a kind heart that it gave him a serenity which won the love of all who knew him." Then on another occasion Eustace said: "The story of Uncle James resembles that of Aunt Ida where the rewards are not in this world, and the justification of the life is to be found rather in its effect on others."

James took a science course at Oxford expecting to be trained eventually as a doctor, but after Father's death at the turn of the century that was not possible. After taking his degree he went as science master, and later mathematics master, when Mr. Badley invited him to help in his new experiment of girl and boy joint education at Bedales school in Hampshire.

In 1905 James married Ilsa von Mollin of Finland, a colleague on the Bedales staff. The second son died as a small child, but the elder, Thomas Eric, became a brilliant mathematician and was appointed lecturer in that subject in Aberystwyth university. After publishing two small papers on his researches involving pure mathematics, he died during a ski expedition on the top of a mountain in Switzerland. Tom's mother was at the time dying in a London hospital and James was advised by her doctors not to tell her.

After Ilsa's death James lived alone in Richmond with the companionship of birds, tamed to come to his whistle for nuts in Kew Gardens; and he was always ready to help everybody on any occasion.

In another letter from Toronto Eustace wrote:

In trying to describe Uncle Jamie to 'Tom the Actor' I said that after a life of tragedy he became a local saint. Think what his presence must have meant to those who knew him.

Though life seems not to come as we hope and expect, it is full of meaning and beauty to those who are capable of appreciating it.

In February 1943 I had a telegram from Mr. Webb, a solicitor friend of Ida's in Lytham, to say that she was desperately ill. I naturally turned to James and by telephone we arranged to go to Lytham without delay. When we arrived we were too late to find her alive. For the first time we then met the family of Fred Garstang Byrne, the son of our cousin Kate and grandson of Uncle Luke. Fred was living quite near the house where Ida and Uncle John had lived and where she had spent her last years alone, and before Fred owned it his house had belonged to his aunt Adelaide, the mother of Bessie who married George Squibb; so Uncle Luke's family had seen quite a lot of Ida and she had not been lonely.

Jamie and I had to stay rather a long time in Lytham to clear up Ida's affairs. After we came home Fred helped me later by sending me information about his side of the family. He was really an artist by profession in his younger days. During the first war, although he had been sent to France as a gunner, he was later posted to G.H.Q. Machine Gun School to make

Pedigree IV.31.

Descendants of Luke Garstang of Blackburn.

Thomas of Lane End. 1803-1864 m.2nd   Susannah Pilkington

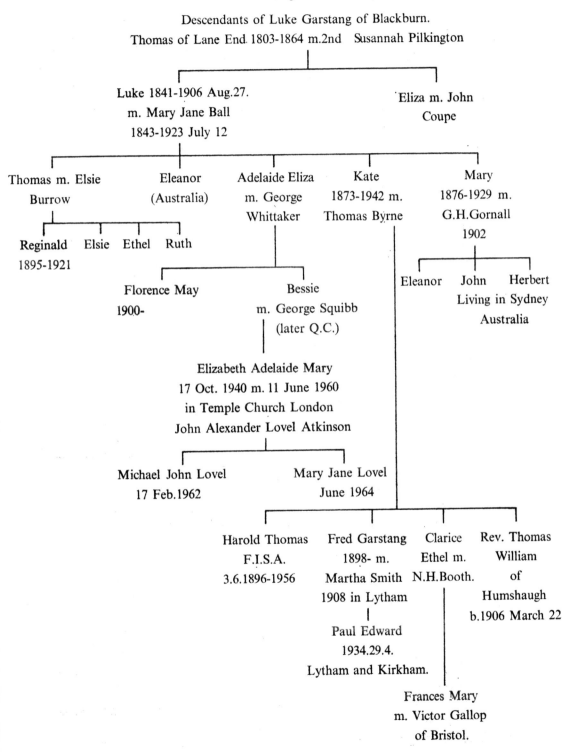

Luke 1841-1906 Aug.27.
m. Mary Jane Ball
1843-1923 July 12

Eliza m. John
Coupe

Thomas m. Elsie
Burrow

Eleanor
(Australia)

Adelaide Eliza
m. George
Whittaker

Kate
1873-1942 m.
Thomas Byrne

Mary
1876-1929 m.
G.H.Gornall
1902

Reginald
1895-1921

Elsie   Ethel   Ruth

Florence May
1900-

Bessie
m. George Squibb
(later Q.C.)

Eleanor   John   Herbert
Living in Sydney
Australia

Elizabeth Adelaide Mary
17 Oct. 1940 m. 11 June 1960
in Temple Church London
John Alexander Lovel Atkinson

Michael John Lovel
17 Feb.1962

Mary Jane Lovel
June 1964

Harold Thomas
F.I.S.A.
3.6.1896-1956

Fred Garstang
1898- m.
Martha Smith
1908 in Lytham

Paul Edward
1934.29.4.
Lytham and Kirkham.

Clarice
Ethel m.
N.H.Booth.

Rev. Thomas
William
of
Humshaugh
b.1906 March 22

Frances Mary
m. Victor Gallop
of Bristol.

sketches of inventions re Lewis Guns, Hotchkiss, and Vickers Maxim. Later he became among other things a cartoonist for the Northern Area of the Railway Clerks' Association.

The preceding pedigree (IV. 31) of Uncle Luke's descendants shows the relationship of Fred and Bessie. Uncle Luke and Father were half brothers as Grandfather Thomas had married twice and Father's mother had been Hannah of Darwen Garstangs. Cf. Pedigree IV (p.34).

When Bessie's grandson, Michael, was born, I sent his mother Elizabeth a copy of the newspaper article "A Long-lived Blackburn Clan, the Garstangs", in case he might be as interested in it as John and I had been as children. George Squibb was very pleased and wrote: "If Michael grows up anything like his grandfather the 1890 cutting he will treasure, and when he is a young man it will be 100 years old."

It is also quite true that without the help of this grandfather this account of the Clan could not have been written.

Next in age to James came Daisy. Of her joy in life and of her contribution to the happiness of all of us it is impossible to give any adequate description. She never married. The following extract from the *Blackburn Times* on April 2nd 1923 written in an article about "The Garstangs of Blackburn", gives some idea of her wide interests: "Many of her old Blackburn friends will be interested to hear that Miss Daisy Garstang has come back to her native town this week and taken up an appointment under the education Committee. I believe Miss Garstang's last appointment was in Macedonia, but the bare record of all the posts she has held in many lands is enough to take away the breath of more stay-at-home folk. As a war nurse she has had many thrilling experiences and fully maintained the fine family traditions of the Garstangs."

In passing I would like to add that one of these war-time tasks was to teach us village women and girls in Ingham the elements of nursing, so that we could pass our Red Cross Examinations and run a Hospital in our grounds in collaboration with the Norwich Hospital, and so help more than a thousand wounded soldiers back to health.

The next member of the family, Florence Elliot, was well known for her eloquence as a speaker and for her power as an actress. I have seen her bring tears or laughter at her will from thousands of Mothers Union members assembled in the huge Guild Hall in Manchester for their Diocesan Festival.

Flo married Ernest Elliot as I have already mentioned and they spent most of their married life in and around Rochdale, but their two children, Joan and Norman Garstang, were born in Whalley.

Joan inherited from both her parents a love of drama. After taking a London degree in English Literature, she chose teaching for a profession, and later studied for the Lambeth diploma in order to qualify in the teaching of Scripture. She loved this work, but used to say that if she had not followed this career she would have chosen to be an actress or a parson.

In all her posts she has enjoyed producing plays, when House-mistress at St. Leonards School, when Headmistress of Queen Anne's at Caversham, and when lecturing to students in Christian Colleges of South India. Some of her happiest memories are connected with those productions—outstanding were the "Chinese Lantern" at St. Andrews, and "The Tempest" at Caversham. But she had a special fondness for religious plays, which included "The Pilgrims Progress" at Caversham and Passion Plays produced in Chapel. In India productions were necessarily simpler; it was exciting to discover unexpected talent and to watch the story of the Nativity played under the stars and moon of a tropical night sky.

Norman was born on January 8th 1901, and took his degree in Civil Engineering at the University in Leeds.

His first job was with Rochdale Corporation Waterworks, repairing reservoirs, building filter plants, and the construction of a new reservoir. In September 1931 he married Dorothy Helen Philips, in Tewin church, Herts. Four years later they moved from the bleak moors near Rochdale to the Devonshire coast on his being appointed water engineer in Torquay. They bought a haunted house and their three children used to hear ghostly footsteps after dark, but the parents changed bedrooms and all was well. "During the second war," wrote Norman later," we could often see the shells bursting over Plymouth, and I used to go there to help with the mending of their water mains. In 1945 I was appointed water engineer for Plymouth and have enjoyed the building of reservoirs on breezy Dartmoor. Our eldest child Dione on August 13th 1955 married Lt. Cdr. Peter Smith, and they now live in Bromley, Kent."

At that time Peter was an Instructor Commander R.N. but he has since retired from the Navy and in 1968 he is a lecturer in Nuclear Engineering at Queen Mary College in London. Dione herself has a Social Science Diploma and is a part-time Child Care Officer in Bromley where they are still living.

Dione's eldest child Penelope and the youngest, Venetia, acted as bridesmaids at their uncle Anthony's wedding on August 24th 1961 when he married Rose Mary Hodgson at the White Eagle Lodge in London. The service was conducted by the bride's grandfather.

Anthony is an electrical engineer and his brother Roger was trained as a librarian, but works in London as a journalist. On July 19th, 1969 Roger married Suzanne, daughter of Mr. and Mrs. F. P. Pendlebury of Victoria, Australia, also at the White Eagle Lodge.

Anthony and Rose now have two daughters, Katherine Elizabeth born in 1965 and Margaret Rose 1966. They live at Liss in Hampshire. So far Dione's Christopher, born in 1957, is the only boy in that generation of the Elliot family and he is now established in the nearby Grammar School.

The one of the seven of us most connected with my mother and her family, the Wardley's of Darwen, I always feel to have been my eldest sister Ida Wardley. It was not only because she received my mother's maiden name at her baptism, or that she spent a year of her school days with Aunt Sarah's family to be educated with our cousin Mary, but mainly because she was so like my memory of Mother and Aunt Martha in her features and manner, in her kindness and devotion to duty. Like Daisy she did not marry, but after Mother died when Ida was only one month from her 21st birthday, I think

Father could not have spared her and may have prevented an early betrothal.

What John and I would have done without her I do not know as she was sister and mother in one for many years, and I am delighted that my school friends can still remember her.

In June 1967 I had a letter from Mrs. Hubert Dixon, my old school friend Connie of 80 years ago!

> I remember the past well—your ugly but faithful little Scottie Scamp, Ida making cocoa for us in your kitchen, and your father making up prescriptions in his surgery, and then telling us most interesting things, also the walks over the Yellow Hills to Pleasington to catch newts and gammarus. Then how we climbed the cannons in the park (they are gone now I think). Do you remember the little curl you and I had over our foreheads, and how Mother called me Dizzy (Disraeli) because of it? Oh! All the delights we enjoyed then! I think on the whole we enjoyed our childhood better than the young people do now because we 'did' things and did not expect every thing to be handed out to us. Do you remember splitting a paint because we had not enough money for each of us to buy a whole one, it cost 7d. and we paid half each!
>
> The poor cotton trade now! It would break your heart! All the men are being made redundant, and their wives at about 50 years of age have to start working. Nobody can think why the Government should squash the poor cotton trade, it is tragic.
>
> Phoebe will try to find out something about the little town of Garstang now, Gertrude and Mab both ended their days there, and Phoebe knows people who could tell about conditions.

Gertrude and Mab were Connie's sisters, and were at our school too, one older and one younger than we were, and Phoebe is Gertrude's daughter, so I suppose she lived in Garstang too. I heard from Connie last Christmas but she did not tell me any more about Garstang. She married Hubert Dixon, like me she is now a widow and lives in Cheshire at Cheadle Hulme.

On November 8th 1968 I have just had a birthday card from Connie to wish me well on my 90th birthday next week. She has just had a party of old friends to celebrate her own in Cheshire.

It was always Ida who kept in touch with Mother's sisters and told us about Grandfather living with Aunt Martha in Lytham, giving us their address and that of Uncle Clifton and Aunt Annie near the pier. I had heard nothing of our Wardley cousins after Uncle Edward and our aunts went to Australia; but on December 1st 1914 Aunt Martha had written to Walter to say that our cousins Fred and Jack had sailed in the first Expeditionary Force "to do their best for the Empire, having joined the Artillery."

Aunt Martha then added that she had married in 1900 John Scott from Glasgow whose brother was sub-editor of *The Times*, so perhaps Walter could meet him. She asked so affectionately after each one of us by name that Walter and John frequently wrote to her, and then Eustace and Meroë corresponded with Verna and Avice, the daughters of James who was Uncle Edward's eldest son.

So in 1962 I wrote to tell Avice about this book. She was most interested and said that Aunt Martha used to love telling them about us all, and her father had very happy memories of the days when we used to meet together in Lytham as children. "It would be wonderful," Avice concluded, "to have the opportunity to meet my cousins in England, but at present I see no prospect of it. However it is a pleasure to meet you thus in a letter." I have recently heard that she hopes to visit me in 1970.

But now I must return to Walter. In 1895 he had married Lucy, daughter of James Ackroyd of Bradford. One of my great treats after my father died was to see them and their three daughters Doris, Sylvia and Ruth in their lovely sea-girt garden with its wave-washed rocks on the estuary of the river Tamar at St. Budeaux near Plymouth. Walter was working at the Marine Biological Laboratory on Citadel Hill. When he was appointed Director of the Laboratory at Lowestoft we had an introduction to the lives of fisher folk, and there Margaret Pauline was born. She was still a baby when Robert and I were married there in 1904, and her three sisters strewed rose petals on my path as I walked along the aisle beside Walter in St. Margaret's beautiful church.

In 1907 Walter was invited to the Chair of Zoology in the University of Leeds, and though very reluctant to give up work in which he was much engrossed, he finally accepted, and while he remained in Leeds he used every opportunity to search out Garstang contacts with George and Bessie Squibb and the rest of our own family still living in Lancashire.

In 1933 Walter retired at the age of 65 when he and Lucy, with their youngest daughter Muriel, came to live in Oxford. The Clan Quest was of necessity then much curtailed, but gardening and his great love of nature and of music filled his spare time; indeed his daughter Doris and our nephew Eustace have often said to me that his eagerness to cultivate the same appreciation in them influenced their developing characters.

Doris Mary (the second name being a tribute to Walter's memory of our mother), took part-time courses at Leeds University, and from 1916-19 was also Demonstrator in Zoology; she then trained and qualified in horticulture at Studley College in Warwickshire, where she returned as Lecturer in 1925 and became Principal in 1949, retiring in 1956.

Sylvia Lucy (the second name this time being a tribute to her own mother) entered Somerville College in 1917 and, like her father, read zoology in the University of Oxford. In 1921 she appeared among the first group of women students to be given degrees in that University. Sylvia then became Research Assistant at Leeds University, and later an Assistant Lecturer at University College, London.

In 1927 Sylvia married Alister Hardy at the church of St. Chad in Leeds; they had been undergraduates together at Oxford and he had recently returned from the Antarctic where he had been Chief Zoologist in the 1925-27 "Discovery" Expedition. He became Professor of Zoology successively in Hull, Aberdeen and Oxford, and is now Honorary Fellow of Merton and of Exeter Colleges and Emeritus Professor of Zoology in Oxford. Among his publications are *The Open Sea, Great Waters, The Living Stream* and *The*

Divine Flame. The two last are essays towards a natural history of religion, and constituted two series of Gifford Lectures on Science, Natural History and Religion delivered in the University of Aberdeen during the session 1964-5. Alister was awarded his Oxford D.Sc. in 1938, elected F.R.S. in 1940 and was knighted in 1957.

Sylvia and Alister have two children: Michael Garstang, born in 1931, and Ailsa Belinda, born 1934. Belinda married Dr. John Dashwood Farley, M.B., B.S., in Oxford on September 28th 1957. Their son, Thomas William Dashwood, was born on October 15th 1962.

Michael was appointed Lecturer in Zoology at Reading University, in 1967 he married Valerie Anne Mather. When I wrote to ask Michael for some news about Trinidad I told him that in 1810 Mary Mather had married Thomas Garstang in Leyland and wondered if Anne's family came from Lancashire. Today Anne wrote: "It would be nice if Mary Mather were of my ancestors' family, but my father was born in Northumberland and his father came from Dunbar in East Lothian. As far as I know there were no Lancashire connections although it is a north country family." Anne enclosed this joint account from herself and Michael.

At first Reading was part of Oxford University, but in a few years it expanded and changed. The centre shifted from the old site on London Road to Whiteknights Park where buildings of concrete and glass transformed the estate, then complete with grotto and artificial lake, into a modern campus. New residential halls fringed the park to cater for the increase in numbers of students, and when Anne took her degree in 1962 there were only eight members in the Honours Zoology class, seven years later there are forty.

"No zoologist is educated until he's seen the tropics", was often one of Michael's warnings to his class. In 1967 he followed his own advice and, said Anne, "four days after our marriage in September 1967 we sailed by banana boat to Trinidad".

Michael was on a year's exchange with a Zoologist from the University of the West Indies.

Trinidad is a detached part of South America, and on a clear day we could see Venezuela, like the mainland the climate is hot and steamy, and the vegetation bright and luxuriant. We lived in the middle of a mixed cocoa and citrus estate, but we seemed to be surrounded by a lush overgrown woodland rather than by a cultivated orchard.

We shared our house with several geckoes, each hotly defending his own territory from innumerable insects and occasional mice; but although outside the tropics may team with life most of it sensibly remains hidden: scorpions and snakes, including some of the largest and most poisonous, are timid and not at all malevolent, much to Anne's relief! There are no large mammals, but the birds are fantastic—minute humming birds darting and hovering around the blossoms, flamboyant scarlet ibis flocking to the mangrove swamps of the west coast to roost, and occasional glimpses of the toucan, immortalised by Guinness, in the high woods of the northern range.

Michael's specialist interest is 'bats', and we caught and kept a few of the sixty-seven species to be found there.

Trinidad, however, is not all jungle and sugar cane. Industrialisation is spreading and white colonialism is gone. There is a refreshing lack of colour consciousness due perhaps to the mingling of African, Indian, European, Chinese, and Syrian families, often with very attractive results. The people are most friendly, gay and extrovert, their favourite pastimes are rum-drinking, dancing, and music. We loved Trinidad and left with regret.

Alister and Sylvia made a short expedition to Trinidad while Michael and Anne were enjoying the sunshine there and here in England we were enduring one of the wettest winters in memory.

Near in age to Sylvia comes Walter's daughter Ruth, born in 1899. After winning a Diploma in Domestic Science at Reading University, she took a secretarial course in Leeds. In 1921 she stayed with my brother John in Palestine as Secretary to the Government Department of Antiquities. Later Ruth became Assistant to the Treasurer at Somerville College, and in 1945 was appointed Bursar, which post she held until her retirement in 1960. On being made a Fellow of the College in 1948 she was awarded an M.A. degree by decree.

Margaret Pauline (known as Polly) was born in 1903 and went to Leeds University, obtaining her M.Sc. degree in Physiology in 1926. During the next three years, whilst helping at home, she taught swimming at her old school. In 1929 she started her nursing career at the Nightingale School, St. Thomas's Hospital, becoming a state registered nurse in 1933 and state certified midwife in 1934. She trained as a Queen's Nurse and worked in the district until 1948, when she became a nurse/secretary to a medical practice of women doctors until she retired in 1963.

The boy came next in Walter's family, but I will leave his career until I have said something about the youngest child, Muriel, born in April, 1911. After leaving school, she attended both the University and the College of Art in Leeds where she gained a Diploma in Textile Industries. Until 1939 Muriel practised handloom weaving and dyeing in a studio at her parents' home in Oxford, at the same time drawing original designs for printed materials.

During the second world war she was absorbed in V.A.D. work, and later for several years in Nursery School teaching, running a small school of her own in the family home. Muriel also then helped her father plan and arrange their new garden and now she can make her borders look prosperous, colourful and happy.

The boy, Walter Lucian, known to us as Tim, was born on September 2nd 1908 in Leeds. After going down from Oxford with a degree in Chemistry and a rowing 'Blue' he joined the Gas Light and Coke Company as a research chemist. While staying with Alister and Sylvia in Hull he met Barbara, the daughter of Dr. S. E. Denyer, C.M.G. They were married in 1933 and lived in Woodford where Peter was born. I have a delightful picture of him playing on the lawn here with coloured balloons while on a visit. At this stage Tim turned to schoolmastering and gave up flying, an enthusiasm which had succeeded his rowing exercises. His first appointment took him back to his old school, Oundle, and while they were living there the second son, Charles

Neville, was born on October 30th 1938. Then came the tragedy of Peter's incurable illness and death. The war years followed at Oundle and on April 18th 1941 Teresa Mary was born.

We know Teresa as Tessa and for some years she was educated at Queen Anne's School, Caversham, while, Joan, my Elliot niece, was Head Mistress. Afterwards Tessa studied Physiology at St. Thomas's Hospital in London and qualified in remedial therapy. In 1965 Tessa married Timothy John Ridley Bullick, a schoolmaster now in Dorset. Their daughter Claire Elizabeth was born on October 31st 1966, and a second daughter, Judith Catherine, on May 27th, 1969.

To return again to Tim and Barbara: for a time while Tim was teaching at Merchant Taylors School they lived a country life in the Chilterns, and their youngest child, Sarah Judith, made her welcome appearance on July 28th 1946. After gaining more experience as science master and then as Head Master in different schools, they settled down in Blackheath where Tim had been appointed Head Master of the Roan school founded in 1677 and financed by a private foundation with an additional grant from the London County Council.

In a report issued by the *Evening Standard* in December 1963 Tim is quoted as saying: "The only thing our six hundred pupils have in common when they arrive is a sound academic ability. Everything is pursued with immense enthusiasm, and we try to create good citizens who can also earn their bread and butter and find their way about the world."

Now, in 1968, he has retired from Roan School to take a part-time teaching job, and is enjoying a rest from the stress of organisation.

The youngest daughter Sarah finished her education at the High School for Girls in Blackheath, obtaining sufficient A levels and knowledge in languages to qualify from there for her entrance to Oxford University, gaining a scholarship at Somerville College. She has now in 1968 been awarded a B.A. degree in French and German, after spending some of her vacations practising the two languages on the continent.

Certainly Sarah has enjoyed the delights of Oxford as much as her predecessors of the Garstang Clan, two of whom were at Somerville and one at Lady Margaret Hall in days gone by.

Both Sylvia and I had previously been to Somerville College, but I have not explained how cousin Bessie also passed her B.A. finals. In December 1924 her mother Adelaide Eliza, who had married George Whittaker in Blackburn, but was then living near Ida in Lytham, wrote to Walter: "It must be forty years since I had the pleasure of seeing you, and I am addressing you as 'cousin' to introduce myself, being the second daughter of Luke Garstang, your father's half-brother." Cousin Adelaide then explains how Bessie had an overwhelming desire to go to Oxford University, and she had been told by several people "that she cannot hope to enter any Oxford College until she has made several attempts and", said Adelaide, "I feel utterly unable to advise her. She would like to try in March for Lady Margaret Hall. Unfortunately she cannot depend on advice from her school; she was a pupil at St.

Anne's High School for Girls until last Easter, when the whole school moved to Windermere. She then transferred to Preston, but unfortunately the Head Mistress was away from school, and has been ill the whole time Bessie was there.

"During the Christmas vacation we would gladly take Bessie to Leeds to see you. If you could see your way to advise her I should be most grateful."

With Walter's advice Bessie went to Oxford to try for the entrance examination in March 1925, and after being called up for an interview she was advised to work at French until the Autumn term when she would get a vacancy. Miss Grier assured Walter that Bessie had done well, and she was advised to take a four years' course in philosophy.

While at Oxford Bessie worked with the Archaeological Society and in 1928 she undertook the drawing of plans and pottery for the excavations at Alchester by the Classical Association.

George Squibb (later Q.C.) was a fellow member of the Archaeological Society, and they were married on February 1st 1936. They began at once to help Walter with the Garstang Quest for members of the Clan, but this was interrupted by the war and when that came to an end Bessie wrote to Walter:

We have a daughter Elizabeth Adelaide Mary, born on October 17th 1940, so nearly five now. His eyes kept George in London, and our first set of chambers blew up the night Elizabeth was born, our second also two years later, then we had an address in Hampstead, but your letter found us at last.

We are both all agog to meet you round the table and see your new finds spread out. I have all the Garstang material here, and out of the corner of my eye I see George has it on the table and is sorting again.

So the Quest began again, but came to a sudden sad end with Bessie's illness and death. In April 1961 Bessie's cousin, Fred Byrne, ended one of his letters:

Martha and I visited George and Bessie at their Paper Buildings flat in London, and when we were leaving, Bessie, only a few months before her death, hugged us as though she had some premonition of impending departure. She was a lovely blonde girl, very slim and always cheerful. We were stunned to learn of her death on May 12th 1954.

George has since married Evelyn May, the daughter of Frederick Richard Higgins of Overleigh Manor, Chester. Bessie's only sister, May, in 1968 married John Gee.

Now we must leave Walter's exploits with George and Bessie Squibb and return once more to his son's family: on the evening when Tessa and her great friend Mandy (Maureen Andrew) were celebrating their success in gaining their certificates in Physiotherapy, Tim's son Charles had just completed his finals in Medicine at Cambridge. He had been registered B.Chir. and after a year's work in hospital the full degree would be automatically added. So how better could they all celebrate their qualifications

Pedigree IV 32.

Descendants of Walter and Matilda Mary Garstang

Walter Garstang, M.D, 1832-1899

m, on February 14, 1866

Matilda Mary Wardley

1847-1886

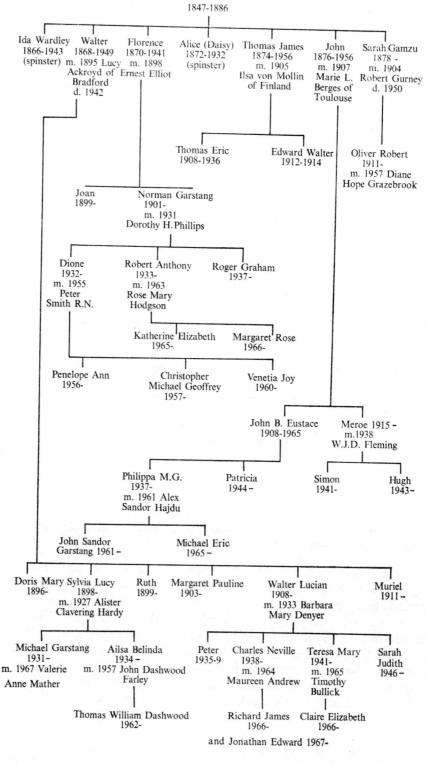

Ida Wardley 1866-1943 (spinster)

Walter 1868-1949 m. 1895 Lucy Ackroyd of Bradford d. 1942

Florence 1870-1941 m. 1898 Ernest Elliot

Alice (Daisy) 1872-1932 (spinster)

Thomas James 1874-1956 m. 1905 Ilsa von Mollin of Finland

John 1876-1956 m. 1907 Marie L. Berges of Toulouse

Sarah Gamzu 1878 - m. 1904 Robert Gurney d. 1950

Thomas Eric 1908-1936

Edward Walter 1912-1914

Oliver Robert 1911- m. 1957 Diane Hope Grazebrook

Joan 1899-

Norman Garstang 1901- m. 1931 Dorothy H. Phillips

Dione 1932- m. 1955 Peter Smith R.N.

Robert Anthony 1933- m. 1963 Rose Mary Hodgson

Roger Graham 1937-

Katherine Elizabeth 1965-

Margaret Rose 1966-

Penelope Ann 1956-

Christopher Michael Geoffrey 1957-

Venetia Joy 1960-

John B. Eustace 1908-1965

Meroe 1915 - m.1938 W.J.D. Fleming

Philippa M.G. 1937- m. 1961 Alex Sandor Hajdu

Patricia 1944 -

Simon 1941-

Hugh 1943-

John Sandor Garstang 1961 -

Michael Eric 1965 -

Doris Mary 1896-

Sylvia Lucy 1898- m. 1927 Alister Clavering Hardy

Ruth 1899-

Margaret Pauline 1903-

Walter Lucian 1908- m. 1933 Barbara Mary Denyer

Muriel 1911 -

Michael Garstang 1931- m. 1967 Valerie Anne Mather

Ailsa Belinda 1934 - m. 1957 John Dashwood Farley

Peter 1935-9

Charles Neville 1938- m. 1964 Maureen Andrew

Teresa Mary 1941- m. 1965 Timothy Bullick

Sarah Judith 1946 -

Thomas William Dashwood 1962-

Richard James 1966-

Claire Elizabeth 1966-

and Jonathan Edward 1967-

for adult life than by Charles and Mandy deciding to succeed in that together!

On January 12th 1964 we all had the pleasure of witnessing their marriage in the beautiful little church of St. Nicholas in Shepperton.

Now in 1968 Charles and Mandy have welcomed to the Clan two of my father's great great Garstang grandsons, Richard James on March 20th 1966 and his brother Jonathan Edward in 1967, and so we pass from generation to generation.

Pedigree IV 33.

Families from Whittle.

In 1498 John owned land in Whittle and Blackburn

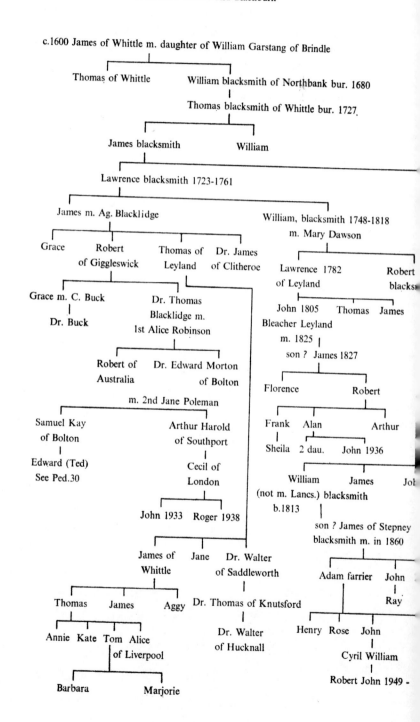

c.1600 James of Whittle m. daughter of William Garstang of Brindle

Thomas of Whittle

William blacksmith of Northbank bur. 1680

Thomas blacksmith of Whittle bur. 1727.

James blacksmith

William

Lawrence blacksmith 1723-1761

James m. Ag. Blacklidge

William, blacksmith 1748-1818
m. Mary Dawson

Grace

Robert
of Giggleswick

Thomas of
Leyland

Dr. James
of Clitheroe

Lawrence 1782
of Leyland

Robert
blacks.

Grace m. C. Buck

Dr. Buck

Dr. Thomas
Blacklidge m.
1st Alice Robinson

John 1805
Bleacher Leyland
m. 1825

Thomas   James

son ? James 1827

Robert of
Australia

Dr. Edward Morton
of Bolton

Florence

Robert

m. 2nd Jane Poleman

Samuel Kay
of Bolton

Edward (Ted)
See Ped.30

Arthur Harold
of Southport

Cecil of
London

Frank   Alan

Sheila   2 dau.

Arthur

John 1936

William
(not m. Lancs.)
b.1813

James   Jol
blacksmith

John 1933   Roger 1938

son ? James of Stepney
blacksmith m. in 1860

James of
Whittle

Jane

Dr. Walter
of Saddleworth

Adam farrier   John

Thomas   James   Aggy

Dr. Thomas of Knutsford

Ray

Annie Kate Tom Alice
of Liverpool

Dr. Walter
of Hucknall

Henry Rose John

Cyril William

Barbara

Marjorie

Robert John 1949 -

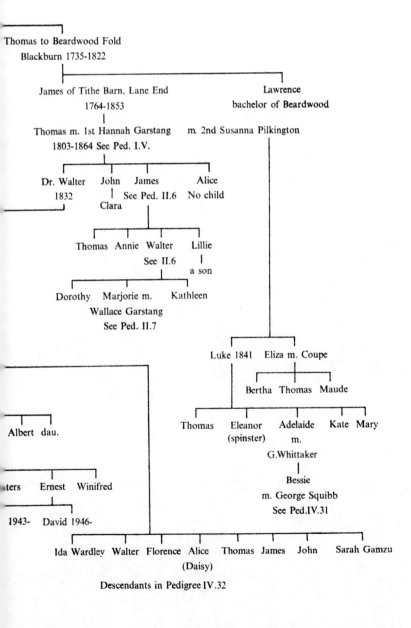

Thomas to Beardwood Fold
Blackburn 1735-1822

James of Tithe Barn, Lane End   Lawrence
1764-1853   bachelor of **Beardwood**

Thomas m. 1st Hannah Garstang   m. 2nd Susanna Pilkington
1803-1864 See Ped. I.V.

Dr. Walter   John   James   Alice
1832   See Ped. II.6   No child
            Clara

Thomas Annie Walter   Lillie
                See II.6
                        a son

Dorothy Marjorie m.   Kathleen
        Wallace Garstang
        See Ped. II.7

Luke 1841   Eliza m. Coupe

        Bertha Thomas Maude

Albert dau.

                Thomas   Eleanor   Adelaide   Kate Mary
                          (spinster)   m.
                                      G.Whittaker

ters   Ernest   Winifred
                                         Bessie
                                    m. George Squibb
1943-   David 1946-   See Ped.IV.31

Ida Wardley Walter Florence Alice   Thomas James   John   Sarah Gamzu
                              (Daisy)

Descendants in Pedigree IV.32